LAGER

LAGER

THE DEFINITIVE GUIDE TO
Tasting and Brewing the World's
Most Popular Beer Styles

VOYAGEUR
PRESS

DAVE CARPENTER

Brimming with creative inspiration, how-to projects, and useful information to enrich your everyday life, Quarto Knows is a favourite destination for those pursuing their interests and passions. Visit our site and dig deeper with our books into your area of interest: Quarto Creates, Quarto Cooks, Quarto Homes, Quarto Lives, Quarto Drives, Quarto Explores, Quarto Gifts, or Quarto Kids.

First published in 2017 by Voyageur Press, an imprint of The Quarto Group, 401 Second Avenue North, Suite 310, Minneapolis, MN 55401 USA. T: (612) 344-8100 F: (612) 344-8692 QuartoKnows.com

Voyageur Press titles are also available at discount for retail, wholesale, promotional, and bulk purchase. For details, contact the Special Sales Manager by email at specialsales@quarto.com or by mail at The Quarto Group, Attn: Special Sales Manager, 401 Second Avenue North, Suite 310, Minneapolis, MN 55401 USA.

10 9 8 7 6 5 4 3 2 1

ISBN: 978-0-7603-5215-1

Library of Congress Cataloging-in-Publication Data

Names: Carpenter, Dave, 1978- author.
Title: Lager : the definitive guide to tasting and brewing the world's most
    popular beer styles / Dave Carpenter.
Description: Minneapolis, MN : Voyageur Press, 2017. | Includes
    bibliographical references and index.
Identifiers: LCCN 2017013886 | ISBN 9780760352151 (hardback)
Subjects: LCSH: Lager beer. | BISAC: COOKING / Beverages / Beer. | COOKING /
    Beverages / General.
Classification: LCC TP577 .C34 2017 | DDC 641.2/3--dc23
LC record available at https://lccn.loc.gov/2017013886

Acquiring Editor: Thom O'Hearn
Project Manager: Alyssa Bluhm
Art Director: James Kegley
Cover Designer: Sussner Design
Layout: Amy Sly

Printed in China

CONTENTS

CHAPTER 5: THE DRY SPELL

CHAPTER 6: THE CRAFT LAGER COMEBACK

CHAPTER 7: TASTING AND ENJOYING LAGER

CHAPTER 8: OLD WORLD PALE LAGERS

CHAPTER 9: OLD WORLD DARK LAGERS

CHAPTER 10: NORTH AMERICAN LAGERS, FOR BETTER AND FOR WORSE

CHAPTER 11: LAGER WORT PRODUCTION

CHAPTER 12: FERMENTATION, CONDITIONING, AND PACKAGING

CHAPTER 13: RECIPES

FOREWORD

BY PETER BOUCKAERT
PARTNER, PURPOSE BREWING AND CELLARS

In 1996, I made the move from Belgium to New Belgium. The brewery had just moved to its current location in Fort Collins, Colorado. It had a very nice German brewhouse and bottling line. At the time, New Belgium was making five beers year-round using just two yeasts. Nowadays, that may sound strange: What American craft brewery would only make five beers? But it was not unusual then. In fact, two yeast strains meant we had one more than most breweries!

In 1997, we started our seasonal program of beers. While we initially intended to make a kettle sour—unheard of at that time!—we ended up making a pilsner for our first release. I had been brewing for over a decade in Belgium and the United States, yet I had never made a lager before the beer we called Blue Paddle Pilsner.

Despite the high-quality brewhouse, the brewery was absolutely not set up to make lagers. The temperature in Fort Collins could be high in the late summer and fall, yet we could only cool the wort with city water straight from the tap. Clearly, I had to work around our system and modify the recipe to get the best results. (As brewers know, you must use the tools you have!) On top of that, pilsners are hard to brew: They are beers where you have to make the malt, hops, and yeast shine and showcase your technical precision. In the end, I pulled it off. I loved it when German visitors tasted Blue Paddle Pilsner and said I should enter it in a German brewing competition. In my opinion, it was not fit for the "Substitutionsverbot," as it used to be called—but, hey, I am not a German.

If you step back, lagers are a blip in history. Just as dinosaurs roamed the earth for tens of millions of years, and humans have existed only for a million, so are lagers within the timeline of fermented beverages. This, of course, comes down to the yeasts used to brew lagers and our ability to control them. Lagers are beers fermented with a different family of yeasts than ales. (Scientifically, the name has changed three times since I have been in brewing, and will probably change again, but the fact remains that lager yeast is different from ale yeast.)

The main difference for brewers is that lager yeast can and should ferment at colder temperatures than ale yeast. This means that breweries in different parts of the world found success with various strategies to keep fermentation temperature under control. There were cliff-hugging breweries with cold cellars built into rock, as the in the Hofmühl brewery in Eichstätt. River ice collection was key at August Schell brewery in New Ulm, Minnesota. Underground tunnels were used by Pilsner Urquell, and can still be seen today. Scientific discoveries (by Louis Pasteur and others) and man-made cooling devices only spurred lager yeasts on, and they eventually conquered the world.

Yet, the past few decades and the rising popularity of craft beer have not been kind to the perception of lager. There are many misconceptions these days. For example, a pale, flavorless beer is what comes to mind for most people when lagers are mentioned. As you will see in this book, however, this is not an accurate representation of lagers today or throughout history. (In chapters 8 through 10, you will see many other types of lager!) Or, for a modern example, look

Vienna lager is just one of many classic lager styles that craft brewers are rediscovering and, in some cases, reinventing.

no further than New Belgium's own La Folie, an oak foeder aged sour brown. Would you believe this beer begins its life fermented with a lager yeast?

While using a lager as the base beer for a wood-aged sour is a fun idea, it also showcases something important: Yeast is a tool in the toolbox of a brewer and a brewer can use multiple tools. Beer is art and the brewer is the artist. We create something beautiful and someone else will put it in a box or style. I encourage you to keep your mind open to this idea as you explore the chapters in this wonderful and engaging book. Lager is likely much more than you imagined.

INTRODUCTION

Beer has come a long way in the last four decades.

Craft brands have exploded as flavor-conscious consumers have rediscovered what it means for beer to delight the senses. Modern brewers have reacquainted us with pale ale, stout, *hefeweizen*, *bière de garde*, *tripel*, and countless other styles. They have introduced us to wild and sour beers that tickle the palate with acidity and funk. And they have developed entirely new kinds of beer, a great number of which have found a home in the ever-expanding family of India pale ales.

Craft beer's ascendency has largely been built on the success of ale, a generic designation for beer fermented at or near room temperature. But for most people, the word *beer* still means one thing: lager. In just about every city in every nation, ordering a beer without further qualification is very likely to get you a lager, an umbrella term for a family of beers that trace their lineage to medieval Bavaria.

For most of the last forty years, however, craft beer consumers have overwhelmingly opted for ales over lagers—save the occasional *oktoberfest* seasonal or summery session pilsner. Fortunately, the tide has begun to turn, and brewers and consumers alike are once again celebrating the joys of lager beer. Some are brewing faithful renditions of Continental stalwarts. Others are reinventing classic styles with an American twist. And still others are creating entirely new kinds of lager beer altogether.

We're on the cusp of a lager revolution, one that's been more than five hundred years in the making. It's time we all started giving lager the respect it deserves.

OPPOSITE: Quaffable Bavarian light lagers are customarily served by the liter.

WHAT IS LAGER?

Nomenclature changes with each passing year, and the beer lexicon is no exception. There was a time when English speakers made a clear distinction between *beer* and *ale*, the modern words themselves deriving from the Old English *bēor* and *ealu*, respectively.[1] In sixteenth-century England, *ale* referred to malt-based libations made without hops, while the word *beer* was reserved for drinks that included cones of the increasingly popular hops plant.

In modern parlance, we consider *beer* to include all fermented drinks based upon malted cereal grains. Hops are usually part of the formula, but we don't hesitate to call *gruit* a type of beer.[2] When we say, "Hey, want to meet for a beer?" we're not being terribly specific about what is or is not present in our drink of choice. About the only guarantee is that we'll be enjoying something made, at least in part, from malted grain.

The word *ale* has changed over the centuries and no longer means beer brewed without hops. Instead, ale has come to refer to beer fermented using a species of yeast called *Saccharomyces cerevisiae*. This type of yeast typically works best at room temperature or slightly cooler, say 62 to 72°F (16 to 22°C), and it usually wraps things up within a week in most cases. Some sources refer to *S. cerevisiae* as "top-fermenting" yeast, for reasons we shall explore later.

Which brings us to lager. Lager differs from ale in two important ways:

1. Lager beers are fermented using a species of yeast called *Saccharomyces pastorianus*. Unlike ale yeast, *S. pastorianus* works well in the cold, usually a frigid 45 to 55°F (7 to 13°C).

2. Lager beers traditionally undergo a period of near-freezing maturation that may last anywhere from a couple of weeks to a year or longer, depending on the beer style and the brewer's intent. In fact, the word *lager* itself derives from the German *lagern*, meaning "to store" or "to keep."

Taking a step back from these two considerations, we observe that three big things define lager:

1. Yeast

2. Temperature

3. Time

Thus, using our modern words, we can classify most beers according to these criteria:

- Ale is a family of beers that are fermented more or less at room temperature with the yeast *S. cerevisiae*. Some are consumed almost immediately, while others are aged before serving.

- Lager is a family of beers that are fermented in the cold with the yeast *S. pastorianus*. Almost without exception, these beers are cold-conditioned for weeks or months before serving.

Note that nothing in the definition of lager implies anything about flavor, color, alcoholic strength, or carbonation. But that hasn't kept us from making up some myths.

FIVE MYTHS ABOUT LAGER YOU NEED TO STOP BELIEVING (AND PERPETUATING)

Legend and myth add mystique and romance to the history of beer. We've all heard how India pale ale and Russian imperial stout developed to withstand long journeys by sea. I admit to having a soft spot for these kinds of stories, even if the evidence to support their accuracy may be embellished, dubious, or nonexistent. The stories and the beers they concern go great with a campfire.

Lager myths are of a different type altogether, though, for they often dissuade the consumer from sampling many of the world's finest beers. In believing such nonsense, even otherwise well-informed beer aficionados dismiss an entire family of classic beer styles outright. Just as we go out of our way to inform the drinking public that not every stout is a meal in a glass, so should we also dispel false information that keeps beer lovers and the beer-curious from discovering what the world of lager has to offer.

Here are five of the most egregious offenders:

1. **Myth: Lager is thin and yellow.** With marketing taglines like "The Great American Lager," "Lager Beer at Its Best," and "A Fine Pilsner Beer," it's no wonder consumers are confused. After all, the brands associated with these slogans are indeed thin, yellow, and unremarkable. But remember, a lager is simply a beer that has been brewed in the cold and allowed to mature for a period of time. The next time you hear someone equate lager with watery yellow beer, do all of us a favor and hand them a Tröegs Troegenator, a Kulmbacher Eisbock, or an Aecht Schlenkerla Eiche.

2. **Myth: Lager is synonymous with pilsner.** This one's just silly. Visit any liquor store with a reasonable beer selection, and even if you never stray from the German imports, you'll discover *oktoberfest*, *dunkel*, *bock*, *doppelbock*, and *schwarzbier*, to name a few. Take a moment to venture to the craft aisle, and you'll likely run across new styles like India pale lager and reimagined classics like Mexican pale lager with lime zest. Some brewers are even straying well beyond the *Reinheitsgebot* and aging lagers on fruit and in barrels.

3. **Myth: Lager is less flavorful than ale.** This myth just won't die. Yes, well-made lagers do not showcase the same yeast-derived characteristics (think fruity esters and spicy phenols) as ales. But lager styles are brewed from the very same malts and hops as other beers, and brewers manipulate these ingredients just as they do when making ale styles. And even though lager yeast tends to stay out of the way, it, too, offers its own understated contributions: sulfur and diacetyl, considered flaws most of the time, can benefit certain well-crafted lagers in measured amounts. Yeast may not jump out of the glass the way it does in a spicy saison, but lager yeasts offer their own pleasures to those who take the time to understand them.

4. **Myth: Lager is easier to brew than ale.** When AB InBev aired its infamous "Brewed the Hard Way" commercial during Super Bowl XLIX, there was a wave of outrage—and rightfully so—within the craft beer community. However, the ads

hinted at a truth that even longtime beer enthusiasts fail to recognize, even if that truth was delivered with the sort of compensatory machismo that makes Dodge Ram commercials look measured and sensitive by comparison. Lager brewing is often harder than ale brewing, especially when the product in question is a light lager that consumers expect to taste the same whether it's made in St. Louis, Houston, or Los Angeles. Professional brewers recognize this fact and respect those who brew light lagers consistently across multiple breweries.

5. **Myth: Lager has less alcohol than ale.** This myth probably has to do with the plethora of light lagers that advertisers endlessly promote during sporting events. But lager can be mild or potent, just like ale. In fact, one of the strongest beers in the world, Samichlaus Classic from Brauerei Schloss Eggenberg in Austria, is a lager that weighs in at a respectable 14 percent alcohol by volume.[3]

LAGER IS DIVERSE

One of the silliest accusations leveled against lager is that it's all the same. When I submitted the manuscript for this book, just four beer archetypes accounted for 90 percent of BeerAdvocate's top 250 beers in the world:

- 34 percent (86) were classified as some kind of IPA.
- 33 percent (83) were classified as some kind of stout.
- 14 percent (36) were classified as some kind of wild, sour, or farmhouse ale.
- 7 percent (18) were classified as some kind of strong ale or barleywine.

The remaining 10 percent included eleven American pale ales, ten American porters, three American fruit beers, and two German-style wheat beers. Just one lager made the list: a 15.5 percent ABV raspberry *eisbock* from Kuhnhenn Brewing Company in Warren, Michigan.[4]

The situation was only slightly better on BeerAdvocate's "Beers of Fame," a collection of 250 top-rated beers that have maintained a presence on the site for more than a decade. These were Death & Taxes, a dark lager from Moonlight Brewing Company in Fulton, California, and Augustiner Bräu Lagerbier Hell, a classic *helles* from Augustiner-Bräu in Munich.[5]

Craft brewers, for all the good they have done, have inadvertently allowed a handful of styles to dominate draft lists at the expense of true diversity. Think of your favorite craft beer bar. How many tap handles are devoted to IPAs, stouts, and sours? How many offer *helles*, *märzen*, *rauchbier*, or *doppelbock*? By no means should we revisit the days when eight virtually identical American light lager brands dominated the beer list, but neither should we let the pendulum swing so far that we limit ourselves to hop bombs and bourbon barrel stouts.

ABOUT THIS BOOK

I was inspired to write this book after hearing "I don't drink lager" one too many times. Avoiding lager because you don't like Bud Light is a bit like eschewing all vegetables just because you don't happen to enjoy asparagus. Having heard more than a few well-educated and experienced craft beer drinkers make such a claim, I felt that it was time to stand up for this misunderstood class of beer.

Lager: The Definitive Guide to Tasting and Brewing the World's Most Popular Beer Styles is, to the best of my knowledge, the first widely available work devoted to telling the story of this family of styles and how they have influenced beer as we know it today. It explains the history of lager, but it is not a history book. It details the technical aspect of brewing lager beer, but it is not a textbook. And it deconstructs diverse lager styles through sensory analysis, but it is not a book of beer reviews. Instead, *Lager* is my attempt to bring together numerous disparate sources to tell the fascinating story of lager beer, one that I don't believe has been told in a comprehensive fashion in English until now.

On that note, please recognize that I don't—I can't—know everything there is to know about lager; except for a few brewing legends with names like Narziß and Kunze, nobody can. I have attempted to make *Lager* accessible to as wide an audience as possible, which necessarily means that some stories have been omitted and some details simplified. That's the price of admission for a book that attempts to cram two millennia of brewing history, an overview of brewing techniques, and a survey of modern craft lagers into 240 pages.

If you'd like to dig further into this fascinating story (and I hope you do), a list of recommended books and articles is offered on page 224. A comprehensive bibliography of all the sources I consulted in writing *Lager* is provided on page 227. And homebrewers interested in creating their own lagers at home will find twenty delightful recipes on page 195.

But for now, I invite you to sit down, preferably with a stocky, dimpled mug of bock or a tall, slender glass of pilsner, and learn why 95 percent of the world's beer drinkers reach for lager.

Prost!

A rich doppelbock counters the notion that lager is synonymous with thin, yellow, flavorless beer.

THE DARK AGES

In the beginning, there was no beer. When twenty-four-hour cable news and Facebook feed feuds leave you yearning for a simpler time, just remember that we have beer, and early humans didn't. So at least there's that.

Yet lager beer is a relatively new phenomenon, one with just a few centuries under its belt. Modern lager as you and I recognize it at the local bar is even more recent. It would not have become the diverse collection of beer styles we enjoy today without the benefit of the Industrial Revolution and the emergence of microbiology as a specialized scientific discipline.

But before there were ale and lager, there was just beer, plain and simple, the product of fermented grain. Understanding, refining, and repeating the process by which grain is transformed into a refreshing alcoholic beverage took millennia, and the story of that journey mirrors that of human civilization. Thus, the story of lager begins with the history of beer itself.

Gruit beer, an early beer style brewed with botanicals instead of hops (see recipe page 200).

THE EARLIEST CONVERTS

Historians disagree on when our ancestors first started turning grain into beer, but most of them (the historians, not our ancestors) seem to acknowledge that we were well on our way by the time of the Neolithic Revolution. The Neolithic Revolution, which took place about ten thousand years ago, was humanity's gradual transition from a nomadic hunter-gatherer life to a more settled existence centered on farming and intentional agriculture.

Why humans decided to make this transition remains a topic of anthropological discussion and research, and scholars have proposed several competing theories that address it. Some hypotheses attempt to explain the shift as a reaction to a change in climate. Others suggest that humans adopted agriculture to support a growing population that hunting and gathering could not sustain on their own.

Some researchers have even suggested that one factor—though certainly not *the* factor—in our conversion from hunting and gathering to an agricultural lifestyle might have been a desire to accumulate enough grain to brew beer. Evidence for such a claim isn't abundant, but the idea seems at least plausible. If you know (or are) a homebrewer, you understand just how powerful the urge to brew beer can be.

Even less understood is how that first beer came about. Wine happens naturally (though the result is not necessarily a great vintage), and one needn't have studied anthropology or oenology to understand how early humans might have come to appreciate it. Fruit contains an abundance of simple sugars, which is why we enjoy eating it: it tastes sweet. Fruit skins also host thriving colonies of naturally occurring yeasts and bacteria.

As it happens, those microbes, like us, have a sweet tooth. When fruit is crushed or starts to turn south, these microbes gain access to the sacchariferous bounty within and ferment the fruit's sugars into ethanol and carbon dioxide. Wait long enough, and crushed grapes become wine. Wait even longer, and that wine becomes vinegar, which isn't nearly as much fun to drink.

Some winemakers today still rely on natural yeasts to turn regular grape juice into grownup grape juice. But, for the sake of control and repeatability, modern vintners usually choose to inoculate crushed grapes with yeast strains that have been selectively pressured over generations and centuries for good performance in the winery.

Mead is an even older beverage than wine and offers the advantage of relying on a sugar source that's easy to store. Left to its own devices, properly cured honey is unlikely to start fermenting because it has a low pH and contains less than 20 percent moisture by weight— inhospitable conditions for spoiling microbes. Diluting honey with water, however, reduces acidity and creates an environment more suitable for fermentation. Thus, ancient meadmakers could have whipped up batches of mead according to need rather than, say, wait for the annual grape harvest.

Cereal grains also offer long-term storage advantages, but unlike fruit or diluted honey, grain must be modified before its innards can be made available to fermentative organisms. Simply adding grain to water results in disappointment. Instead, the starches that lie within a kernel of barley, wheat, rye, or maize need to be unlocked and transformed into simpler sugars that yeasts can metabolize into alcohol and carbon dioxide. How on earth did we figure that out?

One clue is to chew on a piece of bread. I mean, *really* chew on it, well past the point at which you would normally swallow. Chew long enough, and that mushy bread will begin to taste sweet. That's because human saliva contains enzymes that begin digesting grain starches into the sugars we use for energy. In fact, a beer style indigenous to South and Central America still makes use of this fun biological quirk.

Chicha de jora, a maize-based beverage of mild strength (typically just 1 or 2 percent alcohol by volume), predates the Spanish conquest of the Inca Empire. It can be prepared through a variety of means, one of which is to allow maize kernels to germinate so that natural enzymes within the kernels start converting internal starches to sugars—just like malted barley or wheat.

A less popular but more romantic method involves chewing raw maize kernels until human salivary enzymes start breaking down the grain's starch. Get enough people together to chew up and spit out ear after ear of field corn, and you can collect enough converted maize to make chicha for the village. It's unclear whether this chew-and-spit process could have directly led to proto-beer, but given the amount of work involved to create a small amount of alcohol, it seems unlikely that it would have been the quantum leap civilization needed. It may, however, have provided the associative mental link we needed to connect starch to sugar and alcohol.

One plausible hypothesis regarding our discovery of starch conversion concerns sprouted seeds gone bad.[1] Under the right conditions of moisture and heat, a cereal grain will sprout in anticipation of becoming a full-grown plant. This is the first step in malting, and it's something that happens in nature all the time: seed falls, seed gets wet, seed becomes plant. It's entirely reasonable to imagine that ancient grain caches might have been kept in varying degrees of germination, depending on the time of year, weather, and storage conditions.

We know that early humans cooked grain to make porridge and ground grain into flour for bread. If the grain they used happened to be at the right stage of germination, and if conditions of temperature, moisture, and time were favorable, then the gruel or dough would have tasted sweeter than, say, last week's version that had been made with raw, dry kernels. Given that ripe fruit virtually demands to become alcohol, humans had probably made a connection between sweetness and alcohol considerably earlier (perhaps using the chew-and-spit method), and then it would have been just a matter of time and trial and error before they started intentionally brewing proto-beer.

This evolution likely did not come about in a single "aha!" moment. Rather, it almost certainly involved many happy accidents punctuated by periods of wondering what the hell had just happened. But with enough trials and the benefit of collective knowledge, not to mention what was probably a more intimate experience of the natural world than most of us possess today, it's not hard to imagine a cascade of evolutionary if-thens that would have led to recognizing that grain plus moisture plus heat plus time equals sugar, which with more time equals alcohol.

We may never know with certainty what path led ancient humans from grain to beer. And unless you're a career anthropologist, it probably doesn't matter all that much. In fact, the infinite monkey theorem may apply just as easily to grain and beer as it does to typewriters and *Hamlet*. But even if we never fully understand how our ancestors made the leap, we have plentiful evidence that, once they did, they made quick work of putting it to good use in building what we today call civilization.

BEER IN ANCIENT MESOPOTAMIA AND EGYPT

If you think back to every history class you've ever taken, you might recall that every single one of them started in Mesopotamia, just as soon as the instructor had wrapped up the course syllabus and grading scheme. Mesopotamia refers to those portions of what are now Syria and Iraq that lie roughly between the Tigris and Euphrates Rivers. The name itself comes from the Greek μέσο (*méso*), meaning "middle or midst," and ποτάμια (*potámia*) meaning "rivers." In casual speech, Mesopotamia is often used synonymously with the wider so-called Fertile Crescent, which also includes the Levant and parts of Egypt.

While we don't fully understand *how* early humans figured out how to transform grain starches into fermentable sugars, there is no shortage of evidence from Mesopotamia indicating that we didn't waste time once we did. We know that barley was first domesticated here, and residue tests on excavated artifacts show that beer was being brewed in the region by about 5000 BCE. One of the oldest known beer recipes found in Mesopotamia, inscribed upon a clay tablet, offers compelling evidence that beer had been brewed perhaps one thousand years earlier than that. In the Sumerian city of Uruk, barley and beer were even used as currency by about 3300 BCE.

Arguably the most famous artifact demonstrating the importance of beer to the ancient people of Mesopotamia is a poem dating to approximately 1900 BCE that honors Ninkasi, the Sumerian goddess of brewing. Commonly called "The Hymn to Ninkasi," modern brewers find its words striking and familiar:

> Ninkasi, given birth by the flowing water, tenderly cared for by Ninhursag!
>
> Ninkasi, it is you who bake the beer-bread in the big oven, and put in order the piles of hulled grain.
>
> Ninkasi, it is you who soak the malt in a jar; the waves rise, the waves fall.
>
> Ninkasi, it is you who spread the cooked mash on large reed mats; coolness overcomes.
>
> Ninkasi, it is you who hold with both hands the great sweet-wort, brewing it with honey and wine.
>
> Ninkasi, you [bring] the sweet-wort to the vessel.
>
> Ninkasi, you place the fermenting vat, which makes a pleasant sound, appropriately on top of a large collector vat.
>
> Ninkasi, it is you who pour out the filtered beer of the collector vat; it is like the onrush of the Tigris and the Euphrates.[2]

RIGHT: Cuneiform inscription on a Sumerian clay tablet defining workers' payment in beer, ca. 3300 BCE (The British Museum).

OPPOSITE: Egyptian figure of a male brewer, ca. 2649–2100 BCE.

ABOVE: Wooden scene of a brewery in ancient Egypt, ca. 2000 BCE.

OPPOSITE: Limestone funerary stele from Tell el-Amarna, Egypt, ca. 1350 BCE, depicting an early beer drunk through a straw (Staatliche Museen zu Berlin).

In the traditional narrative of the history of beer, the Mesopotamians taught the Egyptians how to brew, which would almost certainly have been a natural result of trading and cultural exchange between two neighboring civilizations. Historians generally date the spread of brewing knowledge from Mesopotamia to Egypt to around 3000 BCE. They also tell us that the Egyptians enthusiastically adopted beer as the drink of choice for occasions both special and mundane.

Brewing beer became an important part of daily life. At the Egyptian city of Nekhen (ιεράκων πόλις, or Hierakonpolis in Ancient Greek), archaeologists unearthed a brewery dating to about 4000 BCE that is estimated to have boasted a weekly output of at least 10 modern-day barrels (317 gallons or 1,200 liters) of beer. Brewers and bakers probably worked alongside one another, but evidence suggests that by the time Egyptians took up brewing, they had refined it into a dedicated practice, not just an extension of bread making as was once thought.[3]

Ancient Egyptians and Mesopotamians malted grain specifically for brewing beer and bypassed the intermediate bread-baking stage altogether. In a remarkably simple but effective system, grains were held in a wicker basket above an open well, and the basket was raised and lowered to adjust the temperature, thereby controlling the rate of germination. Lowering the basket nearer the water cooled the developing malt, while elevating the basket raised the temperature and accelerated the process. Once modification was complete (or as complete as would have been possible in those days), the malt was sun-dried to be used at any time the brewer desired. Technology has improved, of course, but the process of malting is fundamentally the same even today.[4]

What the Mesopotamians and Egyptians brewed was technically "beer" in that it was made from fermented grain sugars, but were you handed a pint of it today, you'd probably send it back. The beer was most certainly gritty and would have displayed a sort of haze that would make even a New England IPA devotee think twice. In fact, Egyptian drinkers used long straws to sip from jars to avoid ingesting floaters and sediment. Some of these straws featured a rudimentary inline filter to help separate out the chunky bits.

A thriving beer culture emerged in Egypt, so, naturally, the Roman Empire came in and screwed it all up. The Romans had little positive to say about beer and those who consumed it, and after Augustus finally claimed Egypt for Rome in 31 BCE, wine displaced beer as the drink of the nobility. Nonetheless, everyday Egyptian citizens preferred beer, and some would argue that this cultural stratification between wine and beer continues even to this day.[5]

BEER IN EARLY EUROPE

While familiar to beer nerds for an entirely different reason today, Pliny—his name rhymes with "Vinnie," not "tiny"—was a Roman historian. He died during the eruption of Mount Vesuvius in 79 CE, but he left us what is widely considered the world's first encyclopedia, *Naturalis Historia* (*Natural History*). In Chapter 50 of Volume 20 of his influential work, Pliny, who must have suffered from a terrific case of writer's cramp, offered one of the first written accounts, perhaps *the* first written account, of the hops plant:

> In Italy, however, we are acquainted with but very few of them [wild, uncultivated plants]; those few being the strawberry, the tamnus, the butcher's broom, the sea batis, and the garden batis, known by some persons as Gallic asparagus; in addition to which we may mention the meadow parsnip and the hop, which may be rather termed amusements for the botanist than articles of food.[6]

It's this reference to hops that has gained Pliny the Elder his posthumous fame among brewers and his namesake beer. But he also offered clues about beer brewing in early Europe. In Chapter 29 of Book 14, Pliny alludes to grain-based drinks found throughout Western Europe, confirming that within a century of the big BCE to CE changeover, grain-based alcoholic beverages had become widespread and well known throughout Europe:

> The people of the Western world have also their intoxicating drinks, made from corn steeped in water. These beverages are prepared in different ways throughout Gaul and the provinces of Spain; under different names, too, though in their results they are the same. The Spanish provinces have even taught us the fact that these liquors are capable of being kept till they have attained a considerable age. Egypt, too, has invented for its use a very similar beverage made from corn; indeed, in no part of the world is drunkenness ever at a loss. And then, besides, they take these drinks unmixed, and do not dilute them with water, the way that wine is modified; and yet, by Hercules! one really might have supposed that there the earth produced nothing but corn for the people's use. Alas! what wondrous skill, and yet how misplaced! means have absolutely been discovered for getting drunk upon water even.[7]

"Indeed, in no part of the world is drunkenness ever at a loss." If only Pliny could see us today.

The exact manner by which beer brewing reached Europe remains a subject of study and debate. Some historians have proposed that Roman conquerors brought beer with them as they marched across Europe, but we know that they encountered and fought Celtic and Germanic tribes who were already accomplished brewers. And excavations near Kulmbach, Germany, have unearthed evidence suggesting that beer was brewed in northern Bavaria as early as 800 BCE. So, it seems clear that early Europeans, whether they developed brewing independently or learned it from elsewhere, were in the habit of enjoying a good (or, more likely, bad) pint or two well before Rome arrived on the scene.

Even if they didn't bring brewing science with them, the Romans *did* bring a period of stability and a snobby predilection for wine. As in Egypt, wine became the drink of the ruling classes, while beer remained popular among the uncouth and unwashed. But after the Roman Empire collapsed, the beer-drinking Germanic "barbarians" had their day, for it was they who filled the resulting power vacuum. And so, beer regained an elevated status as the drink of peasants and nobility alike.

Pliny the Elder lived from 23 to 79 CE.

For the first several centuries CE, brewing remained very much a household chore, as common and pedestrian as cooking and cleaning. But as Christianity spread, brewing knowledge gradually moved out of houses and began concentrating in the monasteries of Europe. In *Beer in the Middle Ages and the Renaissance*, Richard Unger notes that this transition marked an improvement in beer production, as well as a consolidation of brewing science and practice.

> The first large-scale production of beer in medieval Europe took place in the monasteries which emerged in the eighth and ninth centuries. In those institutions the first signs of a new level of beer making included using more and better equipment and the best of techniques, as well as having artisans who developed special skills to produce beer. The political revival of the eighth and ninth centuries associated with the Carolingians, and especially with the reign of Charlemagne, was critical in promoting the development of estate or official production.[8]

In what is now St. Gallen, Switzerland, a monastery dating to ca. 590 CE became an imperial abbey around 800 CE, at roughly the same time Charlemagne was crowned the first Holy Roman Emperor. Plans were drawn up shortly thereafter to build a state-of-the-art brewhouse in the abbey, the first of its kind in Europe. The new facility housed three separate breweries for making different kinds of beer for guests, pilgrims, and the monks themselves.

Der xlvj bruder der do starb hieß
herttel wnepreiw.

Researchers estimate the brewery's output at approximately 10 to 12 hectoliters per day, or about 8.5 to 10 modern US beer barrels.

Throughout the first millennium CE, brewing increasingly became a concern of the Church. Sources indicate that monks in some monasteries imbibed as much as 5 liters per day of medieval beer. This makes more sense when one considers that beer was often safer to drink than water (boiling kills disease-causing microbes), and it provided vital nutrients that monks needed, especially during long periods of fasting. But beer's real allure in the eyes of the Church ultimately came down to cold hard cash.

THE INTRODUCTION OF HOPS

One of the most important developments in medieval brewing—and certainly that which has most organoleptically influenced what we today call beer—was the introduction of hops to the brew kettle. A beer with no bitterness strikes the palate as cloying and syrupy, and modern ales and lagers derive bitterness from hops to deliver the international bittering units (IBUs) that brewers often proudly announce upon their labels.

Early European brewers didn't have hops. Well, they *had* them, but they hadn't yet figured out how to apply them to beer. Instead, they relied upon gruit. A mixture of various botanical ingredients, gruit was to early European brewing what hops are to us today. Some gruit ingredients are familiar to us, like yarrow, heather, rosemary, juniper, and anise. Others have fanciful names that would seem quite at home in a novel by Tolkien or Rowling: bog myrtle, horehound, wormwood, and mugwort all found their way into gruit-based ales.

Gruit lent bitterness and flavor to barley libations. It helped cover up the inevitable flaws in medieval brewing and conferred some preservative properties. And, as it happens, gruit also supplied a lucrative source of revenue to the ruling classes.

In feudal Europe, gruit blends were controlled by the state (i.e., the Church), which enjoyed the exclusive right to forage the botanical ingredients that went into beer. Governments also reserved the exclusive right to sell gruit to brewers, as well as the intellectual property concerning the specific blend for the gruit that brewers, by law, had to use. This gruit right, or *Grutrecht*, was an opportune and monopolistic way for the state to exert control over an industry and line the royal coffers.

Brewers have always been a frugal lot, and with time they learned to exploit a convenient loophole in the form of hops. Hops were plentiful. They weren't taxed. And they conferred bitterness, flavor, and aroma. Hops allowed early brewers to distance themselves from the restrictive gruit monopolies of the state, which at that time was also the Church. Dick Cantwell observes in *The Oxford Companion to Beer*, "With the Catholic Church having widely held a monopoly on the sale and taxation of gruit, the use of hops in brewing was nothing short of a revolutionary act."[9]

But hops did much more than just bitter and flavor medieval beer. Hops also offered antibacterial advantages that extended a beer's shelf life. Hop cones contain substances called alpha acids, which, when boiled in sweet wort (or even in water), transform into a modified form called isomerized alpha acids, or simply iso-alpha acids.

OPPOSITE: Medieval brewer displaying the traditional *Zoigl* star, ca. 1425 CE.

Iso-alpha acids are responsible for what we perceive as bitterness in beer. In fact, the famous IBU is, in its most fundamental form, nothing more than a measure of the concentration of iso-alpha acids in a sample of beer (specifically, 1 IBU is equivalent to 1 milligram of isomerized alpha acid in 1 liter of beer). Homebrewers and small commercial operations usually rely on formulae to estimate IBUs based on boil time, wort strength, hop quantities, and other process variables, but most large professionals measure IBUs directly using spectrophotometry or high-performance liquid chromatography (HPLC).

As it happens, the same iso-alpha acid compounds responsible for bitterness are also antagonistic against certain kinds of bacteria. Even today, lambic brewers use small quantities of hops that have been intentionally de-bittered to gain favorable properties of the hops without overwhelming the colonies of *Lactobacillus*, *Pediococcus*, *Acetobacter*, and other bacteria that define these styles of beer.

Adopting hops not only helped early brewers escape the monopoly of state-controlled gruit supplies; it also allowed beer to be stored for longer periods of time before turning sour. This ability to preserve beer for weeks or months would go on to be a key contributor to the development of lager beer.

THE POWER OF SELECTIVE PRESSURE

Most beer today is fermented using pure cultures of yeasts and, in some cases, bacteria. But medieval brewers in Europe didn't even understand how wort turned into beer, much less how to isolate microorganisms. How did they brew beer? And what was that beer like?

As mentioned earlier, sugars, be they from grapes, honey, or malt sugars, will spontaneously ferment if left exposed to the elements. So-called wild yeasts and bacteria, which is to say naturally occurring yeasts and bacteria, are everywhere—in the air, on fruit skins, and on malt kernels. Spontaneous fermentation is simply what happens when naturally occurring microbes grow into colonies large enough to deplete a given food supply.

Spontaneous fermentation is unpredictable by nature, and even early brewers would have sought ways to stack the odds in their favor. Most true spontaneously fermented beer will develop a layer of foam called *Kräusen* (pronounced CROY-zen) on its surface during active fermentation. And when fermentation subsides, a layer of sludge called cold trub (rhymes with *tube*) will collect on the bottom of the vessel, consisting of coagulated proteins, bits of malt and hops (or, in the case of gruit beer, herbs and other botanicals), and most importantly, yeast.

It's common practice today to either skim the foam from an actively fermenting batch of beer (called "top cropping") or collect the dregs from the bottom of a finished batch (called "bottom cropping"). In either case, brewers collect yeast cells that can be reused in another batch. Indeed, in today's professional breweries, it's not uncommon to repitch yeast for several generations.

Even though medieval European brewers wouldn't have had the scientific knowledge to describe what was going on, they probably understood that there was magic in the trub and in the Kräusen. Just as one can save a piece of sourdough bread dough to start a future batch, brewers would have learned to add a portion of one batch to another, a process called back-slopping. Early brewers did not need microbiology, though their beer would have been better for it.

fun fact

The beechwood that Anheuser-Busch InBev famously employs in the aging of Budweiser has very little to do with the wood itself. In fact, Bud's beechwood chips (more accurately, beechwood strips) are boiled with sodium bicarbonate before use, which sterilizes them and removes potential flavor contributions.

The real purpose of the beechwood is to add surface area to the bottoms of the horizontal lagering tanks the brewery uses. When Budweiser's yeast cells flocculate, they don't just fall to the bottom of the tank; they also collect on the three-dimensional matrix of beechwood spirals. Promoting contact between the yeast and the maturing beer encourages the cells to fully attenuate and clean up byproducts of fermentation like diacetyl.

Most importantly, choosing to remove yeast from the top or bottom of a batch of beer introduces a type of selective pressure. *Selective pressure* is the term for a stimulus that encourages a species to evolve in some fashion over time. Most of the organisms we encounter on a day-to-day basis—birds, dogs, cats, other people—have lifespans measured in years, so selective pressure occurs so slowly that we don't notice it. But a hypothetical brewer who brews once a week for ten years, repitching yeast from one batch to the next, will go through more than five hundred generations of yeast. That's a lot of opportunity to apply selective pressure.

When brewers remove yeast cells from the top of an actively fermenting vessel of beer—that is, from the Kräusen—they are preferentially choosing for certain characteristics. Such yeasts are more likely to remain in suspension and to continue fermenting after other cells have gone dormant. Continuing this practice over multiple generations will gradually encourage beers that are hazy (yeasts remain in suspension), well attenuated (yeasts remain active and consume wort sugars), and dry.

Similarly, harvesting yeast from the bottom of a vessel after fermentation means preferentially selecting for yeasts that drop out of suspension. Such yeasts are more likely to fall to the bottom of the fermenter before fermentation is complete and may leave behind a sweeter beer with more residual body. Additionally, yeasts tend to clean up after themselves, and flocculent strains are more likely to leave behind fermentation byproducts like diacetyl and acetaldehyde.

Today, we see the long-term results of such selective pressure in the yeast strains we use to ferment various kinds of beer. Broadly speaking, English ale strains tend to be highly flocculent and lower attenuating than, say, German *hefeweizen* and *kölsch* strains, which tend to remain in suspension and attenuate more thoroughly.

Selective pressure is a powerful force. To the degree that today's beer styles are defined by the yeasts used to ferment them, it's the most powerful arrow in the brewer's quiver. And when the sixteenth century rolled around, brewers in Europe unknowingly wielded it in a way that changed beer forever.

2

DUKING IT OUT IN BAVARIA

Pick a German beer. Any German beer.

If you can get past the intimidating blackletter script and heävy metäl diäereses, there's a good chance you'll find a certain phrase prominently emblazoned upon the label: "Gebraut nach dem deutschen Reinheitsgebot von 1516."

"Brewed according to the German Purity Law of 1516," the tagline proclaims. It sounds so clean, so efficient, so, well, *German*. Germans brew some of the finest lager in the world for good reason: they invented it.

Sixteenth-century Bavaria was the crucible of modern brewing, and most beer brewed in the world today owes its existence to events that took place in Bavaria in the 1500s. The so-called Beer Purity Law may be the most famous outcome of the day, but a lesser-known decree that came a few decades later forever changed what most of the world considers "beer."

Prague After Dark, a Czech dark lager (see recipe page 202).

A GUILDED AGE,
BUT NOT WITHOUT CONTROVERSY

As cities throughout central Europe grew in the centuries following the fall of Rome, specialized labor, and the division thereof, became an increasingly important fixture of daily life. Then, as today, skilled workers banded together to form organizations to promote trade and to lobby for protections. Merchant guilds and craft guilds popped up to advocate for everything from shoemaking and blacksmithing to baking and brewing.

The earliest records of brewers' guilds date to the early thirteenth century, and by 1300, such guilds appear to have been well established from London to Munich. Guilds were particularly successful in northern Germany, where brewing increasingly became a concern not of church or state, but of private citizens of the merchant class. Merchants in northern Europe gained power throughout the thirteenth and fourteenth centuries, fueled in part by strategic partnerships that facilitated trade. The best known such trade organization, the Hanseatic League, dominated areas along the northern coast of Europe from Bruges in the southwest to as far northeast as Novgorod, Russia, about 100 miles (160 km) south of St. Petersburg.

Things were different in Bavaria to the south, which was a feudal mishmash of principalities, lordships, and territories of the Holy Roman Empire, which, as Voltaire (and later Linda Richman) observed was neither holy, nor Roman, nor an empire. There, the Catholic Church exerted greater influence over the citizenry, and brewing remained very much a monastic concern. But a pivotal event late in the eleventh century served to diminish the power of the Church and, along with it, the Church's control over breweries.

The investiture controversy between Pope Gregory VII and Holy Roman Emperor Henry IV was the most important kerfuffle between the papacy and nobility in medieval Europe. The controversy surrounded who could appoint bishops, who weren't mere affiliates of the Church but de facto civil leaders who wielded tremendous power and influence. (They also happened to raise a lot of money.)

Since the fall of the Roman Empire, ruling nobles had enjoyed the privilege of appointing bishops. Simony, or the practice of selling positions within the Church to those with means, had become widespread by the time Henry was crowned Holy Roman Emperor at the age of six in 1056. But when Pope Gregory came to power in 1072, he initiated a series of reforms, known today as the Gregorian Reforms, one of which was to assert that the Church alone had power to appoint bishops. Henry responded by withdrawing his support of the pope and, going one step further, calling for a new one.

In the ensuing controversy, the pope and the emperor alternately gained the upper hand in a sort of medieval Ping-Pong power play. The pope excommunicated Henry, who regained favor after making a pilgrimage to Italy to apologize for having been so insistent. But Henry ultimately prevailed just a few years later, when he returned to Italy, sacked Rome, installed a new pope, and sent Gregory into exile.

One outcome of the controversy was diminished papal influence within the Holy Roman Empire. Monastic brewers, who had enjoyed almost exclusive rights to brew beer, found themselves gradually stripped of their privileges as the aristocracy decided that the Church had been reaping the benefits of brewing for far too long and that it was time to cash in. Breweries increasingly became a concern of the state, and eventually, being a duke meant having your very own brewery.

The effects of this power shift remain visible and relevant even today. Visitors to Munich may not realize that when they step into the famous Hofbräuhaus, they're stepping half a millennium into the past. For it was Duke Wilhelm V of Bavaria who, in 1589, founded the Staatliches Hofbräuhaus, or state court brewery. Its purpose? To brew beer and funnel revenue to the nobility of Bavaria. It remains a property of the government to this day.

IN WHICH BAVARIA FINDS ITSELF IN DEEP DUCHY

By the sixteenth century, Bavaria had been variously partitioned and reshaped according to the birth orders of sons and cousins for nearly four centuries. The House of Wittelsbach had taken power in 1180 and would remain in control until 1918. But despite the brewing power wielded by the state, wine remained the preferred tipple among the secular. The local grapes were good, and the best beers were understood to come from cities in the Hanseatic League anyway.

That might have been fine had circumstances not conspired to shift preferences from wine to beer. In the early sixteenth century, temperatures began to fall as the world entered what would come to be known as the Little Ice Age. While the cause isn't clear—some sources point to increased volcanic activity, which could have reduced solar irradiance—we do know that temperatures in Europe decreased enough to cause glaciers to advance upon villages in the Alps. The cooling trend was pronounced enough to push grape-growing territory further south, rendering winemaking in Bavaria an increasingly futile prospect. And as wine production fell, demand for beer grew.

With income from wine falling, the state increasingly looked to brewers to make up the lost tax revenue. At the same time, Europe's population was growing, partially triggering what has come to be known as the sixteenth-century price revolution.[1] The overall cost of living increased, including the price of grain, which was used to make both beer and bread. State regulators started restricting the types of grains that could be used for brewing to favor bread, which offered greater caloric density and nutritional value than beer. Strike one.

Beer quality suffered not just at the hands of baking, but also from a lack of quality overall. When Bavarian nobles took over brewing privileges from the monasteries, they had gained a lucrative source of income. Unfortunately, that income stream did not come with an instruction manual—brewing knowledge and techniques remained in the hands of the monks, who, as one might imagine, were not terribly keen on sharing it. That showed in the quality of the beer. Strike two.

Brewers tried all kinds of things to improve their inferior products. According to beer historian Horst Dornbusch, brewers commonly featured such adjuncts as "tree bark, rushes, and poisonous mushrooms, as well as hallucinogens like mandrake root" in their brews, while other additions included "pith, soot, chalk, and oxen bile."[2] With such dubious additives, beer quality became not just an issue of taste but one of public health. After all, the surest way to kill a business is to kill the customer. And when beer quality and consumption declined, so did revenue. Strike three.

There was already a precedent for state intervention. In 1156, the Holy Roman Emperor himself had stepped in. Frederick I, nicknamed Barbarossa for his red beard (Kaiser Friedrich "Rotbart" in German), issued the *Justitia Civitatis Augustensis*, a civil ordinance for the city of

Augsburg, said to be the oldest such proclamation in what we now call Germany. Among other things, Frederick specified that one who brewed bad beer would pay a fine and either have his beer donated to the poor or dumped outright.

In 1363, the city council of Munich took over the regulation of beer in that city, and in 1447, they made it law that beer brewed in Munich could only be made from barley, hops, and water. In 1493, Munich's ordinance was also adopted in the duchy of Landshut, setting the stage for regulatory directives across the whole of Bavaria.

PROHIBITION, BAVARIAN STYLE

By the early sixteenth century, regulation had won over in Bavaria, and the time had arrived to make it the law of the land. On April 23, 1516, at a meeting of the Assembly of Estates in the town of Ingolstadt, Dukes Wilhelm IV and Ludwig X issued the proclamation we now call the Reinheitsgebot. The English translation reads approximately as follows:

> We hereby proclaim and decree, by authority of our province, that henceforth in the Duchy of Bavaria, in the country as well as in the cities and marketplaces, the following rules apply to the sale of beer:
>
> From the Feast of St. Michael to the Feast of St. George, the price for one Mass or one Kopf is not to exceed one Pfennig Munich value, and
>
> From the Feast of St. George to the Feast of St. Michael, the Mass shall not be sold for more than two Pfennig of the same value, the Kopf not more than three Heller.
>
> If this not be adhered to, the punishment stated below shall be administered.
>
> Should any person brew, or otherwise have, other beer than March beer, it is not to be sold any higher than one Pfennig per Mass.
>
> Furthermore, we wish to emphasize that in the future, in all cities, market towns, and in the country, the only ingredients used for the brewing of beer must be barley, hops, and water. Whosoever knowingly disregards or transgresses upon this ordinance, shall be punished by the court authorities' confiscating such barrels of beer, without fail.
>
> Should, however, an innkeeper in the country, city or market towns buy two or three pails of beer and sell it again to the common peasantry, he alone shall be permitted to charge one Heller more for the Mass or the Kopf, than mentioned above. Furthermore, should there arise a scarcity and subsequent price increase of the barley, we, the Bavarian Duchy, shall have the right to order curtailments for the good of all concerned.[3]

Now, it's important to recognize that this proclamation wasn't just about specifying what could and could not be used in the brewing of beer. In fact, most of the text concerns the price for which one could sell that beer, as well as the punishments for failing to obey the law. There's

OPPOSITE: Duke Wilhelm IV of Bavaria.

ALBERTVS · DVX · BAVARIÆ

Fun Fact

The German word *Reinheit* means "purity" or "clarity." *Gebot*, in turn, translates as "order" or "command." Thus, the Reinheitsgebot, regularly called the world's oldest still-in-effect food regulation, literally refers to a regulation of purity, which sounds noble enough. But the word *Reinheitsgebot* didn't come along until 1918, when, during a parliamentary debate about the taxation of beer, a representative gave it the name by which we know it today.

Prior to 1918, this sixteenth-century decree was variously called the *Substitutionsverbot* or *Surrogatsverbot*, meaning "substitution prohibition" and "surrogate prohibition," respectively. These terms more accurately describe the intent of the law, but they don't have the same ring as "purity law." Thus, the word *Reinheitsgebot* has stuck, and it remains on German beers as both a mark of pride and a marketing gold mine.

no mention of purity, cleanliness, or quality. All it says is that beer could only be brewed using barley, hops, and water. (It doesn't even require that the barley be malted.) Yeast, of course, wasn't yet understood.

The attention that beer literati have paid Wilhelm's edict is well out of proportion to the effect it has had outside of modern Germany. As we shall see in later chapters, nineteenth-century German and Czech immigrants to North America would go on to brew with maize (corn). Japanese lagers would incorporate rice. Oats would work their way into English stouts. And Belgian Trappists would rely on sugar and spice to craft the monastic ales for which they have become so famous. The Reinheitsgebot is historically important, to be sure, but it was a lesser-known edict that ultimately set the stage for the most widely brewed beers in the world today.

While the Reinheitsgebot limited brewing ingredients to barley, hops, and water, it placed no restrictions on yeast because yeast hadn't even been identified, much less understood. The finest barley, hops, and water in the world are of little benefit if one does not have at least a rudimentary understanding of microbiology. And that's pretty much where sixteenth-century Bavarians found themselves.

Of particular consequence was the observation that beer brewed in winter improved under the new regulation, but summer beer continued to suffer. In hindsight, we know that without artificial refrigeration and an understanding of sanitation, summer beer would have been prone to contamination by souring bacteria, wild yeast, and other nasties that thrive at elevated temperatures. Winter beer would have been cleaner. The reason for this dichotomy remained elusive to sixteenth-century brewers, but that didn't stop Bavarian nobility from doing something about it.

We human beings have a history of banning that which we do not understand. Thus, the solution to bad summer beer came in 1553, when Duke Albrecht V, son of and successor to Wilhelm IV, simply outlawed brewing altogether from April 23 to September 29, which is to say

OPPOSITE: Duke Albrecht V of Bavaria.

between the Feasts of St. George and St. Michael. All brewing would now have to take place from early autumn to early spring. Simple as that.

This Bavarian ban on summer brewing would remain in effect for nearly three centuries. The unintended consequences of this decree have had a far greater effect on the world of beer than the Reinheitsgebot. By prohibiting the brewing of beer in summer, Albrecht unknowingly propelled the brewers of Bavaria along a path that would cultivate the most popular family of beers in the world today.

LAGER IS BORN

Ales ferment at relatively warm temperatures, typically in the range of 60 to 72°F (16 to 22°C), what we would today call room temperature, or slightly cooler. Ale yeast, *S. cerevisiae*, has been selectively pressured over millennia to thrive at such temperatures. In fact, *S. cerevisiae* can work in much warmer environments, as it often does in the rising of bread dough. But hot fermentation of grain-based wort—above 75°F (24°C) for most strains—coaxes flavors from the yeast that most beer consumers consider unpleasant, not to mention hangover inducing.

A different species of yeast altogether, however, is responsible for the fermentation of lager beers. Like ale yeast, lager yeast, or *S. pastorianus*, can tolerate warm temperatures. But it also has a unique ability to work in environments much colder than *S. cerevisiae*, near the freezing point of water in some cases. We now know that *S. pastorianus* is a hybrid of the species *S. cerevisiae* and *Saccharomyces eubayanus*, a yeast that was only recently discovered in Patagonia, though studies suggest it may have origins in what is now Tibet.

Why does fermentation temperature matter? There are a couple of reasons.

First, yeast production of flavor and aroma compounds largely depends on the temperature at which fermentation takes place. The warmer the fermentation, the more likely it is that yeasts will produce fruity esters, spicy phenols, and solvent-like fusel alcohols in their metabolism of sugar into ethanol and carbon dioxide. Lager fermentation typically occurs at temperatures below that at which such compounds are created in appreciable concentrations. For this reason lagers are often described as clean—yeast expression is minimized, allowing the natural flavors and aromas of malt and hops to dominate.

Sixteenth-century glass from Bohemia or Saxony.

Second, the environment in which lager yeasts ferment wort into beer is usually cold enough that other microbes either become incredibly sluggish or go dormant altogether. Ale yeast activity drops off dramatically at lager temperatures, but more importantly, spoiling bacteria like *Lactobacillus*, *Pediococcus*, and *Acetobacter*, and wild yeasts like *Brettanomyces*, simply don't thrive. A cold environment slows spoilage, a basic tenet of modern refrigeration.

Lager yeast, however, is all too happy to continue working in the cold, and once it takes hold and has outcompeted other species for nutritional resources, it's unlikely that the resulting beer will spoil, as long as it remains sufficiently cold. Including hops in the recipe, which had been codified into law by Wilhelm IV, provided additional antibacterial protection.

Winter beer had staying power and could successfully be stored in cool caves and cellars all summer long.

When Duke Albrecht V prohibited Bavarian brewers from making beer in the summer, he unintentionally forced them into placing selective pressure upon the microbes with which they fermented beer. Prior to 1553, Bavarian beer could have been divided into two broad categories:

- Summer beers would have been the product of mixed fermentation, which would have included multiple strains of *Saccharomyces*, *Brettanomyces*, *Lactobacillus*, *Pediococcus*, *Acetobacter*, and other microbes that thrive in mild to warm temperatures.
- Winter beers would have primarily been the product of *S. pastorianus*. Other microorganisms would certainly have been present, but cold fermentation would have limited their activity.

While the rest of Europe continued brewing ales, Albrecht's summer brewing prohibition favored the brewing of lager in Bavaria. This would have tremendous consequences for the world of beer, for it created an entire class of beer styles that would find tremendous popularity worldwide.

There's no reason that the great brewing traditions of the British Isles or of Belgium could not have taken off the way that lager did. But as we will see, empire, immigration, technology, and historical timing made all the difference.

HISTORICAL AND CULTURAL IMPLICATIONS

Once Bavarian brewers realized that cold fermentation was the key to reliably brewing quality beer, it was only a matter of time before lager cemented itself in the culture of southern Germany. Visitors to Germany today might be surprised to learn that two of the country's most venerable institutions owe their very existence to the development of lager beer and the sixteenth-century prohibition on summer brewing.

The Biergarten

A hallmark of lager is the long period of post-fermentation cold cellaring, during which the beer stabilizes, matures, and clarifies. As mentioned earlier, the very word *lager* comes from the German *lagern*, meaning "to store." Cold storage may have developed, in part, because warming the beer would have meant potential contamination by souring bacteria and wild yeast. Keeping the beer cold increased its shelf life, just as it does today.

Because brewing was outlawed in summer, brewers scrambled in late spring to have beer available during the warmer months to follow. To solve the issue of keeping beer cold even as ambient temperatures rose, breweries excavated vast underground cellars in which to store barrels of beer. Yet Munich's water table lies near enough to ground level—only about thirteen feet (four meters) down—that cellars could only be sunk so deep.

As a solution, breweries dug relatively shallow cellars and compensated for their diminutive depth by extending them above ground and covering the structural framework with dirt and gravel. Planting a few chestnut trees shaded the space and shielded the beer below from the direct heat of the sun, even at the height of summer. Before long, these shady, leafy gardens became gathering places for the public, and it didn't take much imagination to start tapping the

Beer garden at Hausbrauerei Feierling in Freiburg im Breisgau, Germany.

underground beer and enjoying it in situ rather than take it home.

Thus was born the *Biergarten*. To say that Munich wouldn't be the same without it would be an understatement of the most egregious nature. According to one reference, the modern city is home to no fewer than one hundred of these outdoor pubs, with the largest, the Königlicher Hirschgarten, able to accommodate eight thousand guests at once.

Oktoberfest

Brewers didn't just have to stock up for the summer, though. Even when normal operations could resume after the Feast of St. Michael in September, weeks would pass before the citizens of Munich could enjoy the latest beer releases. Thus, brewers concocted special spring batches to be stored all summer long and consumed as autumn fell. Because alcohol is a natural preservative, these beers were brewed to a higher strength so that they would remain potable come September.

This March beer, or *märzenbier*, lagered beneath the Biergartens all summer, and tapping these special kegs most certainly would have called for a celebration, or so the legend goes. The modern oktoberfest as we know it dates only to 1810, when a public party was organized to celebrate the marriage of Crown Prince Ludwig to Princess Therese of Sachsen-Hildburghausen. However, it is likely that autumnal festivals were already part of daily life and that the grand celebration was simply a larger-than-life take on an established institution.

All these events in sixteenth-century Bavaria set in motion a fermented rift between southern Germany and the rest of northern Europe. (Southern Europe continued to favor wine, heathens that they were.) While the British, the Belgians, and even the northern Germans would continue to brew ales, brewers in the foothills of the Alps would forever favor cold-fermented lagers. Once modern science and technology figured out what was going on in those frigid caves, the world of beer would never be the same.

Oktoberfest parade in Munich.

BAVARIAN BEER NOSH

The Theresienwiese is the kidney-shaped fairground in the center of Munich where Oktoberfest revelers down liters of lager within cavernous-yet-cozy beer tents. Called the Wiesn in the local Bavarian dialect, "Therese's meadow" is the very same spot upon which Princess Therese's wedding in 1810 started the beer festival that continues today.

While hefty mugs of festival-strength helles are the event's main attraction, even the sturdiest Bavarian will eventually clamor for something with which to soak up all the hops and malt. Here are a few sure bets.

- **SCHWEINSHAXN:** Roasted pork knuckle is the quintessential Oktoberfest treat. Don't knock it till you've tried it (and after a few liters of helles, you probably will).

- **HENDL:** If pork isn't your thing (or knuckles, for that matter), dig into a whole spit-roasted chicken instead. Picking apart a chicken while swigging a tankard of beer offers the festive cheer of a medieval European party without the threat of smallpox.

- **KNÖDEL:** Giant dumplings are just the thing for soaking up the sauce from your choice of roasted meat. They also stick to the roof of the mouth in a not-unpleasant fashion.

- **OBATZDA:** This luscious mélange of Camembert, butter, paprika, and beer is conveniently spread on rye bread or scooped up with radish slices. It's health food, Bavarian-style.

- **BREZELN:** Bavarian pretzels are deservedly famous, and the varieties on offer at the Munich Oktoberfest are famously large. They deliver valuable salt to help you maintain your thirst, which in turn helps you part with your Euros.

- **LEBKUCHENHERZEN:** Giant gingerbread hearts are conveniently strung around the neck and usually embossed with frosted messages of love. You're meant to give them to your sweetheart, but nobody will judge you for snapping off bites here and there. (Nobody except your sweetheart, of course.)

OPPOSITE: A liter of Bavarian helles is the perfect pairing for hearty Bavarian fare.

CHAPTER 3

BREWERS SEE THE LIGHT

Beer changed forever on November 11, 1842.

In the small town of Plzeň, in what is now the Czech Republic, on what is now Armistice Day, the local citizens' brewery tapped a beer. Had you been a thirsty Bohemian or Bavarian in those days, you probably would have expected a brown liquid—perhaps drinkable, perhaps not. The beer that had been brewed just five weeks prior might not have arrived with much fanfare.

But what emerged from that brewery in the autumn of 1842 was unlike anything the world had ever seen. Fizzy yellow lager had arrived.

Weyermann® Specialty Malts Josef Groll Pilsner 1842 (see recipe page 203).

DARK DAYS IN BAVARIA

Lager fermentation had probably been practiced in Bavaria for some time before Duke Albrecht's summer brewing prohibition in 1553. Some historians posit that the Czechs had originally developed the lager technique and taught the Bavarians how to do it sometime in the fifteenth century. But without an understanding of microbiology, promoting lager at the expense of ale required favorable circumstances. The ban on summer brewing and the increasingly frigid grip of the Little Ice Age supplied just that.

For the next three centuries, brewers in Bavaria unknowingly skewed their house yeast cultures toward *S. pastorianus*. Generation after generation of repitched lager yeast outcompeted ale yeast, wild yeast, and souring bacteria for nutritional resources just a little more each time. Fermenters and aging casks still harbored other bugs, of course, but brewing and aging beer in the cold ensured that *S. pastorianus* was given the competitive advantage it needed to thrive.

In the beginning, all lagers—all beers, for that matter—were dark because brewers couldn't create pale malts with the technologies available to them. Munich dunkel, which remains a widely consumed favorite in Bavaria and around the globe, would have been about as pale a beer as brewers could envision. Furthermore, it's likely that medieval drinkers would have been accustomed to discerning at least some smoky aspects in many, if not most, beers because wood fire was the state-of-the-art heat source for drying malt.[1]

Meanwhile, brewers up north, free to carry on without seasonal restrictions imposed by Bavarian dukes, continued brewing ale. The cities of Düsseldorf and Köln (Cologne) would carry this ale tradition forward, eventually giving us *altbier* and *kölsch*, respectively. And brewers in the town of Einbeck, located two-thirds the way from Munich to the North Sea, made a strong ale that gained quite a following in Bavaria.

Thanks to a unique system in which citizens could only brew with city-owned equipment and under the oversight of a licensed city official, beer from Einbeck enjoyed an excellent reputation. At the Diet of Worms in 1521, Martin Luther himself is said to have exclaimed, upon receiving a glass from Duke Erich, "Der beste Trank, den einer kennt, der wird Einbecker Bier genennt." (The best drink known to anyone is called Einbecker beer.) The claim may or may not be true, but the Einbecker brewery continues to capitalize on Luther's alleged statement to this day.

Wealthy Bavarians in the sixteenth and seventeenth centuries were all too eager to import beer from Einbeck for their own personal enjoyment. They favored the beer so much, in fact, that Duke Wilhelm V (and later, his son, Maximilian I) found sales of the popular beverage siphoning away revenue that otherwise would have gone to their own state brewery, the Staatliches Hofbräuhaus.

Thus, in 1612, Maximilian convinced an Einbeck brewer named Elias Pichler to join the Hofbräuhaus in Munich and brew a homegrown Einbeck-style beer for the city's people. While the original from Einbeck had been brewed as an ale, Bavaria's position as a crucible for cold fermentation transformed the southern German into a lager. As the story goes, the local dialect corrupted the name of the beer from *Ainpöckisch* to *ain Pock*, which then transformed into *ein Bock*. That *bock* also happens to mean "goat" in German has made the beer's name the subject of visual puns on bottle labels ever since.

A century and a half later, around the same time that Britain was imposing the Intolerable Acts upon thirteen of its North American colonies, Benedictine monks of the order of St. Francis of Paola near Munich brewed the world's first doppelbock. A Bavarian original, doppelbock became the strong liquid bread the Paulaner monks needed to make it through Lent. The beer continues to be known as Salvator today.

Doppelbock's invention in 1774 could very well have represented the ultimate triumph of Bavarian lager. But, the victory was to be short-lived thanks to developments 140 miles (220 km) to the northeast.

MALTED ENLIGHTENMENT

Plzeň is a city of one hundred seventy thousand inhabitants located about two-thirds the distance from Nürnberg to Prague. Historically speaking, it lies within the region known as Bohemia, which along with Moravia and Czech Silesia, comprise what we now call the Czech Republic. From 1526 to 1918, the Habsburg dynasty ruled Bohemia, which meant that German, not Czech, was the official language for several centuries.

Beer had been brewed in Plzeň for ages, going back at least to 1295 when Wenceslaus II, King of Bohemia founded the city and granted its citizens the right to brew and sell beer. Records from as far back as 1307 indicate the presence of a central brewery in the town, which ought to have offered a significant improvement over homebrewed concoctions. As in other parts of central Europe, brewers in the city formed guilds charged with protecting their crafts.

Bust of Josef Groll outside city hall in Vilshofen an der Donau.

By the end of the eighteenth century, Plzeň enjoyed an enviable reputation as a center for brewing, as did all of Bohemia. In fact, a Czech brewer named František Ondřej Poupě (1753–1805) is often credited as the first brewer to have used a thermometer. A technical approach improved things in general, but brewers in Plzeň, like brewers everywhere, continued to have their ups and downs.

A particularly bad down in the mid-nineteenth century proved pivotal. Although technological developments and an increasingly scientific approach had improved the quality of the local brew, the town brewery still delivered inconsistent results. In 1838, such inconsistency culminated in the city's brewers' declaring thirty-six barrels of beer undrinkable before unceremoniously dumping them right in the town square. Something had to be done, so they did what all fledgling concerns do just before they go under: they hired a consultant.

Josef Groll was, by most accounts, a miserable man. He was variously described as "coarse" and "having no manners," and even his own father called him "the rudest man in Bavaria." But he must have been one heck of a brewer because, at the ripe young age of twenty-nine, Groll was invited to leave Bavaria for Plzeň (presumably to the delight of Bavarians). His new role? To serve as head brewer

for a new, state-of-the-art brewery intended to return the city to its former brewing glory.

Groll's new position placed him within reach of the finest raw materials for brewing. Moravian barley was then, and remains today, some of the best in the world. Locally grown hops known as Žatec in Czech, or *Saaz* in German, with their earthy, spicy flavor and aroma, were part of a Continental dynasty that continues to be known as the noble hops. The yeast, it is said, had been smuggled in by a monk from Bavaria a couple of years prior.

Perhaps most critically, the water in Plzeň was soft. With a hardness of less than 50 parts per million dissolved solids, it was about as close as one could get to distilled water straight from the ground. Such water is ideal for brewing a pale beer with lots of hops because certain ions—sulfate, for example—accentuate hop character. Using the soft water in Plzeň, Josef could pack more hops into his beer than would have been possible in areas with harder water.

The beer Groll delivered to the citizens of Plzeň on November 11, 1842, was satisfyingly malty with a delicate caramel sweetness. It was delightfully hop-forward, with a slightly spicy aspect. It was crystal clear. Above all, it was *pale*. The people of Plzeň—Pilsen in German and English—couldn't have known it at the time, but their new golden lager, pilsner, would go on to inspire more than 95 percent of the beer consumed worldwide.

In German, the word *Pilsner* simply means someone or something from the city of Pilsen, just as Münchners are from Munich, Hamburgers are from Hamburg, and Wieners are from Wien (Vienna). The popularity of the new lager from Pilsen spread so quickly that brewers worldwide started using the term *pilsner* to describe

Entrance to the Plzeňský Prazdroj (Pilsner Urquell) brewery in Plzeň, Czech Republic.

their own interpretations of the style. The word ultimately became a generic trademark that refers to any pale lager, which is how Miller Lite gets away with calling itself a "fine pilsner beer" despite bearing no resemblance to the original.

Pilsner was by no means the world's first lager. As we have seen, Bavarian brewers had been brewing lagers since at least the summer prohibition of 1553, probably even earlier. But those lagers had been dark. What emerged in Plzeň was light. In fact, it was so light that nothing quite like it had been seen before on the Continent, though light-colored malt had, by the mid-1800s, become all the rage in England.

The very lightly kilned malt we today call pilsner malt was itself a direct product not of German or Czech ingenuity, but of the British Industrial Revolution. In his excellent book *IPA*, Mitch Steele describes how pilsner malt came about thanks to "an apparent industrial espionage mission by Czech brewers into England's best malthouses. The malt used to brew the very first batch of Pilsner Urquell was kilned in an English kiln that had been sent to what is today the Czech Republic."

The English, you see, had been developing ever-lighter malts, which eventually culminated in the so-called "Burton white malt" that brewers in Burton-upon-Trent favored for some of the very first India pale ales. Remember, in 1842, the British were on the cusp of establishing direct rule in India. And whatever mysteries remain in the history of the IPA, there's no denying the association between British India and pale ale brewed in Burton.

The popularity of the new pilsner beer quickly spread beyond Bohemia. Within two decades of its birth, it was being shipped to thirsty drinkers around the world. And if imitation is the sincerest form of flattery, then pilsner would go on to become the most flattered beer in history.

The citizens' brewery would have been known in Czech as the Měšťanský pivovar Plzeň, but because German was the official language, it was called the Bürgerliches Bräuhaus instead. And the beer? In Czech, it is Plzeňský Prazdroj, "pilsner from the original source," better known by its German name: Pilsner Urquell.

In the mid to late nineteenth century, the new beer from Plzeň became all the rage in Europe, and Bavarian brewers wanted in. Gabriel Sedlmayr of Munich's Spaten brewery and Anton Dreher of the Klein-Schwechat brewery near Vienna had already been working on lightening up their own brews, and in 1833 they paid a visit to England to learn from British

Fun Fact

Today, Pilsner Urquell claims to brew its famous beer according to Josef Groll's original recipe from 1842. And while some things have changed—notably its corporate ownership—it remains a defining example of Czech pilsner style and a modern classic. Recent improvements to packaging and shipping (including the use of brown bottles and opaque cartons) have better protected the iconic lager in its transatlantic travels, and we can only hope that it successfully weathers future mergers and acquisitions just as well.

Devil's Backbone Brewing Company Vienna Lager (see recipe page 204).

Munich's Spaten brewery played a pivotal role in the development of modern lager beer styles in the nineteenth century and remains an important part of today's Oktoberfest.

brewmasters' most recent innovations. Of particular interest to the two Continental brewers was the new ultra-pale malt made possible by advances in malting and kilning technology.

Returning to Munich and Vienna, respectively, Sedlmayr and Dreher set out to implement what they had learned in England, applying new Industrial Revolution kilning techniques to the Continent's darker malts. Thus were born what we still today call Munich and Vienna malts, which became the basis for modern Munich dunkel and Vienna lager.

Munich dunkel and Vienna lager got a bit lighter, but they remained, at their core, dark European lagers by today's standards. Always looking for the next great thing, however, Sedlmayr set his sights on an even lighter beer style and in 1841 developed an amber lager. Brewed in March and conditioned in cold cellars all summer long, the beer was known as

märzenbier, or March beer and released at the 1841 Oktoberfest, where it took the place of the standard dunkel that had been the customary tipple.

Sedlmayr and Dreher took measured approaches, making ever-lighter beer using the technology of the day. But the introduction of the pale lager from Bohemia caught them off guard. In Munich in particular, local brewers had long operated with virtually no threat from brewers beyond the region's borders. They were, after all, masters of the craft.

Pilsner was different. Pilsner was new. It was refreshing, hoppy, and flavorful. And it looked damn good in the increasingly affordable glassware of the day (traditionally, Bavarian beers had been consumed in stoneware mugs that effectively hid the clarity and color of the beer within). Drinkers in southern Germany were clamoring for the new brew, and Munich's brewers had no choice but to respond with their own pale lagers.

In 1872, the Franziskaner-Leist brewery, which happened to be run by Gabriel Sedlmayr's younger brother Josef, reformulated the märzen style to take advantage of ever-lighter malt.

fun fact

Calling it *ur-märzen*, meaning "original March beer," he followed the tradition of brewing in March and released it at the Munich Oktoberfest that autumn, presumably to much acclaim, for it survives today as Spaten Oktoberfest, still brewed using the original recipe from 1872. The close association between märzen and the Munich Oktoberfest has made *oktoberfest* a synonym for the style, although what is today served at the event is more a high-octane helles than it is a traditional oktoberfest.

Amber lager was an improvement over dark lager, but it still wasn't the pale lager over which consumers had been fawning. More than two decades would pass before the Hacker-Pschorr and Spaten breweries would release their Münchner Gold and Helles LagerBier, respectively, but neither had staying power.

Finally, in 1895, more than half a century after the first pilsner appeared in Bohemia, Munich would finally have its own pale lager: Munich helles. It happened at Spaten, under the guidance of Gabriel Sedlmayr's sons Anton, Johann, and Carl. In 1894, they tested a batch on the citizens of Hamburg. Apparently, the Hamburgers rather liked it,[2] and on June 20, 1895, the people of Munich got their first taste. Similar in appearance to pilsner, helles, which simply means "light in color," delivered a softer, rounder glass of beer. The water in Munich could not support the same high levels of hops as Plzeň's water, so the Bavarian interpretation became more malt-focused and milder than pilsner.

Although Munich's association of brewers initially resisted helles (they insisted that the future of beer would remain dark), they eventually succumbed to public pressure, and the triumph of light lager in Bavaria was assured. Today, helles remains the daily session beer of the Bavarians, and it is traditionally served by the liter in a large dimpled mug called a *Maßkrug*.[3]

Louis Pasteur, ca. 1870.

Carl von Linde, ca. 1880.

SCIENTIFIC AND TECHNOLOGICAL ENLIGHTENMENT

By the nineteenth century, lager brewing had become commonplace in Europe, fueled in part by consumer preference, but also by the accomplishments of science and the Industrial Revolution. Riding the waves of the Enlightenment, intellectuals and industrialists created a favorable climate in which lager beer could reach its full potential. And brewers used these developments to improve the quality, efficiency, and cost of brewing.

Brewers had come to understand that yeast was associated with the transformation of wort into beer, even though the evidence was purely empirical. Until science demonstrated otherwise, early brewers considered yeast a byproduct of fermentation rather than the driving force behind it, a chemical that precipitated out of solution as part of the process. The dominant theory of life had been one of spontaneous generation, in which life forms simply emerged. Only with the birth of microbiology could brewers finally bring lager to its triumphant conclusion as the world's dominant family of beer styles.

Late in the seventeenth century, Dutch scientist Anton van Leeuwenhoek had laid human eyes on yeast cells with the aid of the first modern microscope. Scientists and brewers gradually came to recognize that these miniscule entities (it took some time before they were identified as organisms) were responsible for the magic of fermentation, but an adequate scientific understanding didn't arrive until the late 1800s. In 1876, Louis Pasteur published his now famous *Études sur la Bière* (*Studies on Beer*), in which he demonstrated that yeast cells weren't a product of fermentation but rather the very engine that drove it.

Perhaps even more importantly, Pasteur showed that other microbes—bacteria—eventually led to the spoilage of beer in the form of souring. Heating beer above a certain temperature killed the microorganisms contained within (including brewer's yeast), yielding a product with

PATENT-URKUNDE

№ 1250

AUF GRUND DER ANGEHEFTETEN BESCHREIBUNG UND ZEICHNUNG IST
DURCH BESCHLUSS DES KAISERLICHEN PATENTAMTES

Professor Carl Linde, in München

EIN PATENT ERTHEILT WORDEN.

GEGENSTAND DES PATENTES IST:

Kälteerzeugungsmaschine.

ANFANG DES PATENTES: *9. August 1877.*

LÄNGSTE DAUER DES PATENTES: *24. Maerz 1891.*

DIE RECHTE UND PFLICHTEN DES PATENT-INHABERS SIND DURCH DAS PATENT-GESETZ
VOM 25. MAI 1877 (REICHSGESETZBLATT FÜR 1877 SEITE 501) BESTIMMT.

ZU URKUND DER ERTHEILUNG DES PATENTES IST DIESE AUSFERTIGUNG
ERFOLGT.

Berlin, den 29. Mai 1878.

KAISERLICHES PATENTAMT.

Beglaubigt durch *Schott*

Sekretär des Kaiserlichen Patentamtes.

GESETZ v. 25. MAI 1877

improved stability and a longer life. This discovery would revolutionize the way brewers make and deliver beer. It was so fundamental, so important, that the process—pasteurization—bears his name today.

Pasteurization wasn't to be Louis's only namesake; lager yeast itself would eventually come to be known as *S. pastorianus*, named for the man whose research made possible the isolation and deliberate, intentional manipulation of yeast. However, lager yeast has historically gone by a handful of names, which seems fitting given the difficulty scientists have had in classifying it. One of those names hints at a further twist in the story of lager.

In 1847, a Danish man by the quintessentially Danish name of Jacob Christian Jacobsen founded the Carlsberg brewery in Copenhagen. In 1875, Jacobsen established the world's very first brewing science laboratory at Carlsberg, where a scientist named Emil Hansen spent several years conducting fermentation experiments with the brewery's house yeast culture. In 1883, Hansen successfully isolated a pure yeast cell from which an entire colony could be propagated. Thus was born the world's first monoculture yeast strain.

That yeast, which Hansen named *Saccharomyces carlsbergensis*, would turn out to be the very same lager yeast that scientists had previously termed *S. pastorianus*. Today, they are considered one and the same. The name *S. carlsbergensis* still shows up with regular frequency, especially in brewing literature, but *S. pastorianus* is now the preferred taxonomic nomenclature.[4]

Interestingly, when Carlsberg first opened its doors, Jacob Christian Jacobsen had obtained his initial culture of yeast from none other than Gabriel Sedlmayr of Munich's Spaten brewery. Speaking of Spaten, back in Bavaria, one Carl von Linde was busy developing a technology that promised to allow year-round production of lager beer. When the Bavarian prohibition on summer beer brewing was finally lifted in 1850, it was because brewers had become adept at cutting large blocks of ice from frozen lakes and using them to keep caves and cellars cool throughout the summer. The process, as one might imagine, involved a great deal of labor and had to be repeated every winter.

Linde's invention, artificial refrigeration, was developed specifically to allow brewers at Spaten to brew throughout the year without the need for large quantities of ice. His original design, based on dimethyl ether, was soon supplanted by an updated version built around the compression and expansion of ammonia. Thus, we have lager beer to thank, not just for pasteurization but also for refrigeration—two technologies without which modern life would be unthinkable.

Pure yeast culture propagation, pasteurization, and artificial refrigeration became key enabling technologies that would allow lager to take the world by storm. No longer were frigid caves in the foothills of the Alps necessary to produce pale lager. Now brewers worldwide could brew cold, refreshing beer regardless of climate. From New York and California to Mexico and Tokyo, things were just heating up. (Or, more accurately, cooling down.)

OPPOSITE: Imperial patent for the first refrigeration machine, 1877.

4

THE LAGER DIASPORA

Canceled flights. Railway strikes. Closed roads. Travelers can't count on much. But no matter where you are in the world—airport bar, hotel lobby, or railway minibar—a thirsty voyager can always find a pale lager. It might not be the best beer you've ever had, but it might be the best beer you can have right now.

Thanks to technological developments, fueled in part by the same Industrial Revolution that had made modern lager possible, people became increasingly mobile in the latter half of the nineteenth century. As immigrants and empires spread citizens further from home, their beer went with them. And with pilsner having just taken Europe by storm, the beer they carried with them was often a pale lager that imitated the original.

From 1820 to 1920, more than seven million Germans made their way to the United States. With political unrest sweeping through the Habsburg-controlled Austrian Empire, Czech immigrants fled their homeland in increasing numbers starting in 1848, and by World War I, more than three hundred thousand had found new homes in America.

Yamanote-Sen, a Japanese-style rice adjunct pale lager (see recipe page 205).

Friedrich Pabst (left) and Frederick Miller (born Friedrich Müller), German immigrants and American lager brewers.

European immigrants brought with them a love of lager beer and the technical knowledge needed to brew it. Their surnames form a who's-who of American brewing: Anheuser, Busch, Jüngling, Kuhrs, Müller, Pabst, and Schlitz. Immigrant German brewers became such a fixture of American life that the Master Brewers Association of the Americas, founded in 1887, initially conducted meetings, published materials, and printed brewing certificates in German. German beer barons transformed the United States from an ale republic to a land of lager.

Revolution in Europe also sent German, Austrian, Swiss, and Czech immigrants across the globe to Argentina, Australia, Brazil, Canada, Chile, New Zealand, and Venezuela. Following the 1871 unification of Germany, the Second German Empire's last-ditch attempt to become a colonial power saw Germans landing in Namibia, Cameroon, Samoa, and New Guinea. The lager diaspora established new breweries where they could and imported Continental beer where they couldn't.

Meanwhile, the French invaded Mexico in 1861 and installed Maximilian I of Austria, a Habsburg, as emperor. His rule lasted just three years, but his brewers traveled everywhere he did and left an indelible mark on the country. Maximilian's brief reign gave Mexican beer an Austrian accent and helped preserve a beer style that might otherwise have been lost.

The movement of people—voluntary and forced—that took place from the beginning of the nineteenth century to World War I firmly cemented, for most citizens of the planet, lager's place as the definition of the word *beer*.

LAGER REACHES AMERICA

Until the mid-nineteenth century, beer in the United States had always meant ale. The thirteen original colonies were firmly rooted in the English tradition, which had remained one of ale, even as most of Continental Europe adopted lager-brewing methods. We still have the recipe for George Washington's homebrew, the charming description of which is perhaps more compelling than the resulting flavor:

TO MAKE SMALL BEER

Take a large Sifter full of Bran Hops to your Taste. — Boil these 3 hours. Then strain out 30 Gallons into a Cooler, put in 3 Gallons Molasses while the Beer is scalding hot or rather drain the molasses into the Cooler & strain the Beer on it while boiling Hot. Let this stand till it is little more than Blood warm. Then put in a quart of Yeast if the weather is very cold, cover it over with a Blanket & let it work in the Cooler 24 hours. Then put it into the Cask — leave the Bung[hole] open till it is almost done working — Bottle it that day Week [sic] it was Brewed.[1]

Ale, however, never really quite caught on in America the way it had in Britain. For one thing, America's summers have historically been much hotter than those of the British Isles. A pint of ale that might seem perfectly refreshing on a 75°F (24°C) rainy afternoon fails to quench the thirst when the mercury approaches 100°F (38°C).

Americans also had a penchant for distilled spirits, beginning with rum, which was readily available and affordable during colonial times. After the country won its independence from Great Britain, increasing restrictions on sugar, as well as an end to the importation of African slaves in 1808, pushed American preferences away from rum and toward whiskey. The graph below illustrates data published in *The Alcoholic Republic: An American Tradition* by W. J. Rorabaugh and suggest that whiskey, not beer, was the libation of choice until the middle of the nineteenth century, which is when lager began appearing in the United States.

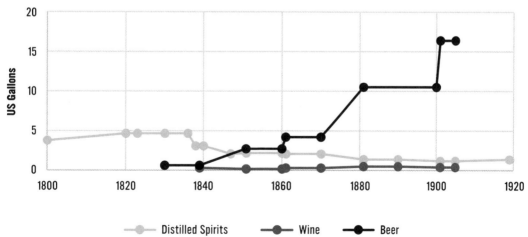

US PER CAPITA CONSUMPTION OF ALCOHOLIC BEVERAGES

ABOVE: Lager propaganda, Mensing & Stecher, lithographers, ca. 1879.

OPPOSITE: Schlitz Brewing Company lithograph, ca. 1888.

Waves of Europeans, mostly from Germany, Ireland, and Britain, began immigrating to the United States in the mid-1800s as part of the second great wave of immigrants coming to the country. An important member of the first wave was David Gottlieb Jüngling, whose name was anglicized to Yuengling upon his arrival in the United States. Originally from the German state of Württemberg, David settled in Pottsville, Pennsylvania, where he established America's oldest continuously operating brewery, D. G. Yuengling & Son, in 1829.

Originally called the Eagle Brewery, David began not with German lagers but with British-style ales. His brewery catered to the numerous workers who immigrated to eastern Pennsylvania to work the anthracite coalmines, and by 1877, it had become America's eighteenth largest brewery. Immigrants like Yuengling came for many reasons: to escape famine, to work in mines, to build railroads, and to farm the land, among others. But many were looking to escape political upheaval in Europe. Among them were the so-called "Forty-Eighters" who fled the instability of revolution and revolt at home in 1848.

One such Forty-Eighter was Charles Bierbauer, who was born in Einselthum, Bavaria, in 1819 and studied brewing in Munich and Vienna before coming to New York in 1848. In 1850, he moved to Utica, where he opened a brewery and introduced the Mohawk Valley to lager beer

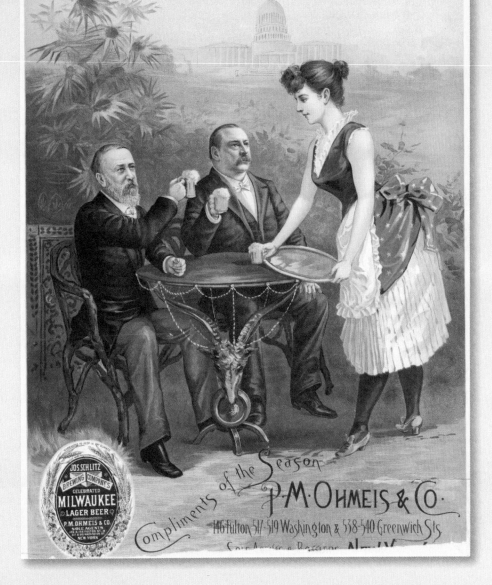

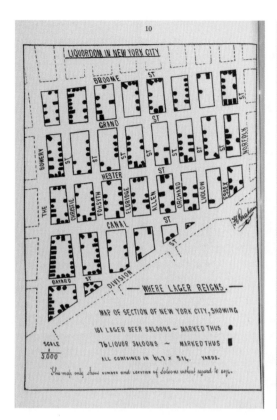
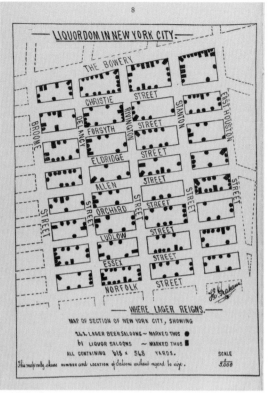

1883 maps locating "lager beer saloons" and "liquor saloons" in Manhattan.

for the first time. According to Daniel Shumway, author of *Utica Beer: A History of Brewing in the Mohawk Valley*:

> Around Christmas time in 1850, he offered for sale the first glass of lager beer ever brewed in Utica. Prior to this time, all the breweries in Utica had brewed ale exclusively. When he began brewing in Utica, lager beer was looked at as exclusively a German drink and wasn't very popular. For a long time, he furnished nearly all the lager that was drank in Utica. The quality of his product did much to make this drink popular.[2]

Bierbauer was one of the first brewers of lager in the United States, but he certainly wasn't the first. Historians have generally credited Johann (John) Wagner for having brought lager yeast with him from Bavaria and subsequently brewing the first lager in America in 1840 in Philadelphia.

Not all historians agree on this matter, though. Some claim the honor should go to a brewer named Adam Lemp of Eschwege, Germany, who arrived in St. Louis in 1838. Alexander Strausz and John Klein are sometimes said to have founded a small brewery in Alexandria, Virginia, in 1838, but Strausz, a Hungarian-born immigrant from Germany, didn't even arrive in the United States until 1851. The two did, however, found Shuter's Hill Brewery in Alexandria, but not until 1858. It seems likely that 1858 might have been mistranscribed as 1838 somewhere along the way.

Regardless of whether it was Wagner, Lemp, or a time-traveling Strausz-Klein duo who introduced America to cold-fermented beer, lager had gained a firm foothold in the country by 1850. And it wasn't just plain immigration that helped, but the methods by which those immigrants arrived in America. In *New Orleans Beer: A Hoppy History of Big Easy Brewing*, authors Jeremy Labadie and Argyle Wolf-Knapp note that new shipbuilding technologies played a role:

> Clipper ships were designed to provide speedy transit, and they did. While the 3,804-mile journey from Bremen to New York took ten to fifteen days by paddle wheeler, a clipper could do it in six to seven days with the right winds. One of the byproducts of this reduced transit time was a lower cost of transport, which made the Europe-America trade routes more affordable. Importing lager also brought lager yeast to the New World. With a viable lager yeast culture to work with, lager beer could be made here.[3]

For German immigrants, lager beer offered a way to maintain their heritage and culture in a foreign land. That included not just beer, but also the habits associated with its drinking. Beer gardens became commonplace, and lager saloons cropped up that were emphatically different from the standard watering hole.

Before the arrival of lager, bars in America were there for drinking. Women weren't allowed entry, and certainly not children. The German beer establishment was different. They were places of civilized discourse, where all were welcome. They allowed women and children. You might even have a meal, and many offered free food with the purchase of beer. According to the *New York Times*, the United States was home to an astonishing two hundred fifty thousand lager saloons in 1897.[4] Garrett Peck, in *Capital Beer: A Heady History of Brewing in Washington, D.C.*, emphasizes the ubiquity of the German beer garden in the nation's capital.

> Beer gardens dotted the urban landscape and provided a major outlet for the city's locally brewed beer. Washington was awash in suds, thanks to the soaring popularity of a German invention: lager. Before the invention of air conditioning, people dealt with muggy summers by drinking lager.[5]

Peck notes that much of the lager consumed in Washington, DC, came not just from local brewers but also from national brewing concerns, which used new technologies to send products much further from the point of production than had previously been possible. By the 1880s, it was common to ship beer in refrigerated railroad cars from a brewery to a remote bottling facility. Another enabling technology, pasteurization, gave beer a longer shelf life. Both refrigerated shipping and pasteurization were pioneered at the Anheuser-Busch brewery in St. Louis, which Peck notes, "had its local office at First Street and Virginia Avenue SW, right along the railroad tracks" in Washington, DC.

Anheuser-Busch has its roots in a St. Louis operation called the Bavarian Brewery, which was founded in 1852 by a man named George Schneider. In 1860, following several years of financial difficulties, he sold it to a pair of businessmen, one of whom was a soap baron named Eberhard Anheuser. The name of the brewery was changed to E. Anheuser & Co.

In 1861, German immigrant Adolphus Busch married Lilly Anheuser, Eberhard's daughter, and in 1869, he purchased the half-stake in the company owned by Anheuser's business partner, William O'Dench. The name of the brewery was changed to the Anheuser-Busch

Brewing Association in 1879, and when Eberhard Anheuser died in 1880, Busch became president of the company.

In 1876, Busch introduced Budweiser, named for the Bohemian town of České Budějovice and known as Budweis in German. It was the first beer to be shipped nationally, thanks to the benefits of pasteurization and refrigeration. For the first time in the United States, beer could travel well beyond its point of origin.

We tend to think of the great brewing cities of the Midwest as the crucibles of American lager. But even as far away as Alaska, lager's influence was being felt at this time. According to Bill Howell in *Alaska Beer: Liquid Gold in the Land of the Midnight Sun*, Skagway's City Brewery "had excellent cold storage rooms, which were kept cool using natural ice, and . . . placed great emphasis on utilizing a proper lagering process."[6]

Northwest entrance to the Anheuser–Busch Brewery, Broadway & Pestalozzi, Saint Louis, Missouri, ca. 1933.

Horse-drawn delivery trucks at the Schlitz Brewery in Milwaukee, ca. 1900–1919.

Also in Skagway, Robert Smith and William Matlock opened the Skagway Brewing Company in 1897, which Howell reports held an open house for a thirsty public. Howell says, "their pure, sparkling lager beer . . . was described as 'clear, amber in color with the most delightful sharp taste . . . a perfect beer.'" [7]

Lager even found widespread adoption in the American South, where climatic conditions did not encourage its production. According to Labadie and Wolf-Knapp, the citizens of New Orleans were so fond of lager beer that the Lemp Brewing Co. in St. Louis started shipping its products to New Orleans in the 1850s. They note that the extremes that the beer had to endure caused barrels of beer to freeze in the winter and explode in summer.

Eventually the people of New Orleans got their own lager brewery, but the city's hot climate did nothing to encourage the brewing thereof. Furthermore, the same low elevation that necessitated its building aboveground graveyards and protective levees meant brewers could not rely on the natural cooling properties of belowground storage.

In *Germans of Louisiana*, Ellen Merrill illustrates just how eager brewers were to make lager:

> In 1864 Georg Merz was successful in brewing the first lager beer in the city, which
> he introduced to open his tavern, Erster Felsenkeller. Merz developed this process
> just before the Civil War broke out, which suspended the importation of beer to New
> Orleans. Since cooling was essential to producing lager beer, Merz attempted to ship
> in 'natural' ice from the state of Maine. Because of time and distance, however, the
> ice melted before it arrived at the docks. [8]

Lager brewing became the first industry in the United States to make use of artificial refrigeration, and by the turn of the century, virtually all American breweries had the means to do so. Refrigeration, refrigerated rail cars, pasteurization, and improvements in bottling enabled national distribution and increased competition. That meant finding ways to cut costs, and in many cases, cutting costs meant sourcing less expensive ingredients.

The pale lagers German immigrants brewed in North America shared some common features with the beers of their homelands. But availability of ingredients—and freedom from Reinheitsgebot restrictions—meant modifying those styles to suit local conditions. European and North American barley varieties differ in their composition and suitability for brewing. Most barley from Europe has just two rows of kernels lining the stalk. American-grown barley had six.

The differences in these two kinds of barley have less to do with their structural properties than with their composition. European barley is lower in protein and has less husk material than American barley, which translates to better performance in the brewery. On the other hand, American 6-row is enzymatically quite gifted. In fact, there are enough enzymes in American 6-row to convert not just its own starches to sugars, but those of other grains as well.

German brewers figured out that while America's native 6-row wasn't great for brewing on its own, combining it with another grain could take the edge off 6-row's grainy, husky character. And because 6-row was so rich in enzymes, it was the perfect pairing for unmalted adjuncts like rice and corn. This realization prompted the creation of two related beer styles that couldn't be more different from one another.

Early formulations were modeled on pilsner itself. Using a blend of 6-row American barley malt and indigenous maize (corn), brewers arrived at a grist that delivered a creamy mouthfeel and pleasant (if slightly corny) flavor. North American Cluster hops are considered the classic choice for the style, but we know from early ads that brewers extolled the virtues of a number of European varieties as well, including Saaz, which was mentioned specifically on early labels for Budweiser.

Classic American pilsner is a full-flavored beer style that can be every bit as satisfying as the original from Pilsen. But that's not what comes to mind for most consumers who think of "American lager." As we'll see in the following chapter, pressures of war and the temperance movement conspired, along with a widespread preference for increasingly lighter beer, to make American lager something else entirely.

In the coming years, American lager breweries would prosper, and American beer consumption would increase with seemingly no end in sight. Beer barons like Busch and Yuengling became household names as production increased and distribution expanded.

And what of Charles Bierbauer, who landed in Utica in 1850? His brewery went on to become the West End Brewing Company, which in 1888 became the F. X. Matt Brewing Company. The Matt Brewing Company's Matt's Premium was named Best American Pilsener Lager at the 1985 Great American Beer Festival, and its Saranac Lager took gold in the premium lager category at the 1991 GABF. In 2011, Matt brewed one of the industry's first white IPAs. Today, Matt Brewing Company remains one of the largest craft breweries in the United States.

MEXICO'S AUSTRIAN INFLUENCE

As we saw in Chapter 3, Anton Dreher developed Vienna lager in 1841, and the style flourished in Austria. But, in an interesting historical twist, Vienna lager wouldn't hit its stride until it arrived in Mexico. And one could argue that Mexico safeguarded the style even as ever-lighter lagers like the pilsner in Europe surpassed it.

Mexico fought two wars with France in the nineteenth century. The first, the so-called Pastry War, lasted from November 1838 to March 1839, and was the cumulative result of French expats' claims that they had suffered monetary losses at the hands of looters and vandals in Mexico. A *patissier* named Monsieur Remontel filed a formal complaint with King Louis-Philippe in 1838, saying his pastry shop had been damaged a decade prior, and could the French government kindly demand that he be compensated?

Remontel's was only one such complaint, but it was apparently significant enough that it (1) prompted action by the French and (2) had a war named after it. In November 1838, France blockaded Mexican ports up and down the country's eastern coast and captured the city of Veracruz. Texas, which was a republic at the time, got involved, as did Texas's old archnemesis, the always-entertaining Antonio López de Santa Anna, who had just settled back into civilian life following his fourth Mexican

Maximilian, emperor of Mexico, ca. 1857–1867.

presidency (he would go on to serve another seven). In the battle of Veracruz, Santa Anna lost his left leg, for which he insisted that a full military funeral be held.[3]

The Pastry War officially ended in March 1839, with the help of British negotiators. The peace agreement included a provision that the Mexican government would pay the six hundred thousand pesos that the French had originally demanded.

Mexico was in no better position to pay the crippling sum than it was prior to the Pastry War, and in July 1861, Mexican President Benito Juárez, barely four month into his term, simply stopped paying. In December of the same year, France once again invaded Mexico, this time with the intent to remain. They arrived at Veracruz and made their way inland. The French were briefly stopped in Puebla on May 5, 1862, which is today celebrated as Cinco de Mayo, but the French ultimately prevailed and reached Mexico City on June 7, 1863. On July 10, Mexico was proclaimed an empire and was given to Maximilian I of the Austrian House of Habsburg.

Maximilian arrived in Mexico in May 1864, but his reign was marked by political unrest, and he didn't last long. In May 1867, he was captured and executed, and Benito Juárez returned to power. Maximilian's time was up, but the era of Mexican beer was just beginning. Maximilian had brought his own brewer with him, and a wave of German, Austrian, and Swiss immigrants followed. Lager reached the country in 1869, when Emil Dercher of Alsace opened Brasserie La Cruz Blanca in Mexico City.

But it was an Austrian brewer named Santiago Graf who arguably had the greatest influence on Mexican beer. In 1875 he purchased the Toluca y Mexico brewery, which had been founded ten years earlier by Swiss immigrant Augustine Marendaz. Graf imported European malts and hops, as well as machines for making ice, and his highly regarded Vienna lager soon took the country by storm. Today's Victoria lager can trace its history directly to Graf, whose brewery was acquired by Grupo Modelo in 1935.

Dos Equis Amber, debuted in 1897 at the Moctezuma Brewery, which was founded in Veracruz by a German immigrant named Wilhelm Hasse in 1890. The beer was originally named Siglio XX in celebration of the forthcoming twentieth century, and it's worth noting that the amber Vienna-inspired lager preceded the lighter, international pilsner-style lager so beloved by the Most Interesting Man in the World. Negra Modelo followed in 1925.

The dark lagers of Mexico have drifted further and further from Dreher's original Vienna lager of 1841. Most now incorporate unmalted adjuncts like maize or rice in the grist, and many rely on caramel malts for color and sweetness. But today's dark Mexican lagers have more in common with Vienna lager than today's light Mexican lagers have in common with Czech pilsner. Visitors to Mexico today may not realize that sipping on one of the country's many dark lagers connects them all the way back to 1841 Vienna.

The craft revolution in the United States has made finding a good Vienna lager relatively easy, and one need no longer seek the Mexican imports section to obtain the style. In fact, many North American craft breweries are brewing examples that are likely much closer to the 1841 original.

LAGER AROUND THE WORLD

Migration and the accompanying spread of lager, of course, weren't limited to North America, and lager beer's appeal was sufficiently universal to make it—especially riffs on pilsner—the preferred type of beer around the world. Unfortunately for the citizens of Pilsen, that popularity came so quickly and so overwhelmingly that by the time they appealed to make *pilsner* a protected term, breweries had co-opted it to mean any light lager. Today, the word *pilsner* appears on labels for beers whose only common features are a light hue and lager fermentation.

As lager reached all points of the globe, brewers applied the new technology to their own beers to suit the preferences of their local drinkers and the ingredients available to them. In North America, that meant pairing 6-row malt with maize. In the Baltic states, it meant using cold fermentation to adapt the popularity of strong porters and stouts to the new approach (see accompanying recipe for Smuttynose Baltic Porter on page 214). And in Japan, it meant augmenting base malts with readily available rice.

At the beginning of the twentieth century, lager was poised to dominate world production. And while production would indeed overtake ale globally, two wars and North American experiments in the prohibition of alcohol would reduce many lager styles to thin, insipid beers with virtually nothing in common with the original pilsner.

OPPOSITE: Generic Green Bottle international pale lager (see recipe page 206).

THE DRY SPELL

At the beginning of the twentieth century, all signs pointed
to lager's continued success with America's beer drinkers.
Breweries reached a per-capita saturation that even in today's
thriving beer landscape remains unmatched. At the end of
2016, even with the number of breweries in the United States
surpassing five thousand—an all-time record—there were just
one-sixth as many breweries per capita as had existed in 1873.
Brewing is bigger than it's ever been before, but not when
normalized to population.[1]

We have the twentieth century to blame. American lager
might have survived World War I. It might have persevered after
Prohibition. It might have weathered World War II. American
lager might have endured any one of these events in isolation,
but it could not survive all three. The cumulative effect proved
too much, and when we came out the other side, American
lager had devolved into a thin, watery shell of its former self
brewed by just a handful of gigantic national brewers. Even
before World War I, the brewing industry underwent a period
of consolidation and reduction, but it took two wars and the
temperance movement to finally destroy full-flavored lager in
the United States.

Fort George Brewery 1811 Pre-Prohibition Lager (see recipe page 207).

After Prohibition, the breweries best equipped to return to their former glory (and profitability) were those that had been able to continue operating during the dry spell. Small mom-and-pop breweries had had to shut down completely. But the nation's largest breweries managed to weather the storm by manufacturing and selling other products.

Consolidation in the industry had begun well before the start of World War I and resumed immediately following the passage of the Twenty-First Amendment. That consolidation, along with rationing during World War II, a general consumer shift toward goods seen as technologically novel, and the decreasing availability of previously mainstream lager styles served to lighten the color and body of the lager beer—and by the mid-twentieth century virtually all of it was lager—that America's beer drinkers consumed.

The decades following the end of the Second World War also brought new advertising channels through the increasingly pervasive medium of television. As TV made its way into more and more American households, breweries that could afford to advertise on a regional or even national scale had a convenient platform with which to promote their products right inside the private space of the consumer.

An increasingly bland lager landscape emerged in the latter half of the twentieth century. The 1900s were not kind to lager beer in the United States, and by the time the craft beer renaissance began gaining traction, small brewers would suffer the heavy burden of trying to undo decades of damage.

WORLD WAR I

Readers who were alive and fully sentient when the administration of President George W. Bush attempted to build a coalition to invade Iraq in the aftermath of the September 11, 2001, terrorist attacks on the United States may recall that the coalition did not include France. France was opposed to the war, and with the benefit of hindsight, many of us would agree they were right to object.

French opposition to the war led to some acts of protest in the United States that even at the time seemed ridiculous. The cafeterias of the United States Congress renamed French fries on their menus to "freedom fries." The French's mustard company became sufficiently concerned about backlash that it released a statement reminding consumers that it was, in fact, an American company through and through.

Such proclamations were, of course, reactionary and childish, but students of history recognized that Americans already had a precedent for such silliness. In World War I, anti-German sentiment led manufacturers of sauerkraut in the United States to rename their products "liberty cabbage." The frankfurter, already on the verge of linguistic extinction, finally made the complete and total changeover to the hot dog. And America's great lager-brewing industry, born of German immigrants, was faced with the harsh realities of xenophobia.

Garrett Peck highlights the situation in *Capital Beer*:

> As Congress debated entering the war, a wave of anti-German hysteria swept the country in early 1917, making things difficult for German Americans. Anyone born in Germany was suspected of sedition and/or treason. Wayne Wheeler of the Anti-Saloon League openly insinuated that the brewers were in league with Germany's Kaiser Wilhelm as part of a propaganda war to marginalize German Americans (the

Petition from 1890 demanding that brewers "Give Us Pure Lager Beer."

largest ethnic group in the country in the time, a group that was also the brewers). Drinking beer became unpatriotic despite the fact that it had been the de facto national beverage since the time of the Civil War. The brewers were thrown on the defensive and never recovered.[2]

That's right—drinking German-style lager became an act of betrayal during World War I. That German was the day-to-day language of the early dealings of the Master Brewers Association of the Americas didn't help.

Businesses with German names traded for more American-sounding titles. Schools stopped teaching German as a foreign language. And countless numbers of loyal German-Americans anglicized their names. The effect of anti-German attitudes on lager beer, both that imported from Germany and that produced domestically, was devastating. From 1914 to 1918, the number of breweries in the United States—most of them lager breweries—decreased from 1,392 to 1,092. A year later, in 1919, the number fell even further to a mere 669.

Despite this decrease in the number of breweries, total national beer production continued to climb, as did the average size of the breweries that made it. In 1870, 3,286 breweries produced a total of 6.6 million barrels, a little more than 2,000 barrels per brewery on average. In 1915, 1,345 breweries produced nearly 60 million barrels, a per-brewery average of 44,461 barrels.

It's hard to overstate how much momentum the temperance movement gained from anti-German attitudes. Most breweries in the United States in the years leading up to Prohibition, which also happened to be the years of World War I, were owned and

Detroit police inspect a clandestine underground brewery during Prohibition.

operated by German-Americans. Those who didn't support Prohibition might as well have been supporting the Kaiser directly (a sentiment that would rear its head a century later in George W. Bush's famous "You're either with us or you're with the terrorists" State of the Union line).

After the war ended in 1918, soldiers returned home to a country gripped by temperance. And, for beer in the United States, the darkest days still lay ahead.

PROHIBITION

On January 16, 1919, Nebraska became the thirty-sixth state in the union to ratify the Eighteenth Amendment to the United States Constitution. The text of that amendment is simple enough:

> After one year from the ratification of this article the manufacture, sale, or transportation of intoxicating liquors within, the importation thereof into, or the exportation thereof from the United States and all the territory subject to the jurisdiction thereof for beverage purposes is hereby prohibited.

The Eighteenth Amendment had nothing to say about the logistics of making intoxicating liquors illegal. It didn't say anything about enforcement. It didn't even define what an intoxicating liquor was. Answers to those questions were left to the Volstead Act.

Brewers had initially aligned themselves with the temperance movement and promoted beer as a safe and healthy drink of moderation in comparison to whiskey, gin, rum, and other hard alcohol. Such a stance may or may not have had as much to do with morality and benevolence as it did with gaining a powerful ally that could limit the manufacture of spirits.

It was, of course, a deal with the devil. On January 17, 1920, national Prohibition became the law of the land in the United States, marking the start of a thirteen-year period during which illegal alcohol would propel organized crime to new heights. For breweries, Prohibition presented an important question: How long would this last? Brewers had to wager a bet as to whether the Great Experiment was a new normal here to stay or a flash-in-the-pan blip that would be reversed in good time.

For small breweries with limited means, the decision was simple: they were forced to shut down completely. But larger brewers with more resources survived by applying the methods of the brewhouse to other products. Some continued mashing malt to make wort, which they boiled, concentrated, and sold as malt extract syrup. Consumers could legally purchase that

Franklin D. Roosevelt signs the bill that legalizes beer and marks the beginning of the end for Prohibition. Looking on are, left to right, Rep. Claude V. Parsons of Illinois, Rep. John W. McCormack of Massachusetts, Clerk of Committee H. V. Hesselman, Rep. John J. O'Connor of New York, and Reps. Thos. H. Cullen and Adolph J. Sabath of Illinois, March 22, 1933.

extract, dilute it in municipal water delivered from a completely legal tap, boil it using a legally obtained heat source, and add completely legal yeast to make their own illegal homebrew, though we can't imagine—*cough, cough*—that anyone would actually do such a thing:

> The Volstead Act, the legislation enacted to carry out and enforce the Eighteenth Amendment, did not prohibit the sale of ingredients used in producing alcohol, and the breweries—those that survived, at any rate—took to selling cans of malt extract syrup. Add water and yeast, wait a period of time and the syrup fermented into beer.[3]

Other brewers produced soft drinks, malt products for the baking industry, and so-called "near beer," beverages with an alcohol content south of the 0.5 percent ABV threshold defined as "intoxicating" in the Volstead Act. Importantly, the nation's largest breweries were awarded special permission by the federal government to continue producing normal-strength alcoholic beverages for the medicinal and religious exceptions provided for in the law. During Prohibition, an alarming number of individuals became sick and pious.

Large breweries also diversified their product portfolios to include new bottling technology, as near beer was almost exclusively sold in bottles and not from casks, as beer had been prior to Prohibition. These breweries also invested in automotive technologies, bought delivery vehicles, and solved complex logistical problems related to the distribution of their products. Relieved of the burden of supplying the nation's beer, these breweries were free to prepare for its eventual return.

Of course, we all know how Prohibition eventually turned out. Organized crime proved to be too powerful, and the lost tax revenue too valuable, to make Prohibition sustainable. When the Great Depression hit in 1929, with the nation approximately two-thirds the way through the Great Experiment (though they didn't know that at the time), cries to repeal Prohibition became more urgent. With nearly 15 percent of taxes nationwide having come from alcohol prior to Prohibition, lawmakers knew that a lucrative source of revenue was only a signature away.

On March 22, 1933, President Franklin Delano Roosevelt signed the Cullen-Harrison Act into law, which legalized the sale of beer with an alcohol content of 3.2 percent by weight (about 4 percent by volume). Two days later, the German Reichstag and Reichsrat passed the Enabling Act, an amendment to the constitution of the Weimar Republic that gave Chancellor Adolf Hitler the power to bypass the German parliament and enact laws unilaterally and without regard for the constitution.

WORLD WAR II AND ITS AFTERMATH

Flavorful American beer had already suffered at the hands of one world war and national Prohibition. World War II would effectively be its death knell. Even before the United States formally declared war in 1941, Americans had already become revolted by all things German, and, in a repeat performance of what had happened a quarter-century earlier, German-Americans once again became the targets of anti-German hysteria.

In *Utica Beer*, Shumway notes that "by mid-1940, anti-German sentiment caused West End [the predecessor to Matt Brewing Company] and other brewers to change any brands and

Citizens of Cleveland obtained beer from outside the city after local brewers announced that their beer needed more time to age, April 9, 1933.

advertising that looked or sounded German. West End removed its slogan 'Hopfen und malz got [sic] erhalts' from its products."[4]

World War II saw rationing of countless products and foodstuffs, including those needed to brew beer. Rations were allocated according to size, and large brewers, which generally had the resources to stay afloat, were able to continue operating. Small brewers went out of business. The lagers that large brewers offered during World War II became lighter and lighter, in part due to brewers' attempts to appeal to female factory workers, as Labadie and Wolf-Knapp describe in *New Orleans Beer*. And as breweries increasingly offered the same bland product, price became the biggest differentiator.

> [American adjunct lager] was initially aimed at the female factory worker market in particular, just as filtered cigarettes were. The success of American pilsner was due to market concentration, with most of the big breweries making variants of the same style and little else; lots of advertising; low prices; and a fading demand for older, more full-flavored traditional beers. An unhappy byproduct of this style dominance was fierce competition between makers of similar products, which made price the single most powerful variable for the market. The consolidation of the brewing industry that flowed from that is similar to Microsoft's consolidation of software in more recent times and has deep effects to this day.[5]

After World War II, the largest breweries in the country grew ever larger. Growth and consolidation, along with a public that increasingly preferred processed foods, convenience, and modernity, served to water down and lighten American lager to the point at which it was no longer recognizable as beer. The white sliced bread and TV dinner generation gravitated toward the bland, and large breweries were more than happy to oblige.

As the largest breweries grew, small breweries continued shutting down. After Prohibition and World War II, small and independent breweries in the United States virtually disappeared. In 1945, the Unites States was home to 476 breweries. Ten years later that figure would fall to 239. And by 1965, it would be down to 163. American brewing reached its nadir in 1978, when only 89 breweries remained in a country that had once supported more than 4,000.[6]

Consumers also changed the way they drank their beer. Before Prohibition, most beer was consumed in the neighborhood bar. But after the Great Experiment came to an end, the public drank less often, and when it did drink it preferred to do so in the privacy of the home. Thus, bottling and canning thrived, and big breweries held the upper hand. Packaging equipment is complex and expensive, but large brewers had invested in those technologies during Prohibition. As consumer demand for traditional, full-flavored lagers fell, breweries produced fewer and fewer of them. This made finding a traditional lager ever more difficult, which, in turn, further reduced demand.

When the war finally ended in 1945, Europe and its breweries were devastated. Pearl Harbor notwithstanding, American soil survived unscathed, and the American populace was ready to celebrate. As soldiers returned home from war, bought houses in the suburbs, and made babies, all they really wanted was to relax with a cold, refreshing beer. And a handful of American breweries stood poised to give them just that.

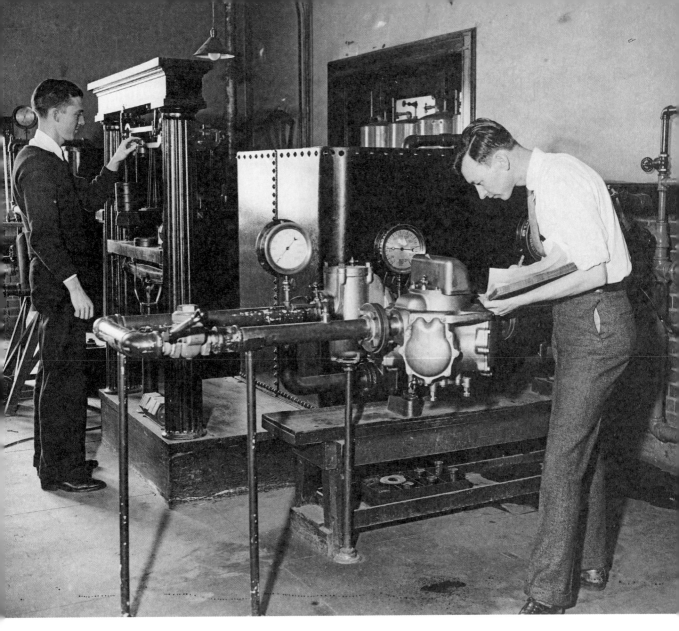

Officials from the National Bureau of Standards calibrate a meter that measures beer volumes for taxation purposes, April 1, 1937.

TASTES . . . GREAT?

In 1967, at New York's Rheingold Brewery, Dr. Joseph Owades invented the product that would come to define American lager at the end of the 1900s. Even today, light lager—light in that orthographically and organoleptcally hideous sense of "lite"—remains the number-one-selling beer style in the United States, despite the continued growth of craft and fuller-flavored beer.

Dr. Owades had been investigating an enzyme that could completely break down malt starches beyond what normal mash enzymes could do. The resulting wort was almost completely fermentable by brewer's yeast, meaning that the final beer would be dry and crisp, with very little residual carbohydrate content.

The beer was a commercial disaster. It was marketed as a "diet" beer with a sort of clinical aura about it. Rheingold ended up giving away the recipe to another brewery that was later acquired by Miller Brewing Company.

In 1973, hoping to cash in on the latest wave of health fads that fitness-obsessed Americans latched onto, Miller launched the beer as Miller Lite. But rather than position it as a beer for those looking to cut calories, it instead associated the world's first commercially successful light beer with professional athletes. Those ads turned Miller Lite into an image and lifestyle product and culminated in the famous "Tastes great, less filling" campaign.

Miller's product took off, and soon many imitators followed. Coors delivered Coors Light in 1978, and Anheuser-Busch, somewhat late to the game, launched its own Bud Light in 1981. Today, Bud Light is the number-one-selling beer brand in the United States and worldwide.

BULLETS, BIKINIS, AND BULL TERRIERS

The 1970s and 1980s saw a meteoric rise in television advertising for the country's largest breweries. Beer brands, especially light lagers like Miller Lite, Coors Light, and Bud Light, became less about the beer the consumer drank than about the perceived lifestyle with which they would associate themselves by drinking it.

Coors Light's iconic silver can became the Silver Bullet, with ads featuring a frigid train blasting through scenes that somehow always managed to feature bikini models. The company developed an image around ice-cold beer, associating cold lager brewing and conditioning with quality. And it developed an aluminum can with a special color-change indicator to let you know when your Coors Light had become "as cold as the Rockies."

For sheer marketing genius, however, one needn't look further than Anheuser-Busch's greatest hits, many of which have come to be so intimately associated with the Super Bowl that, for many fans, the ads are more compelling than the games themselves. AB's Spuds Mackenzie ad campaign, which featured an anthropomorphic bull terrier who loved nothing more than hanging out on the beach and sharing a Bud Light with his harem of swimsuit models, drew criticism for appealing too much to children (Spuds Mackenzie plush toys did nothing to refute this assertion). AB withdrew the ad campaign after two years, but only after it had become firmly entrenched in the mind of the public.[7]

In the 1990s and early 2000s, Budweiser and Bud Light featured some of the most memorable advertising in sports history. The famous *Bud-weis-er* trio of frogs, said to have initially been met with skepticism within AB's boardrooms, turned out to be one of the company's most successful. The "whassup" guys changed how an entire generation of young men greeted each other. And the stunning imagery of AB's iconic Clydesdales has even been known to bring viewers to tears.

Throughout all of this, the one thing that is rarely mentioned in these national ad campaigns is the beer itself. Sports figures, gimmicky packaging, and scantily clad women sell a lifestyle, an image, an attitude. The big brewers know their target demographic, and they go after him with fervor.

By the time President Jimmy Carter legalized homebrewing at the federal level in 1978 (a year in which the United States could boast a mere 89 breweries), an entire generation of Americans had grown up in a beer landscape dominated by a handful of large national brands that offered little diversity of flavor. Light American lager's rapidly increasing ad-fueled

THAT ONE TIME I DRANK A LIGHT BEER

I toured Anheuser-Busch InBev's Fort Collins production facility in 2013 and marveled at the scale and science of it all. On what turned out to be a two-hour behind-the-scenes tour that included time on the brewhouse and packaging floors, I had the opportunity to sample Bud Light at various stages of production, from sweet wort to end product.

Like most large breweries, AB InBev uses a technique called high-gravity brewing to maximize the output of its brewhouse. It's a little bit like extract homebrewing but without the extract. Rather than mashing, lautering, and sparging to yield a wort that has the original gravity of the desired beer, brewers create a higher-gravity beer and then dilute it prior to packaging. Bud Light goes into the packaging area with more than 7 percent alcohol by volume. It comes out the other side at 4.2 percent. The full-strength version is a strong, flavorful American lager. The watered-down version tastes, well, "light."

No matter what you drink, and no matter what you think of ABI and its business tactics, every beer lover should make a point of touring the impressive cathedrals of fermentation found within the walls of the world's largest brewers. It's impossible not to be impressed at the massive scale at which these facilities turn out beer.

popularity stole shelf space from even the full-strength originals from which they derived their names. The trajectory of American brewing in the late 1970s pointed firmly toward less flavor and less diversity.

Out of this grim environment the modern craft beer movement emerged. Homebrewers, finally out in the open, started brewing flavorful alternatives to the bleak, flavorless American macro-lager. They shared them with friends. They entered them in competitions. They resurrected nearly forgotten styles. And some of them started their own breweries. Most brewed ale, partly because it was easier, but also because it was a definitive rebuke of the status quo. But a few reclaimed lager from the clutches of insipid macro-brew.

Craft was a response to a beer culture that had become more about advertising and image than about taste. The pioneers of the modern beer revolution—and, indeed, of the modern lager revolution—brought flavor back to America. And in doing so, they improved flavor worldwide.

THE CRAFT LAGER COMEBACK

We live in an era when even airport bars and roadside cafes—not traditional hotbeds of fermented flavor—tap kegs of local craft beer, or at least crack open a bottle or two from widely distributed brands like Samuel Adams, Sierra Nevada, and New Belgium.

An entire generation has come of age during the craft beer renaissance, having known nothing different, but it wasn't always this way. In 1979, the United States could lay claim to just ninety breweries, fewer than two per state on average. To have increased the brewery count by more than 5,000 percent in fewer than four decades was not mere happenstance. Today's craft brewers owe their successes to beer pioneers of the late twentieth century who challenged the status quo of industrial light lagers.

Hoppy Pilsner inspired by Russian River's STS Pils (see recipe page 209).

In 1976, Jack McAuliffe opened New Albion Brewing Company in Sonoma, California, serving up such ales as stout and porter. One hundred miles north and east, Ken Grossman and Paul Camusi gave us Sierra Nevada Brewing Company and its namesake Pale Ale in 1979. Ale would dominate craft beer in the coming decades, but two pioneering brewers, whose achievements and influence remain powerful to the present day, achieved success not with ale, but with lager. Today, craft brewers continue to innovate on the lager front, even as they respect the past.

One of my reasons for wanting to write this book was to dispel the notion that the word *lager* automatically means bland, fizzy, yellow beer. The European classics offer enough evidence to the contrary, but if even more proof is needed, one need only look to the innovative and interesting things that craft brewers are doing with lager today.

As we have seen, there's a long tradition of lager in North America, and were it not for Prohibition, that heritage might have continued through to the modern day. Advertising, consolidation, and a general lightening of the American palate may have been inevitable, but be that the case, Prohibition accelerated our descent into watery oblivion.

Today's craft brewers are proudly reclaiming lager and asserting its rightful place alongside ale. Some are reinterpreting classic styles with an American twist, while others are inventing new beer styles altogether. We might never get back to lager's pre-Prohibition heyday. But if modern craft lager is any indication, what we've lost in volume we've made up for in flavor.

WHEN YOUR BREWERY RUNS OUT OF STEAM, JUST CALL THE MAYTAG REPAIRMAN

The term "craft beer" wasn't on anyone's lips in 1965. But San Francisco's Anchor Brewery would, in that very year, transform from what might have been America's last craft brewery of a bygone era into what is frequently heralded as the first craft brewery of the American beer renaissance. Its flagship beer would be a lager. And it was in need of serious help, for the history of the old Anchor Brewery reads like a country song.

The Anchor Brewery dates to 1871, when it was originally known as the Golden City Brewery and owned by a German immigrant named Gottlieb Brekle. Twenty-five years later, in 1896, a German brewer named Ernst Baruth and his son-in-law Otto Schinkel Jr. purchased the brewery and renamed it Anchor for reasons that remain unclear. Ernst died suddenly in 1906, leaving Otto as the sole owner. Otto's brewery might have been a success had the great earthquake of 1906 and the ensuing fire not destroyed it just two months later, along with most of the city.

The brewery was rebuilt and reopened in 1907, immediately after which time Otto was run over by a streetcar and died. More German investors came to the rescue, though we can only imagine they might not have been clued in to the entire history of the brewery. Nonetheless, they managed to keep the operation going for another thirteen years—a new record for the longevity silver medal—until Prohibition came along and shut down the brewery. After Prohibition was repealed in April 1933, part owner Joseph Kraus reopened, and within ten months, Anchor went up in flames.

Undeterred, Kraus reopened Anchor in another building, this one made of brick, with a new business partner named Joe Allen. This time, the brewery managed to stay open, even surviving Joseph Kraus's death in 1951, until Joe Allen decided he'd had enough and shut the whole thing down in 1959. The brewery once again reopened in 1960, but it continued to suffer ups and downs for the next five years, by which time owner Lawrence Steese was ready to call it quits. One could have been forgiven for siding with him.

Enter Fritz Maytag—no, quite literally, he *entered* the Old Spaghetti Factory in San Francisco's North Beach neighborhood, where he was a regular. Fritz came from a family of successful inventors and entrepreneurs. His great-grandfather, Frederick Louis Maytag I, had in 1893 founded the Maytag Washing Machine Company in Newton, Iowa. In 1941, Fritz's father, Frederick Louis Maytag II, had founded Maytag Dairy Farms, whose award-winning wheels of Iowa-made blue cheese remain highly regarded today. And Fritz, having received a degree in American literature from Stanford in 1959, had started grad school but decided he wanted to do something different.

As it happened, the owner of the Old Spaghetti Factory, Fred Kuh, kept exactly one beer on draft: Anchor Steam. His restaurant was one of just a few accounts around town that still carried it. Steam had become a favorite of Maytag's, too, in the five years he had lived in San Francisco. As the story is usually told, Kuh encouraged Maytag to pay a hasty visit to the Anchor Brewery, as it was scheduled to shut down in a few days' time.

Maytag toured the Anchor Brewery the very next day. The brewery was in disrepair, there was filth everywhere, and much of the beer that the brewery turned out went sour. So, he did what any rational human being would do and purchased a 51 percent majority stake in the company. Fritz's legacy was not to be washing machines. It was not to be blue cheese. It was to be beer.

Fritz used his inheritance to pay off the brewery's debts and began investing in the company. In doing so, he saved not just Anchor but also one of the few styles of beer that can truly be called American. Steam beer, or as it's better known today, California common (Steam® is a trademarked brand of Anchor Brewing Company), had emerged from West Coast breweries around the time of the California Gold Rush. Several competing theories abound regarding the name *steam*, all of which seem as equally plausible as they are refutable.

What's important is that this beer style is a lager, but not your traditional "brewed-in-a-cave" Bavarian lager. Those require a consistently cold place, such as an artificially refrigerated space or a cave or cellar lined with bricks of ice. San Francisco had neither of those in the nineteenth century, but what it did have was a mild climate. Mark Twain is often falsely quoted as having said, "The coldest winter I ever spent was a summer in San Francisco." The attribution may be wrong—Twain never said it, and we don't know who did—but the sentiment is spot on.

California common yeast is a lager yeast that has adapted to perform well in the moderately cool, but never too cold, climate of San Francisco Bay. The yeast is as unique as the beer it's associated with, and we very nearly lost it. But when Maytag staked his claim in the company, Anchor's Steam beer had been reduced to a shell of its former self, with various sugars and coloring agents doing who knows what.

Fritz went back to the drawing board and reformulated it as an all-malt beer, which had become all but unheard of in the United States in the late 1960s. He acquired woodsy, spicy, herbal Northern Brewer hops, which he backed up with a generous measure of crystal malt. The result is the beer that is still brewed today, one which has become so, well, common, that it can get overlooked in an increasingly competitive and diverse craft landscape.

Anchor Brewing Company would go on to make many other important contributions to the American craft brewing movement, but it all started with Steam. Today, Anchor still brews

Steam exclusively with Northern Brewer hops. It is still fermented in large open vats, a rarity in an industry dominated by closed, stainless-steel cylindroconical vessels. And it is still naturally carbonated using the technique of kräusening. It is a beer that is quintessentially American and quintessentially craft. And it's a reminder that the craft revolution started with a quintessentially American craft lager.

SHOTS HEARD 'ROUND THE WORLD (OR AT LEAST FROM COAST TO COAST)

When Jim Koch, founder and chairman of Boston Beer Company, launched Samuel Adams Boston Lager in 1984, lager in the United States was virtually synonymous with mass-produced, nationally distributed domestics and pricy imports. But Jim comes from a long line of brewers—six generations—going back to the 1830s and the beginning of lager brewing in the United States. So when it came time to brew up something different for the American beer consumer, he went with what his family did best: lager.

When Jim announced his decision to leave a lucrative consulting position to continue the family tradition of brewing, his dad Charles, who had graduated from Chicago's prestigious Siebel Institute in 1948, guided him to the attic and opened the trunk containing the recipe for Louis Koch Lager. Charles had brewed it once at Wooden Shoe Brewing in Minster, Ohio, in the 1950s, in an attempt to save the struggling operation. Wooden Shoe closed

Hops growing in front of the Samuel Adams brewery.

Jim Koch with a glass of Samuel Adams Boston Lager.

in 1953, but Louis Koch lager was ahead of its time.

It was a challenging beer to brew, one that made use of techniques that had all but disappeared from American brewing by the time Boston Beer Company came along. Decidedly German techniques like decoction mashing and kräusening, along with dry hopping—de rigueur now, but unusual then—produced a distinctive amber lager that was unlike anything else at the time. Despite the challenges, Jim's gut said to go with this beer.

Rather than build a new brewery from the ground up that could accommodate the technical demands, Koch decided to initially contract brew. In contract brewing, a brewer "rents" time on a brewing system from a brewery that has more capacity than it needs. For example, some breweries, when they expand, size their new brewhouses according to the production they expect to see a few years down the road. Until production catches up to that estimate, brewing equipment is underused.

The situation in the 1980s was a bit different as regional breweries closed down or scaled back production. Breweries that had formerly operated at full capacity to meet consumer demands found themselves with time on their hands. Contract brewing allowed these brewers to earn revenue from equipment that would otherwise have gone unused. And such an arrangement offers a startup brewery the opportunity to brew on proven equipment without incurring the enormous costs of building a new brewhouse.

Some brewers at the time disparaged contract brewing as somehow less real than cutting one's teeth building equipment and starting from scratch. But it is worth noting that in contract situations, the usual arrangement is for the contract brewer to bring in all of its own raw materials and staff. It's the brewing equivalent of renting your neighbor's extra coffeemaker until you can buy a new one. You're still brewing the coffee; you're just doing so on borrowed equipment.

In *Ambitious Brew: The Story of American Beer*, Maureen Ogle offers context on the decision to contract brew in the beginning:

> He wanted to brew from superior ingredients; he wanted to provide Americans with an alternative to skunky imports, bland corporate beer, and sour amateur microbrews; and he wanted it to be lager. In that he was nearly alone. Most craft brewers made ale, either because they shunned corporate lager's reputation or because ale required

less fermenting time. Lager brewing also demanded an investment in storage space and expensive cooling equipment.

Those two goals—to brew lager rather than ale and to produce a high-quality, fresh beer—led Koch to another conclusion. The means mattered less than the end, and . . . all he needed was access to professional-grade equipment and a professional brewmaster.[1]

Jim found his professional brewing equipment at Pittsburgh Brewing Company, best known for its Iron City brands. And he engaged the expertise of Dr. Joseph Owades, who had invented light beer in 1967 when working for the Rheingold Brewery in New York. The first bottles of Samuel Adams Boston Lager rolled off the line in December 1984, and today Samuel Adams is a household name that extends well beyond craft beer enthusiasts.

Jim attributes much of the success of Boston Lager to its flavor profile. Its malt backbone includes sugar molecules small enough to be tasted as body and complex sweetness, but large enough that yeast has trouble digesting them. This gives it a unique and characteristic body and sweetness that can support relatively high levels of hops. Dry hopping and a touch of sub-threshold diacetyl add to the complexity.

The foundational beers of craft—Sierra Nevada Pale Ale, Samuel Adams Boston Lager, and Anchor Steam—were an ale, a lager, and a hybrid lager, respectively. These are the beers that awakened Americans' taste for good beer. They remain successful to this day.[2]

CRAFT LAGER ELEVATED, AMERICAN STYLE

Anchor Steam and Samuel Adams Boston Lager pioneered craft lager in the United States, setting the stage for cold-fermented delights to come. From the West Coast to New England, America's small and independent brewers have brought American lager full circle, resurrecting it from the bland, blonde watery mass-market lagers that thrived in the wake of Prohibition.

Chuckanut Brewery & Kitchen in Bellingham, Washington, opened in 2008, though co-owner Will Kemper has been brewing much longer than that.[3] When he and his wife founded Chuckanut, the plan was always to focus on lagers. A devotee of Ludwig Narziß, Will believes his brewery's scientific approach shows in the finished beer. Chuckanut uses classical German brewing techniques and cold conditions its lagers below the freezing point. Will naturally carbonates his beer by using a spunding device, a kind of pressure relief valve that vents excess carbon dioxide after a certain level of carbonation has been achieved in the brite tank.

This attention to detail has earned Chuckanut an impressive battery of awards. Chuckanut Brewery & Kitchen won Small Brewpub of the Year at the 2009 Great American Beer Festival with a lineup that included nothing but lager: helles lager, Vienna lager, pilsner lager, and dunkel lager. Two years later, Chuckanut won Small Brewery of the Year at the 2011 Great American Beer Festival with two lagers and two ales. And the brewery is expanding.[4]

Chuckanut has a long and enviable history as a lager-focused brewery, and a handful of other American breweries have maintained a focus on traditional lager styles, including Bierstadt Lagerhaus, Gordon Biersch, Heater Allen, Moerlein Lager House, Von Trapp Brewing, and Zwei Brewing, among others. Increasingly, though, breweries rooted in other brewing approaches have come to embrace lager and are changing the face of American craft beer in the process.

Vinnie Cilurzo, owner and head brewer at Russian River Brewing Company, is known for many things, but most of us know him for just two of them: IPAs and Belgian-style ales. Pliny the Elder, a double IPA, is consistently rated one of the best beers in the world, and readers of *Zymurgy* magazine named it the best beer in America for the eighth year in a row in 2016. Pliny has medaled four times in the imperial IPA category at the Great American Beer Festival[*]—two gold and two bronze—and has taken a gold medal at the World Beer Cup[SM].

Pliny the Younger, an even stronger relative of the Elder, draws lines that stretch around the block when it is available for a short time every February. The Sonoma County Economic Development Board even conducts an annual assessment of the beer's local economic impact and estimates that the 2016 tapping generated 4.88 million dollars from attendees who traveled to Sonoma County from forty states and eleven foreign countries specifically for the beer release.[5] At press time, Pliny the Younger remained in top position on BeerAdvocate's "Beers of Fame" list, which ranks top-rated beers that have been represented on the site for more than a decade.

Russian River's Belgian ales program, including its barrel-aged and sour beers, are no less accomplished. The brewery's Supplication, Damnation, Salvation, and Consecration are classics that, unlike the two Plinys, can gracefully stand up to aging. Thanks to Russian River's limited distribution (at present, only in California, Oregon, Colorado, and Philadelphia), beers like Pliny the Elder and the numerous variations on the suffix *-ation* are regularly the quarries of Internet beer traders.

So, when the founder of Russian River Brewing Company admits to having a thing for pilsner, we should take it as a clue that the craft lager revolution is well underway. Cilurzo says brewers have been interested in making high-quality lagers for a long time, but the craft beer industry has needed time to mature and to allow consumers to create demand.

Craft drinkers haven't been exposed to craft lager on a larger scale until recently, in part because the extra capacity just hasn't been there. For a small, up-and-coming brewery, it just doesn't make sense to tie up a tank with lager for thirty days when an ale can be done in eighteen. Even now, Cilurzo admits that Russian River doesn't have that kind of capacity, but he has made it a priority to perfect a flagship lager. With a new brewhouse in the works, he wants to have three rooms devoted to open fermentation: one for ales, one for Belgian styles, and one for lagers.

After coming back from a trip to Germany, where he had been inspired by Schönramer Pils, he decided to take a serious stab at an authentically snappy, dry, hoppy pilsner. He had brewed two lagers before. One of those, White Apron, was brewed exclusively for Thomas Keller's upscale restaurants. The other, HUGE Large "Sound Czech" Pilsner was available exclusively at the brewery's Santa Rosa brewpub. What he learned from brewing those early examples informed the decisions he made in developing STS Pilsner.

Step mashing, a custom water profile, and an improved understanding of lager yeast have been crucial to the success of STS. Vinnie admits that the hardest part was managing the water in a brewery focused on IPA and Belgian-style ales. At first he considered using a fermenter as a temporary hot liquor tank to hold water for STS, but in the end, he bought a separate tank exclusively to hold water for STS Pilsner. That's how important the water is.

Yeast turned out to be the other major obstacle. With years of experience brewing wild and sour styles, Russian River's brewers understood *Brettanomyces* better than *S. pastorianus*. So

OPPOSITE: Avery Brewing Company The Kaiser (see recipe page 210).

Vinnie and his team became obsessed with yeast. They pulled gravity samples every day over numerous brews, meticulously collecting data to build accurate profiles for how their yeast performed in the brewhouse.[6]

The obsession paid off. STS Pils won a gold medal at the 2015 and a silver medal at the 2014 Great American Beer Festival.

STS is just one member of a lineup of hop-forward American riffs on Continental pilsner that are wowing drinkers in North America and worldwide. One of the first and most influential, Prima Pils, was introduced by Victory Brewing Company of Downingtown, Pennsylvania, in 2001, at a time when craft beer was exploding with IPA. Victory recognized the need for a refreshing pilsner but used a hefty dose of European hops in its formulation, much more than most American drinkers were accustomed to at the time. The result was a pilsner of uncompromising flavor that continues to impress.

A year after its release, none other than the great Michael Jackson named Prima one of the best pilsners in America. (He ended up giving the award for best pilsner to Tupper's Hop Pocket Pils of Old Dominion so that he could name Victory's St. Victorious the best doppelbock. Mr. Jackson was kind and generous in that way.) Prima won silver and bronze medals at the 2007 and 2008 Great American Beer Festivals, respectively.

Prima was one of the first and remains one of the best, but it has been Firestone Walker's Pivo Hoppy Pils, which debuted in 2013, that has led the way in recent years. Firestone Walker brewmaster Matt Brynildson cites Birrificio Italiano's Tipopils, a dry-hopped pilsner brewed about 19 miles (30 km) northwest of Milan, Italy, as inspiration for Pivo (Vinnie credits both Tipopils and Pivo as inspiration for STS). Pivo debuted in 2013 and was considered avant-garde at the time for the way it combined traditional German ingredients and brewing processes with a West Coast American attitude to hops.

In the 2013 press release for Pivo's debut, Brynildson says, "A lot of pilsners have the malt element down, as well as the dryness and drinkability, and even the bitterness—but they lack hop aroma. We're trying to elevate that hop aspect, but we don't want to beat you over the head with it. I think it makes for a very interesting beer that remains true to the pilsner style with a lot of drinkability."

Pivo took gold in the German-Style Pilsener at the Great American Beer Festival for three straight years, from 2013 to 2015.

INVENTING NEW LAGERS

Not content simply to improve upon existing styles, some craft brewers have taken it upon themselves to invent new ones altogether. Avery Brewing Company in Boulder, Colorado, enjoys a well-deserved reputation as a brewer of high-alcohol beer, and its Dictators and Demons series were known for pushing the boundaries of how much flavor—and alcohol—could be packed into a single beer.

The Kaiser, a self-titled "imperial oktoberfest," emerged from the brewery in 2004 as a fall seasonal. Avery's nod to German tradition included an American craft twist in that it boasted an alcohol content of more than 9 percent by volume. The Kaiser went on to win gold and silver medals at the 2009 and 2014 Great American Beer Festivals, respectively, but because of The Kaiser's strength, it medaled not as an oktoberfest/märzen but as a doppelbock.[7]

In addition to "imperializing" everything under the sun, American craft brewers love stuffing hops, hops, and more hops into their creations. So, it was just a matter of time before someone decided to combine the hoppiness and strength of India pale ale, which remains the best-selling craft category, with the smoothness and crispness of a lager. Thus was born the India pale lager (IPL).

The style remains elusive and somewhat hard to pin down. Coney Island's Sword Swallower was one of the first when it appeared in 2007, but it took a few years for the idea to catch on. Perhaps nobody knew quite where to place these hybrids, which were brewed like a lager but hopped like an IPA. As of the publication of this book, the Beer Judge Certification Program had not officially recognized IPL as a distinct style category.

Why bother brewing IPA as a lager? Why not just stick with what works? Well, lager offers some distinct advantages when it comes to hop-forward beers. For one thing, yeast doesn't get in the way. IPL offers a mostly pure expression of malt and hops, and in the case of IP-anything, those hops stand front and center. But what really makes lager the perfect vehicle for these kinds of beers is the slower, less vigorous fermentation.

All that bubbling carries away precious hop aromatics. The quieter the ferment, the more of those aromatics remain in solution. Thus, a cold lager fermentation is ideal for preserving those hoppy qualities that drive us to brew India pale beers in the first place. And the cold helps too. We all know that IPA should be kept cold to keep it fresh. With IPL, that cold begins in the brewhouse.

Jack's Abby Craft Lagers in Framingham, Massachusetts, has made a name for itself for several reasons. One is that it exclusively makes lager. Another is that it has mastered the art of the IPL with offerings like Hoponius Union IPL, Excess IPL, and Calyptra Session IPL. Drinkers lucky enough to live near the brewery can also find 3× Hoponius Union and Sibling Rye-valry as taproom-only specials.

Excess IPL, one of Jack's Abby's newer offerings, pairs a traditional lager approach with such American hop-bomb techniques as kettle hopping, whirlpool hopping, and three rounds of dry hopping. The brewery also uses a "proprietary hop-dosing technique" to introduce the massive quantities of Citra, Chinook, Equanot, Calypso, and Simcoe that define this beer. Drinkers who gravitate toward fruit-forward, hazy New England IPAs are finding that Jack's Abby delivers lagers that can compete on equal terms.

The movement shows little sign of slowing down. As craft brewers increase production and expand operations, more room is opening up in the fermentation tanks for lager to make itself known to modern drinkers. Craft malt, which has grown into an industry of its own alongside craft beer, promises to deliver even more choice to consumers. Hoppy pilsners and India pale lagers have shown us what craft lager brewers can do with hops. Craft malt promises to show us what they can do with barley.

Lager has come a long way since 1553. What began inadvertently when a Bavarian duke outlawed the brewing of beer in summer has become an international phenomenon, one that, for most of the world, continues to define what *beer* is.

TASTING AND ENJOYING LAGER

A beer in every glass and a glass for every beer. This very easily could be the mantra of the modern craft beer movement. Not only have we become more accustomed to a diverse selection of beer styles, but we've also come to learn how the right glassware can accentuate the desirable characteristics of the beer we drink.

The corollary to this might very well be *Death to the shaker pint!* The ubiquitous conical pint glass is familiar to us all, but it was never really intended to be a serving glass (it's just one-half of the Boston cocktail shaker). Bars love them, but the shaker pint glass will do nothing to enhance the enjoyment of your beer, and enjoyment is what it's all about. Well, almost.

Enjoyment is what it's all about if you never have to answer the question: "What kind of beer do you like?" For this, a vocabulary is needed, which is where sensory evaluation comes in. Sensory evaluation is *not* about sitting around and frowning and scratching your chin while saying things like "a bouquet of rancid petunias flummoxed by a cacophony of herbal cherubs." OK, some people will say things like that, but you don't have to.

A pilsner flute is the ideal glass for Czech pilsner, German pils, and other light lagers.

Sensory evaluation is about *describing* the beer you taste so that you can (1) tell others what you like and (2) tell others what you don't like. That's really it. The approach and language used to evaluate beer is the same whether you're staring down a dark doppelbock or a crisp kölsch, but analyzing lager does present a few unique aspects, which we'll cover here.

Glassware and sensory evaluation go hand in hand. The right glass can highlight a beer's strengths. The wrong glass can make it fall flat. Spend some time getting to know your beer and the glass from which you drink it, and your lager experience will be richly rewarded.

GLASSWARE FOR LAGER BEER

Glassware can be a complicated topic, but it doesn't have to be. Generally speaking, the higher in alcohol the beer, the smaller, shorter, and squatter the glassware should be. This doesn't apply to the stem, just to the bowl itself. Using a smaller glass for high-alcohol beers does a few things. First, it takes advantage of the old culinary trick of serving small portions on small plates to make them look more generous than they really are. High-gravity beers are usually served in smaller quantities, and it just makes sense to do so in a smaller glass.

The short and squat aspect, which correlates with capacity, also assists by giving high-gravity beers more surface area with which to open up. They lend themselves to swirling and sipping more than do their larger counterparts, which are more for boisterous swigging and swallowing. Furthermore, those short, squat glasses can be cupped in the hand, and the heat from one's palm helps to warm the beer. High-alcohol beer is usually best served a little warmer than more sessionable styles.

What follows are my personal glassware recommendations for a wide range of lager styles. Your own choice should always be dictated by personal preference. If you prefer to drink all of your beers from a favorite Denver Broncos 2016 World Champions souvenir mug, then by all means, do so! Consider these recommendations as suggestions, not gospel. Let experience guide you.

Willi becher

If you want to keep things ridiculously simple, here's all you need to know: If you can keep only one kind of lager glass in your cupboard, let that glass be the 0.33 liter *Willi becher.*[1]

The Willi becher (pronounced VILL-ee beh-cher, where the *ch* is an aspirated sound similar to the English *sh*—think of the initial sound in *humor* or *Hugh*) is, in my opinion, the single best all-purpose beer for serving lager. It can handle everything from light American lager to eisbock, and it looks good to boot. Taller and narrower than a shaker pint, the Willi becher flares outward as the glass ascends from base to lip, but then curves slightly inward again

The Willi becher is the workhorse of the German brewpub and a great all-purpose lager glass.

before getting there. Unlike the shaker pint, which is virtually designed to eliminate head and volatilize aromas, the Willi becher's elegant shape holds on to foam and concentrates aromas as you drink. It's the workhorse of the German pub for a reason.

The Willi becher most commonly comes in 0.33-liter and 0.5-liter volumes, and I like to keep both around. Actually, that's a lie: I keep around 12-ounce and 0.5-liter glasses because American beer comes in 12-ounce bottles and cans, and European beers are more commonly packaged in 0.33-liter bottles and 0.5-liter bottles and cans. Those 0.33-liter (11.2 ounce) bottles will still fit into a 12-ounce glass, but an American 12-ouncer won't quite fit into the 0.33-liter volume. Until the United States goes metric, we simply must live with this dichotomy.[2]

If you can choose just one of the sizes, I say go for the 12-ounce or 0.33-liter glass. Why? Because I'd rather pour a refill from a larger bottle than use a glass that's too big for the bottle I'm pouring. That's strictly a personal preference, and you're, of course, free to do what you like.

Use a Willi becher for any lager style you like. Of course, there is no one ideal glass for every beer, and if you have room for several kinds of beer glassware, you'll discover that you gravitate toward certain shapes for certain beers. Following are some other classic beer glasses and the beers that pair well with them.

Stange

The *Stange* (sh-TAHNG-uh) is a short, perfectly cylindrical glass that usually holds just 2 deciliters (6.8 fl. oz.). It is the preferred glass for kölsch, which is traditionally served in a *Kranz*, or wreath, of a dozen Stangen at a time. Altbier is normally served in the Stange as well, though these can be larger, up to about 4 deciliters (13.5 fl. oz.). In North America, the larger Stangen are more common.[3]

Lagers aren't traditionally served in the Stange (kölsch and altbier are both ales), but I think they're great for dortmunder-style export beers and helles because (1) they deliver a good balance of malt and hop aromatics and (2) the diminutive size ensures that your beer doesn't get too warm. They also do a great job with standard bock. If you already maintain a battery of glassware for cocktails, a Collins glass is a good substitute for the Stange.[4]

Use a Stange for:

- Dortmunder Export
- Helles
- Bock
- Pilsner

The Stange is traditional for kölsch and a great choice for pale and amber lagers.

Pilsner glass

The pilsner glass (PILZ-ner), is the perfect glass for, well, pilsner. Both German and Czech examples are great in this tall, slender glass that gradually tapers from a narrow base to a slightly less narrow (I wouldn't call it wide) mouth. It captures the delicate hop aromatics of true pilsner-style beers admirably and shows off the fluffy white head that exemplifies these classics.

In a pinch, a North American or modern German *weizen* glass is a reasonable substitute for the pilsner glass, and some glassware manufacturers actually market the same glass for both styles. There are some similarities, and some pilsner glasses do taper a bit toward the top. The traditional vase-shaped German weizen glass, which tends to have a much narrower middle and wider top, isn't the best choice for pilsner.

Use a pilsner glass for:

- American lagers
- Czech pilsner
- German pilsner
- Generic "green bottle" Euro lagers

A relative of the pilsner glass, the *Pokal* (POH-kull) features a stem that separates the main glass from the base. The two can be used interchangeably.

Augenkanne

The *Augenkanne* (OW-gen-kahn-uh) is an excellent all-purpose mug for a wide variety of beers to accompany feasting and festing. It's the quintessential Bavarian and Austrian mug for swinging back and forth to the beat of an oompah band at long tables in a dimly lit tavern. These are usually built like a tank and can stand up to the abuse of toast after toast after toast.

A variant on the Augenkanne is also a favorite of many a British pub, and you can very easily use the same glass for your mild ale as for your Munich dunkel. A true Augenkanne has a slight inward taper near the mouth so as to resemble a barrel, while the British dimpled beer mug usually lacks this additional bit of curvature.

Use an Augenkanne for:

- Czech pilsner
- Czech Dark Lager
- Dunkel
- Helles
- Dortmunder Export
- Schwarzbier
- Rauchbier

OPPOSITE: The Augenkanne might look frumpy, but it's an excellent glass for dunkel, Czech dark lager, and schwarzbier.

Maßkrug

The trusty Maßkrug (MAHSS-krook) is the standard for Oktoberfests worldwide. If the Augenkanne is the quintessential mug, then the Maßkrug is the quintessential "stein," and if an Augenkanne is built like a tank, then the Maßkrug is built like a fortress. It's possible to break one of these, but you really have to put your mind to it. They're fabricated from extra-thick glass, and the bases are specifically designed to bear the brunt of boisterous revelry. Conveniently, you can hang a pretzel off the handle in an emergency.

A drawback of the Maßkrug is that the last few swallows of beer can get kind of warm, so as charming as it can be to drink from one on a hot day in a beer garden, keep in mind that you might not enjoy the end of your first serving. Once you've made it through that first liter, though, you won't care.

Use a Maßkrug for:

- Helles
- Festbier
- Dunkel

Flute

The word *flute* can apply to a variety of glassware pieces, perhaps the most famous of which is the Champagne flute. But the diminutive size of these makes them impractical for beer. Instead, look for flutes that are a little shorter and a little wider. These are, in my opinion, the ideal glassware for the entire bock family, as they really highlight the malty aromas of these styles. A flute is also an excellent choice for schwarzbier and rauchbier.

Use a flute for:

- Bock
- Maibock
- Doppelbock
- Eisbock
- Rauchbier
- Schwarzbier

LEFT: A flute is perfect for a diverse range of styles, but bock and doppelbock are particularly nice.

TOP: A Maßkrug is the traditional glass for Bavarian helles lager and is the quintessential Oktoberfest mug.

Tulip

As much as I am happy to see more and more breweries eschewing the shaker pint, it's disappointing that so many have flocked to the tulip as the next be-all, end-all glass. A tulip is an excellent choice for the Belgian styles with which it is most intimately associated, and it's also a great choice for certain lagers. My beef with the tulip as an all-purpose beer glass is that it isn't ideal for really spritzy, bitter, hop-forward beer like pilsner. Even IPA, I think, loses something when served in a tulip.

The tulip is, however, a great choice for dark, malty lagers. Use a tulip for:

- Dunkel
- Rauchbier
- Schwarzbier
- Bock
- Baltic porter

The tulip is a great choice for dark, malt-forward lagers like Baltic porter.

Snifter

Snifters are traditionally reserved for very strong ales, and the same is true for very strong lagers. Baltic porter and eisbock are great choices for a snifter. As brewers increasingly barrel-age their beers, it's inevitable that a lager is going to make it into the barrel now and then, like Jack's Abby's Barrel-Aged Framinghammer and Lakefront Brewery's Barrel-Aged Cherry Lager. A snifter is the perfect vehicle for these strong, woody libations.

Use a snifter for:

- Baltic porter
- Doppelbock
- Eisbock
- Malt liquor[5]

Use a snifter for small pours of high-alcohol lagers that need room to breathe. It's the perfect vehicle for eisbock.

Teku

A relative newcomer to the world of craft beer, the Teku is becoming the new tulip in some circles. It's a fantastic beer glass, but I think it falls short of advertisements that bill it as the world's best. I like to think of the Teku as a jazzed-up tulip or snifter, and in most cases, they're pretty interchangeable. The only time I might recommend a Teku over the tulip is for eisbock or very strong doppelbocks like Samichlaus. I think this glass really shines for strong, malty styles.

Use the Teku glass for:

- Baltic porter

- Eisbock

- Rauchbier

- Showing off

Shaker

OK, the shaker pint clearly isn't my favorite, but if I'm invited to someone's house and served beer in a shaker pint, I'm going to thank him or her and enjoy the beer. It's important to respect your beer, yes, but it's more important to respect your friends. Don't be a jerk.

Actually, there is one very good use for a shaker pint, and that's keeping hangovers at bay. Every time you order a beer, make sure you have a shaker pint full of water next to you. You can't order another beer until your shaker pint of water is empty. Your trips to the bathroom will be more frequent and voluminous, but you'll feel much better the next day.

Use the shaker pint:

- To be polite to your hosts

- To stay hydrated

- To hold pens

OPPOSITE: A Teku glass highlights smoky rauchbier with elegance.

SENSORY EVALUATION

Sensory evaluation is the process of identifying what you detect in beer and putting that into words. To the uninitiated, it can come off as incredibly froufrou and elitist, and sometimes it is. Done with the right attitude, though, it's a valuable opportunity to learn more about beer of all kinds.

If you really get into sensory evaluation, you can become a credentialed beer judge through the Beer Judge Certification Program (BJCP), or you can enroll in classes through the Cicerone® Program and become a Certified Cicerone®. Most homebrewers who get into beer judging do so through the BJCP because it's the same organization that sets the standards for homebrew competitions around the world. Cicerone tends to cater more to beer service and education, and in fact, Certified Cicerones are sometimes called "beer sommeliers" in casual conversation.

The process of evaluating beer uses all five senses. Taste, smell, and sight are the most obvious, but touch plays a role in feeling the texture of the beer on your tongue, and sound comes into play when you listen to the beer being poured. The pop of the bottle cap or cork and the subsequent fizz (or lack thereof) may be your first clues about the beer you're about to taste.

In the BJCP framework, it's customary to evaluate beer according to the following criteria, in order of which they are considered.

Aroma

Aroma, obviously, is what you smell, and it can be incredibly fleeting or long lasting. But aroma does more than that. It is actually responsible for most of what we perceive as flavor, which you can confirm by holding your nose when you eat or drink. When we say that different kinds of glassware are best suited to different kinds of beer, what we really mean is that different kinds of glassware are best suited to highlighting various aromas. It's the aroma that is accentuated or muted when we select one kind of glass over another.

When discussing aroma, we're looking for three big things:

- Malt-derived aromas
- Hop-derived aromas
- Yeast-derived aromas

Of course, if spices, barrel aging, or other things are at work, then those will play into the nose as well, but these are outliers that other authors have treated much better than I can here.

Malt aromas in lager span a wide range from the crackery, doughy, grainy characteristics of pilsner malt to the raisin-like, toasty, bready depth of Munich malt. There might be notes of chocolate or coffee from roasted malt or suggestions of toffee and caramel from caramel malt. The goal is not to identify the specific malts used in a beer, but rather to use specific language that evokes what you pick up. Some malt-related elements you might detect include:

- Grain
- Dough
- Bread
- Corn
- Rye
- Honey
- Toast
- Biscuits
- Caramel
- Toffee
- Dried fruit
- Coffee
- Chocolate

Malt aromas are somewhat easier to describe than hops aromas because most of us eat—or have at one point eaten—breads, crackers, and other grain-based foods. Not many of us have eaten hops, and those of us who have, have sworn never to do so again. Hops can deliver a wide range of characteristics, some of the most common of which are:

- Herbal
- Spicy
- Floral
- Citrus

- Tropical
- Berry
- Minty
- Woody

- Piney
- Resinous

Each of these can be broken down into more specific terms. What kind of coffee? French roast, espresso, or Sumatra? What kind of dried fruit? Prunes, raisins, or figs? How about citrus? Is it grapefruit, orange, lemon, or lime? And are those tropical notes more akin to mango, pineapple, or passion fruit?

These are terms that apply equally to ales and lagers. Yeast is where things get a bit different. Ales might have terms like:

- Fruity
- Spicy

- Peppery
- Banana-like

- Bubblegum-like

If you're drinking a well-made lager, such terms should not appear. They're the sign of a warm fermentation and almost always a flaw. If you taste bubblegum in your helles, something has gone horribly wrong.

On the other hand, there are aromatic terms that are appropriate for some kinds of lager that would be rather out of place in most ales. Sulfur, for example, is a natural byproduct of lager yeast fermentation, and a whiff of sulfur is not necessarily a flaw in a light lager. If it's strong enough that rotten eggs dominate the flavor, then yes, it's a problem, but if a subtle memory of Yellowstone thermal features gives way to malt and hops, then it might be completely appropriate. Some yeast strains produce more sulfur than others.

Speaking of yeast strains, certain American lager strains are known to confer a green apple–like fruitiness upon the finished beer. Green apple character can come from esters or from acetaldehyde. Green apple esters are a little "cleaner," while acetaldehyde comes off more like a cider or a Jolly Rancher. I personally don't perceive acetaldehyde as green apple. Instead, it strikes me more as the raw innards of a freshly cut pumpkin.[6]

Diacetyl, a compound most commonly described as "movie theater popcorn" or butterscotch, is generally a flaw, but certain styles, especially Czech pilsner, can include a small (and I mean *small*) amount of diacetyl as part of their profile. This seems to be a love-it-or-hate-it kind of quality. If you find that you're sensitive to diacetyl, avoid classic Czech pilsner and steer toward German and American examples.

Alcohol can present on the nose in higher-gravity lagers just as it does with strong ales. In a well-crafted lager, it's never an overpowering kind of alcohol that burns your nose hairs, but rather a comforting warming sensation that invites you to explore the glass in front of you. It's okay to be reminded of whiskey, but paint thinner and nail polish remover are signs of a problem.

A common lager off-flavor is the dreaded skunky byproduct of a beer that has been exposed to ultraviolet light. This isn't an issue with lager specifically, but one commonly associated with it because so many European lagers are packaged in green glass. Green glass and clear glass admit the wavelengths of light that interact with hop compounds to create skunk aromas. The characteristic is so intimately associated with brands like Corona, Heineken, and Grolsch that some consumers have come to believe that skunk is a desirable aspect. It certainly is not.

When possible, purchase beer in brown bottles or, even better, cans. Cans really are the best vessels for transporting beer long distances. They're shatterproof, impermeable to light and oxygen, and far easier to ship. They're better for your beer and better for the planet.

Appearance

It is said that we drink with our eyes first, and there's a certain truth to that. There's a reason that blind taste tests are conducted using opaque glassware, and much of pilsner's original appeal was rooted in the simple fact that glassware had become more affordable and more readily available when it emerged in the mid-nineteenth century.

Lagers span the same range of colors and hues as ales, from the lightest straw blonde to the darkest shade of black, with heads of foam that vary accordingly. Generally speaking, the more alcoholic the beer, the smaller and shorter-lived the head will be.

One defining aspect of virtually all lager styles is their brilliant clarity, which is in part a byproduct of the extended cold aging period. The longer a beer sits in refrigeration, the more it promotes yeast dropping out of suspension. If that yeast isn't roused during the racking process, the resulting beer is likely to be crystal clear. Commercial examples are often filtered, which further aids in clarity.

An important exception to this is the *zwickel* (TSVICK-ul) or *kellerbier*. These unfiltered masterpieces are historically what the brewer gets when he or she draws a sample directly from the maturation tank. In Germany, they're considered a delicacy, and they're becoming increasingly available in the United States, both as imports and as domestic craft examples. The suspended yeast in a zwickel/kellerbier leaves the beer hazy, though rarely as hazy as a German hefeweizen.

Flavor

After examining the beer's aroma and appearance, it's time for the main event: tasting. Virtually all the same descriptors we use for aroma apply equally to flavor. If you're taking notes on the beer you're drinking, it's worth jotting down some words at several points: when you first pour the beer, when you're about halfway through the glass, and when you're just about finished.

The way we perceive beer changes as it gets warmer and loses some of its carbonic bite. By sampling beer at various temperatures, you learn which serving temperature is right for you. Generally speaking, the fizzier and yellower the beer, the colder it should be served, and the darker and more alcoholic the beer, the warmer it should be served.

Flavor introduces a few new variables. In addition to all of the aromatic considerations, we also have to deal with sweetness, sourness, bitterness, saltiness, and umami-ness. A well-brewed lager should almost exclusively have sweetness and bitterness. A touch of acidity can be okay in some light styles, but never to the point that the beer tastes sour. Saltiness is also generally frowned upon, although adding a little salt to the mix, as I have done in the recipe for Una Más (see page 218), can introduce complexity.

Umami is that brothy, meaty, savory sensation we associate with things like soy sauce, beef stock, mushrooms, certain cheeses, and Vegemite. Highly trained tasters might detect a hint of umami in certain dark styles, but any perceptible umami in a lager is almost always an off-flavor indicative of yeast autolysis. In general, if you pick up umami in a lager, something has gone wrong.

So that leaves us with sweetness and bitterness, both of which play into a beer's finish. The finish is everything that comes after you swallow, including the aftertaste, and if you pay attention, you'll notice that most beers change as they go down the hatch. Bitterness comes in varying levels, from the soft bitterness of the helles to what can be quite an aggressive bitterness in India pale lager. Generally speaking, bitterness is there to offset malt sweetness, and the two play off one another. Sweetness should not be confused with malt flavor. A beer can have a robust malt character and still finish dry. As you taste more beer, you'll be able to pick these things apart.

Mouthfeel

Mouthfeel is the final sensory component we consider when we evaluate beer. It's a combination of tactile sensation (does the beer feel heavy or light on the tongue?), viscosity (is it syrupy and thick or light and fluid?), carbonation (is the beer spritzy and prickly or creamy and smooth?), and astringency (does the beer make you pucker at all?).

Most of these are qualities with which we are familiar from our daily lives. Skim milk is thinner than cream. French press coffee feels fuller in the mouth than a cup of pour-over drip. Sparkling water and still water leave different impressions on the tongue. Astringency is an aspect we don't always think about, though.

The best definition I've seen for astringency is the sensation one gets from sucking on a tea bag, which, thankfully, one need not have actually done to get the idea. It's a puckering sensation that's qualitatively different from acidity. Astringency can come from grain husks and may show up more in lagers built on American 6-row malt than on those formulated around 2-row: think classic American pilsner.

The same diacetyl that one might observe in the aroma and flavor can also offer a textural component. It presents as a slickness on the tongue, and for many tasters, including me, the oily slickness is more apparent than any aroma or flavor of butterscotch. I find that low concentrations of diacetyl are more textural, and only in high concentrations do I pick up on the movie popcorn aspect.

Overall Impression

The overall impression is your chance to say how well you like or dislike this beer in spite of, or because of, how well it fared in aroma, appearance, flavor, and mouthfeel. Your homebrewed light American lager might not hold a candle to Annie Johnson's Mow the Damn Lawn on the sensory descriptors, but if you enjoy drinking it nonetheless, this is where you say so.

Your overall impression of a beer might be as colored by the circumstances under which you drink it as by the individual sensory qualities that comprise it. You might be more willing to forgive blandness in a pale lager you drink on a hot day at the ballpark than you would at home with dinner. If you're a homebrewer, knowing that you brewed a beer yourself can make up for flaws you wouldn't otherwise tolerate in a beer you purchased commercially.

In describing these sensory aspects of beer evaluation, I have deliberately left out the idea of evaluating a beer for *style*. This is something beer judges necessarily do for competitions because style guides are the rules of the game. Those rules don't apply when you're simply evaluating beer for the purpose of describing what you do and don't enjoy.

Your overall impression of a beer, lager or otherwise, is ultimately what convinces you to drink another pint or (in the worst case) not finish the one you're on. It's what matters most.

OLD WORLD PALE LAGERS

Lager was born in Europe, and European brewers—especially from Germany and the Czech Republic—have had several centuries to get it right. It is therefore only appropriate that we begin our survey of lager styles at the source.

European pale lagers are genteel classics, and like aristocrats throughout history, they enjoy the benefits of noble lineage, even while bearing its burdens. At their best, European pale lagers are rich and refined, complex and contemplative, delicate yet dangerously drinkable. At their worst, they can be tired and complacent. And some are so ubiquitous that they suffer from the curse of familiarity—it can't be good if it's popular, right?

There's also a quality control issue. The lightest examples of these classic styles simply don't travel well. Many a traveler has experienced temporary elation when a favorite beer enjoyed abroad becomes available at the local liquor store, only to suffer grand disappointment when the imported example fails to live up to the standard held in one's memory.

Fort Collins Brewery Maibock (see recipe page 211).

Psychology plays a role, of course, but beer is food first and commodity second. The helles enjoyed in a Munich Bierkeller is already at a romantic disadvantage when packaged and sent overseas. But the very act of sending it on that journey, despite the best efforts of brewers and freighters, adds further insult that serves to degrade the experience of the first impression.

The positive side of this situation is that the opposite is also true: a Czech pilsner that one experiences as pedestrian and uninspired when poured from a bottle in your neighborhood bar may become a feast for the senses when you sample it directly from a cask in Prague. Don't let one bad experience limit your exploration.

Fortunately, we're no longer confined to obtaining European classics from European breweries. Increasing numbers of craft brewers in North America and around the world—indeed, in Europe itself—have acknowledged the eternal appeal of these classic styles, and finding a well-brewed *helles*, *pilsner*, or *maibock* among a small or regional brewery's offerings is far more common now than it was even two years ago.

I encourage you to seek out the pale classics in this chapter—and the darker Old World classics in the next—not just from the green (and increasingly brown) bottles whose journeys around the world mirror those of the immigrants who first popularized them, but also from a small, independent brewery in your own town. You might just discover that your favorite new craft beer has been around a really, really long time.

CZECH PILSNER

We kick things off in the Czech Republic. Lager wasn't invented in Bohemia, but it was most certainly perfected here (no offense to my Bavarian friends). The Czechs drink more beer per capita than anyone else in the world, and it's easy to understand why. Brewers here may not win many points for stylistic diversity, but they hold their own for historical innovation and consistent quality.

Czech pilsner really is in a class all its own. Plenty of beer drinkers *think* they know pilsner, only to discover upon tasting an authentic Czech example that there's far more to this pilsner thing than they first thought. "I thought pilsner was just industrial macro-lager," they might say. No. No, it's not.

As we saw in Chapter 3, Pilsner Urquell was the world's first pale lager, and it remains very much the archetype for this beer style today. Just as a true citizen of France won't call any old sparkling wine *champagne*, the Czechs are protective of the appellation *pilsner* and reserve that designation for the beer that actually comes from Pilsen. Everything else is simply beer. We'll be a little more relaxed about it and extend the term "Czech pilsner" to mean pale lager brewed in the style of that from Pilsen.

The first clue as to the geographic origin of your pilsner may be the color of the beer. While most "pilsner" brewed outside the Czech Republic is usually straw blonde to light gold, Czech versions tend to be a shade darker, borderline copper even. The richer color is a product of the intensive decoction mash regimen and an extended boil in the kettle that conspire to darken the wort and slightly caramelize malt sugars.

The right ingredients are critical to this style. One can brew an entirely satisfactory pale lager without Moravian barley, Saaz hops, and very soft water, but it won't be the same. Yeast selection is important as well (the Urquell brewery has historically used a blend of strains and a complex culturing process to maintain performance of each constituent member) but malt, hops, and water are the keys to the castle.

If you enjoy lager—hell, if you enjoy *beer*—this is a beer worth coming back to again and again. It isn't the loudest and most attention-seeking style out there, nor is it one that sits in the corner and fades behind the din. But when you taste a good Czech pilsner, you'll experience the entire history of beer right in your glass. It's there if you listen.

TYPICAL COMPOSITION

ORIGINAL EXTRACT: 11–14°P (1.044–1.057 SG)

ALCOHOL: 4–5.5% by volume

BITTERNESS: 30–45 IBU

COLOR: 3–6 SRM

SENSORY PROFILE

Gold to light copper and crystal clear, with a thick, pillowy, white head and bountiful lacing. The nose often includes a bready malt aspect and an assertive bouquet of spicy hops. A sip reveals malt that's more complex than the pale color might imply. There's a grainy sweetness, yes, but also a suggestion of caramel. Some examples might contain a touch of diacetyl too, which you may perceive as either a textural sensation of slickness on the tongue, or as a suggestion of butterscotch. Hop flavor is powerful but not in an audacious American IPA sort of way. It's a refined spicy and herbal hop flavor that is as intoxicating as it is substantial. The finish is typically well balanced between hop bitterness and malt sweetness.

SERVING SUGGESTION

Serve by the half-liter in a pilsner glass (Pokal) at 40 to 45°F (4 to 7°C).

OUTSTANDING EXAMPLES

Pilsener, New Belgium Brewing Company, Fort Collins, Colo., USA

Grainy Pils background with hints of corn and a bit of sulfur. Spicy, slightly herbal hop aroma. Brilliantly clear, classic Pils golden color, fluffy white head with good retention and outstanding lacing. Sweet, bready malt backbone. A bit of sulfur and sweet corn backed up by a firm but balanced bitterness that lingers well into the dry finish. Hop flavor is spicy and herbal. Medium body, no astringency.

New Belgium's Pilsener (called Blue Paddle prior to 2017) straddles a line between Czech- and German-style pilsner. A great, widely available pilsner that will pair well with any number of backyard barbecue dishes, Thai satay, or corn chowder.

Budweiser Budvar (Czechvar) Czech Lager, Budějovický Budvar, České Budějovice, Czech Republic

Spicy hops; crackery, bready malt; a touch of diacetyl; and a whiff of green-bottle skunk dominate the aroma. The body is deep gold with brilliant clarity and displays a white head that fades quickly. Rich bready malt, balanced by a firm but not-at-all-overwhelming bitterness, plays foil to a pleasant spicy and floral hop character. There's also a hint of diacetyl, which is appropriate in this style of beer. Budvar is soft on the palate but has a pleasing carbonic bite. Bitterness lingers into the finish and leaves an impression of crispness.

Despite the slight skunk that is virtually inevitable with green-bottle imports, this remains a definitive example of a Czech pale lager. Refreshing and imminently drinkable, this is a fine lager and one to seek out as fresh as possible.

Heater Allen Pils, Heater Allen Brewing, McMinnville, Ore., USA

Oskar Blues Mama's Little Yella Pils, Longmont, Colo., USA

Pilsner Urquell, Plzeňský Prazdroj, Pilsen, Czech Republic

Floral, spicy hop aroma atop a bready malt backbone with notes of caramel. Deep gold body borders on copper and showcases a pillowy white head and good lacing. Initial sip of spicy hop flavor gives way to a deep malt foundation that offers hints of caramel. A bracing bitterness extends through the taste and into the dry finish. The level of hops is on par with some of the newer hoppy American pilsners. Detectable but not over-the-top diacetyl offers both a tactile sensation of slickness and a bit of buttery popcorn flavor that complements the spicy hops. Long finish is decidedly bitter and imminently refreshing.

Can a beer be simultaneously rich and refreshing? This one is. Equally at home as a summer patio sipper or next to a hearty plate of roast pork in the darkness of winter, there's a reason this pilsner is a classic.

The brewery asserts that Pilsner Urquell is brewed to the same recipe originally conceived by Josef Groll in the nineteenth century, and while that claim is great for marketing, brewhouse modernization and variation in ingredients virtually guarantee that this is a different beer than that of 1842. Certainly, recent changes to packaging and shipping have ensured a better product by the time it reaches foreign shores.

An oldie but a goodie, this beer is one to seek out if you've never had it, and if you have, it's one to revisit. You might just fall in love with pilsner all over again.

Smiley Blue Pils, Stevens Point Brewery, Stevens Point, Wis., USA

Fresh cracker-like pils malt with a whiff of corn-like sweetness that fades quickly. Spicy, somewhat grassy hop character has a sharpness that initially surprises and is a testament to the freshness of this sample. Brilliantly clear yellow body that is slightly darker than straw blonde but not quite into golden territory. Fluffy white head shows good retention and leaves behind good lacing. Initial impression is of the almost grassy notes that give the impression of wet hops. There's also a peppery character that's unusual for a Czech pilsner. Lots and lots of dry hop character. Next up is crisp pils malt that is really just there to support the hops. Firm bitterness lingers well into the bone-dry finish. Pleasantly carbonic. This beer will make you burp! A touch of astringency works well in this beer.

A surprising take on a Czech pils that will have hopheads dancing for joy. This beer successfully manages what so many session IPAs attempt but fail. It delivers aggressive fresh hop character in a low-alcohol vehicle. The dryness of this example is particularly refreshing. If Steven's Point distributed where I live, this would be a staple in my fridge all summer long.

HELLES

A brewer who can turn out a good Bavarian-style helles is a brewer who knows what they're doing. Complex enough to delight a sophisticated palate, but straightforward enough to quaff by the liter, helles (pronounced "HELL-iss") may well be the most refined expression of malt, hops, water, and yeast on the planet.

EIN PROSIT, EIN PROSIT DER GEMÜTLICHKEIT: EINS, ZWEI, DREI, G'SUFFA!

With these words, countless tourists, wanderers, and college students have hoisted hefty dimpled mugs into the air, locked eyes with lederhosen-clad strangers, and taken deep draws of the golden elixir of the Munich Oktoberfest. The eye contact is critical, for failing to do so, it is said, leads to seven years' bad sex. (Whether the penalty accumulates over subsequent eye-averted toasts remains unclear.)

Germany is traditionally *the* destination for those who enjoy beer, or at least festive gatherings involving its mass consumption. The craft beer explosion has leveled the imbalance somewhat, and sampling a generous selection of well-made beer styles no longer necessitates vacationing in Bavaria. Still, Germany has held its own; for lovers of lager, a pilgrimage to the land of *Hopfen und Malz* continues to occupy prime position on the brewer's bucket list.

Germany's relevance and individuality derive from the elevated position that beer occupies in the national culture. Hairy hipsters of the Pacific Northwest have fixie-biked their way to craft beer festivals for a few decades now, but Bavarians have celebrated the Oktoberfest for more than two centuries. Beer is as central to the German psyche as tea is to the British.

Elegant locations are the norm—those accustomed to imbibing in a glorified garage will delight in the ubiquitous *Biergartens* and *Gaststätten*. Sometimes cheesy, but always charming, such locales offer respites from the day-to-day and envelop customers in the *Gemütlichkeit* for which Germany is so famous. It is entirely possible—expected, even—that a day's hike in the Black Forest will include pausing at one or two opportunities for liquid refreshment along the way.

What Teutonic beer lacks in stylistic diversity it more than makes up for in brewing precision. With more than five hundred years of Reinheitsgebot under its belt, Germany continues to set the mark to which all other lagers aspire.

Because helles is best served fresh, does not travel particularly well, and is difficult to brew, finding outstanding examples outside Bavaria remains challenging, despite craft brewers' noble attempts to master the style. It's a *tough* style to brew well, and the Bavarians have had more than a century during which to perfect it.

As we have seen in Chapter 3, helles is Bavaria's answer to pilsner, an adaptation of the light lager to the local brewing conditions of Munich and its environs. Brewmaster Gabriel Sedlmayr II of Munich's Spaten brewery introduced LagerBier Hell in 1894—a dramatic change from Bavaria's traditional darker beers—and helles has remained the everyday beer of Bavaria more or less ever since.

While the almost distilled softness of Pilsen's water could support large quantities of hops without rendering pilsner excessively bitter, Munich's somewhat harder water forced brewers to use restraint. Thus, while helles may, in the glass, appear indistinguishable from light lagers with more assertive hop character, this quintessentially Bavarian style is a showcase for soft pilsner malt, with spicy, floral noble hops playing a supporting role.

TYPICAL COMPOSITION
ORIGINAL EXTRACT: 11–12.5°P (1.044–1.051 SG)

ALCOHOL: 4.5–5.5% by volume

BITTERNESS: 18–25 IBU

COLOR: 3–6 SRM

SENSORY PROFILE
Straw-blonde and brilliantly clear body, with a fluffy white head that lasts and lasts. Sometimes, but not always, a shade lighter than German pils. Pilsner malt is the name of the game here. Look for a grainy sweetness up front, with a whiff of noble hops in the background. You might also pick up a light sulfur quality, which isn't a flaw in small amounts. In the flavor, as in the aroma, you'll first notice a pleasantly grainy soft malt sweetness from the pilsner malt that forms the backbone of the style. Noble hop flavor offers subtly spicy or floral overtones, but the focus always remains on the malt. A malty-soft yet thirst-quenching dry finish invites another sip. Or, as is customary, another liter.

SERVING SUGGESTION
Serve by the liter in a dimpled Maßkrug, or by the half-liter in a Willi becher, at 40 to 45°F (4 to 7°C).

OUTSTANDING EXAMPLES
Andechser Vollbier Hell, Klosterbrauerei Andechs, Andechs, Germany

Augustiner-Bräu Lagerbier Hell, Augustiner-Bräu, Munich, Germany

Augustiner-Bräu Edelstoff, Augustiner-Bräu, Munich, Germany
This is the export version of Augustiner's impressive Lagerbier Hell. Light hay-like hop aroma complemented by a soft, rounded pilsner malt depth. A straw-blonde body with exciting effervescence is topped by a small head with acceptable lacing. Flavor combines cracker-like pils malt sweetness with delicate floral hop flavor. Crisp carbonation and a smooth finish makes for an easy-drinking brew. The quintessential Munich helles, made half a percent stronger for the foreign market.

fun fact

Helles is the nominative form of the German adjective *hell*, which means "light." Thus, the name of the beer style translates roughly as "a light one." That the homophonically and orthographically identical English word refers to the lair of Mephistopheles has led to endless, often tiring wordplay. The most famous of these may well be Fucking Hell, which is brewed in Germany and named for the Austrian town of Fucking, a town that, as it happens, experiences some difficulty holding on to road signs.

Golden Export, Gordon Biersch Brewing Company, San Jose, Calif., USA

House Lager, Jack's Abby Brewing, Framingham, Mass., USA

Beautiful crisp pils malt and a light kiss of floral hops with hints of lemony citrus. Crystal clear light gold; initially dense white head falls to a small film of bubbles, but lacing is decent. Grainy malt with hints of sweetness and very light touches of floral hops. Restrained bitterness is appropriate for the style and cleanly executed. A slight hint of sulfur from the lager yeast. Moderate carbonation with a slightly creamy quality. No astringency. Light to medium body. Soft malt sweetness glides smoothly over the tongue and leaves behind just the faintest trace of hop flavor, followed by a restrained bitterness.

    Thirst-quenching and refreshing, this lager clearly demonstrates how a well-crafted American example can stand shoulder-to-shoulder with European imports. And with the freshness of this sample, it's in much better shape than much of what makes it here. An outstanding American craft example of a Munich-style helles.

Paulaner Original Münchner Hell, Paulaner Brauerei, Munich, Germany

Prost Brewing Helles, Prost Brewing Company, Denver, Colo., USA

Light noble-like hop aroma supported by doughy, bready pils malt and hints of honey. Very light gold body with a robust head that dissipates quickly. Grainy pils malt with very subtle floral hop highlights. Bitterness is apparent, but only just so. Just enough to support the malt. Soft, moderately carbonic palate. The perfect summer thirst quencher. Helles should be drinkable by the liter, and this one does not disappoint. At 5 percent ABV, this one is a little too strong to be sessionable, but it would make for an outstanding Radler.

Spaten Münchner Hell, Spaten-Franziskaner-Bräu, Munich, Germany

Victory Helles Lager, Victory Brewing Company, Downingtown, Pa., USA

Saltine cracker-like pils malt sweetness, a light hint of sulfur, and faint floral hops. Brilliantly clear, straw-blonde body, moderate head that drops fast, good lacing. Light water cracker-like sweetness, understated bitterness, very light floral hops. Light and spritzy, moderate carbonation, no astringency. One of the best readily available domestic examples of a classic Bavarian helles. A well-crafted light lager that will appeal to beer drinkers of all backgrounds and preferences. Round, soft malt sweetness dominates with only the lightest nod to delicate hop flavor and aroma.

Weihenstephaner Original Bayrisch Mild, Bayerische Staatsbrauerei Weihenstephan, Freising, Germany

Sweet, crackery pils malt with faint floral, herbal hops. Crystal-clear, straw-blonde body. Fluffy, pillowy, white head with excellent retention and great lacing. Classic Bavarian malt flavor: crackers and bread dough—and a touch biscuit-like—with a sweet, round aspect. Hop flavor is herbal and slightly lemony. Finish is just barely this side of dry, with a firm but balanced bitterness. Full bodied yet light—the classic *Vollmundigkeit* so desirable in this style. Lovely carbonation that is at once robust and mild. Just a very slight astringency that complements rather than distracts.

There's a reason Weihenstephan's helles is a classic, and not just because the brewery claims a lineage dating to 1040. Augustiner helles sets the standard for the citizens of Munich, but Weihenstephaner's wider availability makes it the standard worldwide. The correct answer to the question "What is a helles?" may very well be "Something that looks, smells, and tastes like Weihenstephaner." You want this. You want several liters of it on a sunny afternoon, sitting at a long table beneath the shade of a chestnut tree.

Weihenstephaner 1516 Kellerbier, Bayerische Staatsbrauerei Weihenstephan, Freising, Germany

Mandarin oranges, spicy pepper notes reminiscent of tequila, medium caramel. Hazy orange; initially fluffy white head fades and leaves behind a thin layer of bubbles. Good lacing. Tequila connotations continue from aroma into the flavor. Suggestions of wood. Soft bready malt character with a gentle but sufficient bitterness. Orange citrusy overtones. A touch of caramel sweetness rounds out the bitterness and begs another sip. Creamy and soft with smooth carbonation and no astringency. Full bodied. Feels heavier on the tongue than the beer actually is.

An interesting kellerbier that offers something a little different from the usual German pale lager. Soft and bready, full bodied and delicious. One might be forgiven for mistakenly thinking this beer was Belgian in origin. The hop character in particular is a departure from what you typically find in German lagers.

GERMAN PILSNER

Leave it to the Germans to take something perfect and attempt to improve upon it. When we say that most beer in the world today is a riff on pilsner, we really mean a riff on *German* pilsner. More aggressively hoppy than its Czech namesake, German pils (the Germans tend to use the truncated name to avoid confusion with the original) spans a range that starts with "Oh, I've had this before in a hotel bar, I think" and ends with "Nice job on the session IPA."

What the helles (see what I did there?) is to malt, German pils is to hops. While not a "hoppy" beer in the modern craft American IPA sense, German pilsner offers a refined, Continental treatment that remains simultaneously familiar (you've tasted this before . . .) and still-exciting.

If scrutinizing lager is new for you, you might wonder how German pils is different from the Czech original. There are two big things to look for. The first is color: German pils tends to be more yellow than gold, while Czech pilsner is a deep gold with an almost copper hue. The color difference is also expressed in the malt character. German examples will have a snappy, clean, cracker-y malt foundation, while Czech versions are rounder, softer, and often include a caramel element.

The second thing to look for is hop character. Czech pilsner is usually brewed with Czech hops, the most famous of which is Saaz (Žatec). German pils, on the other hand, leans more heavily on Bavarian hops like Hallertauer Mittelfrüh, Tettnanger, and Spalt. As a general rule, the further north you go in Germany, the bitterer and more assertive the pils—some say much like the German people themselves.

TYPICAL COMPOSITION

ORIGINAL EXTRACT: 11–13.5°P (1.044–1.055 SG)

ALCOHOL: 4.5–5.4% by volume

BITTERNESS: 25–40 IBU

COLOR: 3–5 SRM

SENSORY PROFILE

Straw-blonde to golden and brilliantly clear body, with a dense, white, long-lasting head. Visually similar to helles, but often leans ever so slightly more toward gold than straw. Noble hop aroma typically jumps out of the glass, backed up by the crisp, malty sweetness of pilsner malt. A faint sulfur note is also common. While helles showcases malt, German pils is more hop-focused. A distinctive noble hop flavor dominates the palate, supported by a clean, crackery pils malt backbone. Bitterness is firm and assertive.

SERVING SUGGESTION

Serve by the third-liter or half-liter in a pilsner flute at 40 to 45°F (4 to 7°C).

OUTSTANDING EXAMPLES

Dry Dock Pilsner, Dry Dock Brewing Company, Aurora, Colo., USA

Heater Allen Pils, Heater Allen Brewing, McMinnville, Ore., USA
Biscuit-like malt and earthy, spicy hops. Some honey-like notes reminiscent of mead. Hazy gold with a robust head and lace that won't quit. Cracker-like malt and floral hops present initially in equal measure, then the malt fades somewhat and allows the spiciness of the hops to shine through. Finish is long, bitter, and dry. Creamy yet prickly high carbonation. Light-medium

body. No astringency. A fine Continental-style lager that toes the line between German and Czech takes on the style. An outstanding pilsner and one that ought to be on your bucket list the next time you visit the Pacific Northwest. You want a session beer? Forget session IPA. Drink this instead.

König Pilsener, König-Brauerei, Duisburg, Germany

pFriem Pilsner, pFriem Family Brewers, Hood River, Ore., USA

Prima Pils, Victory Brewing Company, Downingtown, Pa., USA

Prost Keller Pils, Prost Brewing Company, Denver, Colo., USA

The aroma offers spicy noble-like hops and clean, crackery pils malt, while the body showcases hazy gold with a white head that dissipates quickly. Bright, spicy hop flavor up front, supported by a light, bready malt backbone. Firm bitterness should satisfy IPA fans without overwhelming newcomers to craft. Good attenuation—finishes dry with a lingering back-of-the-throat bitterness. The natural carbonation is evident and delivers a softer, rounder impression than is found in a standard Pils. A great example of a keller/zwickel beer, as good as you're likely to find without taking it directly from the bright tank yourself.

pFriem Family Brewers Pilsner (see recipe page 212).

Radeberger Pilsner, Radeberger Exportbierbrauerei, Radeberg, Germany

Crisp, clean, spicy noble-like hop aroma. One whiff and you know it's a northern German pils. No skunk. Blonde to light gold; brilliant clarity; initial fluffy white head fades to a thin layer of bubbles. Noble-like hops make the first impression, followed immediately by soft pilsner malt and a suggestion of sweetness. It's only a suggestion, though, as the beer finishes dry. Very faint sweet corn-like notes in the middle. Crisp and moderately carbonated. A very light touch of astringency. For me, this is the standard for what German pilsner should be. Spicy hop aroma up front draws you in and sets the stage for a crisp, dry, hop-forward (though not "hoppy" by North American craft standards) sip that rides on a wave of grainy malt flavor. The dry finish makes for an exceptionally drinkable pale lager. Other German breweries would do well to take a cue from Radeberger and package in brown glass!

Rothaus Pils, Badische Staatsbrauerei Rothaus, Grafenhausen, Germany

Sunshine Pils, Tröegs Brewing Company, Hershey, Pa., USA

Lager-appropriate sulfur, a bit of soap, some floral hops, pils graininess. Mostly clear, very slightly hazy, straw-blonde body. White fluffy head that drops to about a pinkie width and leaves behind good chunky lace. Sharp, noble-like hop aroma followed by crackery malt. Assertive bitterness stays on the back on the tongue long after the sip. Crisp, clean, spritzy, moderately high carbonation. A fantastic American interpretation of the German pilsner. Noble hop flavor is slathered onto a good pils foundation, with the yeast introducing a bit of its own character. At 45 IBU, this is a bitter pilsner that satisfies.

Trumer Pils, Trumer Brauerei, Salzburg, Austria and Berkeley, Calif., USA

An initial whiff of green bottle skunk upon opening dissipates somewhat after being poured but never completely disappears. A bit of floral noble hop aroma and subtle grainy malt. Trumer Pils is brilliantly clear blonde with an initially fluffy white head that dissipates into a thin raft of bubbles and displays decent lacing. Initial impression is of noble-type, herbal, floral hops and a respectable bitterness that, while firm, leaves enough room for malt sweetness to show its face. The finish is dry, but the impression of malt sweetness helps maintain balance. Bitterness doesn't stick around in the aftertaste at first but manages to come back for a reprisal after the beer goes down the hatch. Crisp, clean, and satisfying. Moderately high carbonation is right on target for this kind of beer. There's a tiny bit of astringency, but it doesn't distract as much as complement the crispness.

Trumer brews a great German pilsner, and the Austrian brewery cemented its dedication to quality by building a second brewery in Berkeley, California, rather than have its beer suffer the indignity and degradation of a trip across the Atlantic. Why they insist on packaging in green bottles, then, is beyond me, and I wish they would rethink it. Get this one on draft when you can, and if you must buy it in bottles, do your best to keep it away from light. Your mileage may vary.

Weihenstephaner Pilsner, Bayerische Staatsbrauerei Weihenstephan, Freising, Germany

DORTMUNDER EXPORT

Dortmunder export is a chameleon style. Somewhere between the round, malty delicacy of the helles and the assertive hop character of the German pils lies the dortmunder export. It's not an easy beer to classify, at least not within what we think of as style guidelines today (In fact, the 2015 Beer Judge Certification Program guidelines absorbed dortmunder into a broader category called German helles exportbier). In some ways, the dortmunder export category has become where we send German-style pale lagers that don't quite conform to the helles and pils archetypes.

Sometimes it acts like a hoppy helles. Other times, it's more like a soft pilsner. Either way, dortmunder is a delightfully drinkable light lager of moderate strength when you can get your hands on it. The German brand DAB is readily available in most markets, and if you can find it on draft or in cans, you'll have a great time. Avoid the green bottles, though, unless you're willing to play light-struck roulette.

TYPICAL COMPOSITION
ORIGINAL EXTRACT: 12–14°P (1.049–1.057 SG)
ALCOHOL: 5–6% by volume
BITTERNESS: 20–30 IBU
COLOR: 3–7 SRM

SENSORY PROFILE
Dortmunder-style lagers are built on mineral-rich water and express a pleasant balance between malt sweetness and hop bitterness. Appearance-wise, dortmunder is indistinguishable from German pils or any other pale lager. The nose has firm but not outspoken hop character—usually floral or herbal—along with cracker-like pils malt sweetness. Flavor is similarly balanced between grainy Continental malt and floral hops, and the finish is often a little sweet but tempered by hop bitterness. The mouthfeel offers a compromise between smooth viscosity and carbonic bite.

SERVING SUGGESTION

Serve by the half-liter in a Willi becher at 40 to 45°F (4 to 7°C).

OUTSTANDING EXAMPLES

DAB Original, Dortmunder Actien Brauerei, Dortmund, Germany

Golden Export, Gordon Biersch Brewing Company, San Jose, Calif., USA

Great Lakes Dortmunder Gold, Great Lakes Brewing Company, Cleveland, Ohio, USA

Soft, bready, almost dough-like malt with herbal hoppy overtones. Deep gold, almost pushing into American pale ale and IPA territory. Initially robust white head fades to a millimeter of foam but leaves impressive lacing. Sweet, bready malt complemented by slightly spicy and herbal hops with a faint musty note. Balanced bitterness leaves a refreshing, long finish. Medium bodied with moderate, creamy carbonation. No astringency. Rounder and a little heavier on the tongue than your typical pale lager. A little darker and stronger than most pale lagers, this dortmunder goes down smooth and virtually demands another sip. The addition of caramel malt and Pacific Northwest hops gives this lager a character that aficionados of old-school American pale ales will appreciate.

Jahrhundert Bier, Brauerei Aying Franz Inselkammer KG, Aying, Germany

Fresh bread dough, honey, a faint whiff of sulfur. Herbal, grassy, slightly spicy hops. Brilliantly clear body, between straw blonde and golden. Thick fluffy white foam that lasts and lasts. Incredible lacing that won't quit. Bready pils malt, suggestions of hay and fresh cut grass. A subtle hint of corn. Spicy. Finish is off-dry and tilted in favor of malt sweetness. Restrained bitterness. Incredibly smooth, creamy carbonation. Beer feels luxurious on the tongue. A hint of astringency. A thoroughly enjoyable pale lager that typifies the catchall export designation conferred upon lagers with enough strength to survive shipment abroad. At 5.5 percent ABV, Jahrhundert Bier is hardly "strong" in today's craft landscape (indeed, it's barely more alcoholic than Full Sail's Session Lager), but it's a solid export worth your attention.

MÄRZEN (OKTOBERFEST)

Oktoberfest beer can be a little confusing because there are two kinds. As we saw in Chapter 3, märzen replaced dunkel as the beer of the Munich Oktoberfest in 1841. Märzen remained the beer of choice for more than a century until it was gradually displaced by a strong golden lager that is more amped-up helles than classic märzen. This lighter lager, called *festbier*, is profiled in the next section and is the official fuel of Munich's Oktoberfest today. But in North America, oktoberfest beer remains virtually synonymous with märzen, and that's the style we discuss now.

As previously discussed, the word *märzen* derives from *März*, the German word for March. When summer brewing was outlawed in Bavaria, märzen was the slightly stronger "keeping beer" that brewers put down in March and lagered throughout the summer. Its association with Oktoberfest comes down to the convenient fact that these beers would have filled the gap between the end of summer (by which time the very last beers brewed in spring would have either been depleted and/or infected) and the arrival of brewers' first batches of autumn after they could resume business on September 29.

Now, märzen as we know it today really didn't come about until the middle of the nineteenth century, but the idea of "March beer" goes back much longer, perhaps even as far back as the summer brewing prohibition of 1553. But it is the amber lager that Spaten debuted in 1841, refined for thirty years and rebranded as oktoberfestbier in 1872, that has defined modern märzen.

TYPICAL COMPOSITION
ORIGINAL EXTRACT: 12.5–15°P (1.051–1.061 SG)
ALCOHOL: 5–6% by volume
BITTERNESS: 20–25 IBU
COLOR: 5–15 SRM

SENSORY PROFILE
Märzen presents with a color that ranges from light copper to reddish brown. American craft examples might run a little darker than their German counterparts, owing to more generous use of caramel and color malts. The head is usually off-white and exhibits good retention. Malt is the name of the game, both in the aroma and on the palate, with a toasted, bready quality. Hop flavor and aroma are both subdued in favor of the bready malt backbone. Bitterness is firm enough to supply balance but yields the floor to malty goodness. Note, however, that malty doesn't mean sweet. A surefire way to ruin a good märzen is to have a too-sweet finish. The best examples are boisterously malty but have a long, dry finish that makes them immensely drinkable.

SERVING SUGGESTION
Serve by the liter in a dimpled Maßkrug, or by the half-liter in a Willi becher, at 45 to 50°F (7 to 10°C).

OUTSTANDING EXAMPLES
Ayinger Oktober Fest-Märzen, Brauerei Aying Franz Inselkammer KG, Aying, Germany

Brooklyn Oktoberfest, Brooklyn Brewery, Brooklyn, N.Y., USA
Moderate toffee, toasted bread, somewhat nutty, faint hops. Suggestions of pumpkin pie spice. Slightly hazy, deep orange-ish amber; moderate off-white head dissipates rapidly, minimal lacing. Toffee carries over from the aroma, as does the interesting spiciness. Plenty of malty goodness to enjoy here and barely a hint of floral hops. Finish is sweet but has enough hop bitterness to keep it balanced. Medium bodied and slightly creamy with a mild carbonic bite; moderate carbonation; no astringency. A solid American oktoberfest. A little "muddy" and heavy on the caramel compared to classic examples, but if you enjoy English winter warmers, this could be your lager!

Märzen Oktoberfest, Prost Brewing Company, Denver, Colo., USA

Oktoberfest, Fort Collins Brewery, Fort Collins, Colo., USA

Oktoberfest, Great Lakes Brewing Company, Cleveland, Ohio, USA

Oktoberfest, Left Hand Brewing Company, Longmont, Colo., USA
Deep melanoidin-like malt aroma with toasted whole wheat bread and very subtle hops. Deep russet and brilliantly clear with an off-white head that fades quickly but leaves good lacing.

Hints of raisins and light toffee; long finish that slightly favors malt sweetness over drinkable dryness. Clean lager fermentation character. Moderate carbonation; light and spritzy on the tongue; a touch of astringency in the finish. Ever so slightly darker and sweeter than traditional Bavarian oktoberfest, but very much in line with American interpretations of the style. Residual sweetness and elevated alcohol make it a little heavy to consider drinking by the liter, but served in a goblet, this would be a great foil for aged or smoked gouda.

Oktoberfest, Stoudt's Brewing Company, Adamstown, Pa., USA

Paulaner Oktoberfest-Märzen, Paulaner Brauerei, Munich, Germany

Toasted bread, light caramel, and herbal hops. Bright copper with a thin white head and acceptable lacing. Toast, biscuits, light toffee, and a bit of yeasty sulfur. Medium bodied, certainly lighter than many North American examples. Light and spritzy on the tongue. I admit to being a little sentimental about this beer. It was the first "real" beer I ever tasted, and even though there are fresher and more complex examples, all those ranks of beer tent servers hoisting impossible numbers of liter mugs make me happy every time.

Point Oktoberfest, Stevens Point Brewery, Stevens Point, Wis., USA

Biscuity, bready malt and a hint of slightly earthy hops. Crystal-clear copper body with a healthy white head but not much lacing. Lovely malty backbone: not too light, not too chewy. On the lighter side as American craft oktoberfests go, but fairly in line with German examples. Focus is on biscuits and toast with only a vague suggestion of hop flavor. Finish is balanced and not too sweet with soft bitterness. Creamy moderate carbonation, a touch of astringency. American drinkers accustomed to heavy malt bomb oktoberfests might feel underwhelmed by this example, but it's right where it should be and a great representation of the style.

Samuel Adams Octoberfest, Boston Beer Company, Boston, Mass., USA

Dark copper body with light red highlights and a creamy, off-white head. Head falls quickly but leaves behind outstanding lace. The aroma is of toasted bread crust, light toffee, and a mild hint of herbal hops. The flavor is decidedly malty, with a pleasant toasted quality, moderate caramel, and light dried fruit. Very slight hop flavor. Mouthfeel is rich, creamy, and full bodied, and the finish is malty-sweet with a light bitterness.

A classic American craft oktoberfest that has gained quite a seasonal following, this example leans a little more heavily on caramel flavor than most German märzen beers and has a correspondingly sweeter and fuller-bodied finish. Its ubiquity, affordability, and freshness make it a great choice for autumn.

Schell's Oktoberfest, August Schell Brewing Company, New Ulm, Minn., USA

FESTBIER

Festbier is a relative newcomer to the world of German lager, having originally been developed by Paulaner in the 1970s as an easy-drinking alternative to the traditional oktoberfest beer, märzen. By 1990, all six of the Munich breweries that serve at the Wiesn—Augustiner-Bräu, Hacker-Pschorr, Hofbräu, Löwenbräu, Paulaner, and Spaten—had switched from märzen to the newer festbier.

OPPOSITE: Festbier, the beer of the modern Oktoberfest (see recipe page 213).

The term *festbier* is mainly used outside Germany because *oktoberfestbier* enjoys protected status in its homeland as the name of the beer served at the eponymous event. For example, the beer that Paulaner sells as Oktoberfest-Märzen in North America is known within Germany as Original Münchner Märzen. But Paulaner's German Oktoberfest Bier is renamed Wiesn when it ships to other countries. This duality of oktoberfest beer can be confusing.

So what, exactly, is this festbier? It's a moderately strong (6 to 6.5 percent ABV) golden lager that lies somewhere north of export strength helles and retains a touch of the deeper malty-ness of märzen without quite getting into maibock territory. Clear, right? The grist is typically a blend of pilsner malt and Munich malt, so it's not quite accurate to call it a kind of helles from an ingredient standpoint. But, from a sensory perspective, festbier has more in common with helles than it does with märzen or maibock.

You know it when you drink it. And when you drink it, you tend to drink a lot of it.

TYPICAL COMPOSITION
ORIGINAL EXTRACT: 13–14.5°P (1.053–1.059 SG)

ALCOHOL: 6–6.5% by volume

BITTERNESS: 20–30 IBU

COLOR: 4–6 SRM

SENSORY PROFILE
Festbier has a crystal-clear, deep gold body and a fluffy white head that won't quit. It's a shade darker than a standard helles but a shade lighter than märzen. Aroma- and flavor-wise, expect a rich malt backbone accented with floral, spicy, noble-like hops. Like all good German quaffing lagers, it has a relatively full body and a dry, crisp finish, though the balance leans more malty-sweet than some other light-colored styles. Unlike märzen, you won't find any of the toasty or slightly caramel notes associated with highly kilned malts, even though Munich makes up a portion of the grist. A well-crafted festbier is dangerously easy to drink by the liter.

SERVING SUGGESTION REQUIREMENT
Serve by the liter in a dimpled Maßkrug, at 40 to 45°F (4 to 7°C). Doing it any other way just misses the point.

OUTSTANDING EXAMPLES
Augustiner Bräu Oktoberfest, Augustiner-Bräu, Munich, Germany

Hacker-Pschorr Festbier, Hacker-Pschorr, Munich, Germany

Hofbräu Festbier, Hofbräuhaus, Munich, Germany

Löwenbräu Oktoberfestbier, Löwenbräu, Munich, Germany

Paulaner Wiesn, Paulaner Brauerei, Munich, Germany
Pours crystal-clear gold with a beautiful fluffy white head that exhibits good retention and lacing. Aroma of light, herbal, floral hops and soft, cracker-like malt. Soft pils malt dominates the flavor, along with notes of light honey adding richness. The same herbal, floral hop character from the aroma plays a supporting role, as well as a touch of light hay. The crisp, smooth mouthfeel helps this beer glide down the throat effortlessly, leaving behind an impression of delicate malt sweetness barely balanced by hop bitterness.

These beers travel a little better than the helles lagers from which they take their inspiration, but they're best enjoyed beneath a tent at Oktoberfest. Nonetheless, it's a real treat to get to enjoy this style beyond its region of origin. Prost!

Weihenstephaner Oktoberfestbier, Bayerische Staatsbrauerei Weihenstephan, Freising, Germany

VIENNA LAGER

Lagerbier nach Wiener Art—lager beer in the style of Vienna—is how Spaten's Gabriel Sedlmayr originally described his new märzenbier, which was based on Anton Dreher's new Vienna lager. It thus makes sense that, even today, the line between Vienna lager and märzen is somewhat blurry.

Fundamentally and theoretically, a Vienna lager is built around Vienna malt, while märzen is built around Munich malt. Munich malts are more highly kilned than Vienna malts, so they tend to be darker in color and offer a deeper malt experience that can include some toasted aspects. Vienna malt is lighter and grainier and doesn't have quite the malty depth of Munich malt. Those differences show in the final beer.

In today's craft landscape, however, where small breweries may only keep a couple of base malts on hand, this distinction doesn't always hold. A brewery that goes through a lot of pilsner and Munich malts might use a blend of these two to brew the occasional Vienna lager rather than maintain a supply of Vienna malt.

Regardless of the grist composition, Vienna lager often (but not always) is a little lighter in color than märzen, has a little more bitterness, and has less malt richness. Phrased another way, on a continuous spectrum with pilsner at one end and märzen at the other, Vienna lager lies closer to märzen than it does to pilsner, but not as close as you might think.

As discussed in Chapter 4, Vienna lager gained popularity in Mexico even as it lost ground to pilsner in Europe. Thus, many of the classic "dark" Mexican lagers today owe their heritage to Vienna lager. Negra Modelo, Dos Equis Amber, Victoria, and Bohemia Obscura are all born of Mexico's Vienna lager heritage. And though most have evolved over the years, not always for the better, Mexico's dark lagers remain a reminder of the influence of Austrian brewers one hundred and fifty years ago.

TYPICAL COMPOSITION
ORIGINAL EXTRACT: 11.5–13.5°P (1.046–1.055 SG)
ALCOHOL: 4.5–5.5% by volume
BITTERNESS: 20–30 IBU
COLOR: 10–20 SRM

SENSORY PROFILE
The nose is typically malty-sweet, perhaps with suggestions of toast or some light caramel. Traditional examples won't have much in the way of hop aroma, but modern craft brewers might not resist the urge to add some late-kettle hops to deliver some floral or herbal notes. Look for a light copper body with a just off-white head that may or may not stick around. The flavor delivers the malty character promised in the aroma, but sweetness is less than one might suspect based on the nose alone. The best examples have a crisp, refreshing, dry finish that nicely balances malt depth with hop bitterness for a supremely drinkable amber lager. Vienna lager tends to be light to medium bodied, with American craft examples leaning a little more heavy than their Mexican counterparts.

SERVING SUGGESTION

Serve by the half liter in a dimpled mug or Willi becher, at 45 to 50°F (7 to 10°C).

OUTSTANDING EXAMPLES

Chuckanut Vienna Lager, Chuckanut Brewery and Kitchen, Bellingham, Wash., USA

Churchville Lager, Neshaminy Creek Brewing Company, Croydon, Pa., USA

Danish Red Lager, Figueroa Mountain Brewing Company, Buellton, Calif., USA

Eliot Ness, Great Lakes Brewing Company, Cleveland, Ohio, USA

Puesta del Sol, WeldWerks Brewing Company, Greeley, Colo., USA

Moderate toffee and toasted bread; light roasted nuts; light caramel. Deep amber with red highlights and a healthy off-white head that drops to about a millimeter thick with good lacing. Pleasantly nutty with moderate caramel and a deep, toasted bread crust flavor. Clean lager fermentation profile and (if this is possible) even cleaner bitterness. Crisp, clean finish. Creamy mouthfeel with lively carbonation; medium-full body; no astringency. Think of your favorite Mexican amber lager and make it fresher and more flavorful. This is a great Mexican-style lager in the Vienna tradition and one worth seeking out. Will pair well with spicy Mexican cuisine, of course, but also with hearty central European specialties like pierogis and goulash.

Schell's FireBrick, August Schell Brewing Company, New Ulm, Minn., USA

Vienna Lager, Devil's Backbone Brewing Company, Roseland, Va., USA

Biscuits, light caramel, toasted bread. Very light hops. Brilliantly clear amber body; fluffy off-white head dissipates to a couple of mm. Lacing is good. Toast and whole wheat crackers, with a little toffee. A touch of earthy hops that do not dominate. Bitterness is sufficient but not overpowering. Crisp, with moderately high carbonation of a creamy quality. No astringency. Medium to full body. A fine Vienna lager that exemplifies the style well. In the same family as amber Mexican lagers but considerably more flavorful. A great accompaniment to a wide variety of foods. A great introductory amber lager for those accustomed only to light lagers.

MAIBOCK

Literally "May bock," maibock is a transition beer that bridges the gap between the strong, malty lagers of winter and the lighter, more sessionable light lagers and *weißbiers* of summer. It's a wolf in sheep's clothing, with a lightness of body and color that belies the strong malty lager that lies within.

Sometimes called helles bock, the only thing *hell* (light) about maibock is its pale golden hue. Otherwise, this is a bock that can easily approach doppelbock territory in terms of strength. It's the perfect après-ski libation for late spring, when a bright sun remains in the sky a little longer each day, even as winter's icy grip remains firmly in control.

TYPICAL COMPOSITION

ORIGINAL EXTRACT: 16–18°P (1.066–1.075 SG)

ALCOHOL: 6–8% by volume

BITTERNESS: 20–35 IBU

COLOR: 5–10 SRM

SENSORY PROFILE

Like all members of the bock family, maibock delivers a malt-forward nose. Unlike standard bock and doppelbock, though, that malt leans more toward grainy, bready sweetness than it does dark fruit and rich depth. This is a style that sneaks up on you, and that begins in the nose. The golden body with its fluffy white head might fool you into thinking you've received a much lighter beer than you ordered, but those misconceptions fly out the door when you take a sip. The malt character lies somewhere between helles and märzen but is usually a little richer than festbier. A bit of toasted character adds complexity, while some floral or spicy hops in the nose and on the palate are often present—certainly more so than in a standard bock or doppelbock. Maibock is heavier on the tongue than its pale color might foreshadow, but again, not as weighty as doppelbock. Creamy, slightly elevated carbonation and a touch more bitterness add to the easy-drinking character of this strong lager.

SERVING SUGGESTION

Serve by the third liter or half liter in a dimpled mug or Willi becher, at 50 to 55°F (10 to 13°C).

OUTSTANDING EXAMPLES

Ayinger Maibock, Brauerei Aying Franz Inselkammer KG, Aying, Germany

Blonde Bock, Gordon Biersch Brewing Company, San Jose, Calif., USA
Toasty malt, light caramel. Delicate. Brilliantly clear, moderate copper body. Robust off-white head with moderate retention and okay lacing. Toasty Munich-like malt with a slightly chewy aspect and notes of honey. Mild bitterness and a slightly sweet finish. Medium bodied. Creamy carbonation, smooth and delicate on the palate. This maibock will sneak up on you. It's a smooth, malty sipper that is all too easy to slam. Take it easy and enjoy this maibock with duck confit on a snowy afternoon.

Einbecker Mai-Ur-Bock, Einbecker Brauhaus, Einbeck, Germany

Hofbräu Maibock, Hofbräuhaus, Munich, Germany

Mahr's Bock-Bier, Mahrs-Bräu, Bamberg, Germany

Maibock, Fort Collins Brewery, Fort Collins, Colo., USA
A rich, bready malt aroma with notes of plums and moderate toffee and a light kiss of spicy hops. The deep amber body is topped with an off-white, almost tan head that develops quickly and falls just as fast. Rich malt flavors of toasted brown bread, golden raisins, light melanoidin character, and maybe a touch of light oxidation (the good kind). A bit of herbal-spicy hops in the finish with a soft bitterness that's just enough to offset the malt. The finish is relatively dry for a beer of this weight and malt depth. Creamy, moderate carbonation. Full bodied with no astringency. An outstanding maibock that leans toward the dark edge of the style and nudges up against standard bock territory without crossing over into it. Attenuation is paramount to making a good bock, and this one doesn't disappoint. The just-shy-of-dry finish makes FCB maibock a hefty beer that's easy to drink.

Maibock, Stoudt's Brewing Company, Adamstown, Pa., USA

Maibock Hurts Like Helles, Jack's Abby Brewing, Framingham, Mass., USA

OLD WORLD DARK LAGERS

The dark lagers of Europe take us back to the beginning of beer itself. The pilsner revolution that took hold in 1842 needed barely a century to change beer all around the world. But before there was pilsner, Europeans had a few millennia of dark beer under their belts. And for several centuries, brewers in Bavaria and elsewhere had been transforming those dark beers into dark lagers through the triumph of cold fermentation.

If European pale lagers epitomize the genteel and the refined, Old World dark lagers remind us of beer's humble provenance. Staring into the dark depths of a dunkel or doppelbock, one is transported to the cold cellar of a medieval monastery, where those who enjoyed the brewing privilege developed libations that would go on to fuel reformation and renaissance. Pale lager is Mozart's *Eine kleine Nachtmusik*. Dark lagers are the introductory measures of Beethoven's Symphony No. 9.

Smuttynose Brewing Company Baltic Porter (see recipe page 214).

In this genre, you'll find comparatively light styles like Munich dunkel as well as obsidian jewels like schwarzbier and the uniquely powerful Baltic porter. But the crowning achievement of European dark lager is arguably bock and its variations. Excepting the black sheep of the family, maibock, bocks are dark and rich with none of the roast character we often associate with beers of such color. Malty depth is the name of the game.

Newcomers to lager are sometimes surprised that dark lager is even a thing. After all, a pint of lager in the United Kingdom is synonymous with the pale. And in North America, the word *lager* is commonly confused with *pilsner*. Perhaps it's because dark lager never quite caught on in the United States (Mexico, of course, is another story), but this family of beers is foreign to many craft beer aficionados and novices alike.

If you've never explored the richness on offer in the European dark lager family, I urge you to make it a priority to seek out dunkel and bock, schwarzbier and Baltic porter. They're not always the easiest beer styles to find, but I can assure you your efforts will be rewarded. The next time you're deciding what to drink, opt for something dark and stormy—not the cocktail, the lager.

CZECH DARK LAGER

There must be some universal truth about light and dark that applies to beer because every great brewing culture has it, and the Czechs are no different. For all the acclaim that has been bestowed upon pale Czech lagers since 1842, dark lager remains as popular as ever.

Arguably the most famous of these is the Flekovský Tmavý Ležák brewed at Prague's U Fleků brewery, which traces its history to 1499 and claims to be the oldest brewpub in Europe. Assertions of longevity in European brewing are as difficult to prove as they are ubiquitous, but there's no denying the popularity and high regard of U Fleků's one and only beer.

Not many breweries in North America make this interesting style, and imports are not all that common. The ones that do get here might not be in the best of shape, owing to the persistence of the Euro import green bottle. If you enjoy German schwarzbier or dry Irish stout, this is an oft-overlooked lager style worth seeking out.

TYPICAL COMPOSITION
ORIGINAL EXTRACT: 12–14°P (1.049–1.057 SG)
ALCOHOL: 4.2–5.5% by volume
BITTERNESS: 20–35 IBU
COLOR: 15–30 SRM

At press time, the Žatec brewery proudly proclaimed on its website that its Žatec Dark Lager was "a truly unique beer, for women and men." The jury is still out on its suitability for children.

SENSORY PROFILE

Although Czech dark lager might appear jet black at first glance, many are very dark brown—you might notice some ruby highlights around the base of your glass in the lighter examples. A big ivory head is appealing and offers the same sort of white-on-black contrast found in a freshly poured Guinness Draught. These lagers are malt-focused and may exhibit a coffee-like roast character along with rich bread and a slight caramel sweetness. Hop aromas and flavors are usually muted, but hop bitterness can be substantial. Some will have a bit of sweetness in the finish, but a dry, bitter finish is more common.

SERVING SUGGESTION

Serve by the half-liter in a dimpled mug at 45 to 50°F (7 to 10°C).

OUTSTANDING EXAMPLES

Budweiser Budvar (Czechvar) B Dark, Budějovický Budvar, České Budějovice, Czech Republic

Pours deep, deep ruby, but not quite black, with a thick tan head that falls quickly. Aromas of soft malt sweetness, light coffee roast, toasted bread, and a slight hop spice greet the nose. The flavor offers a coffee-like roasted character with a bit of roast bitterness, some hints of cola, and a faint nuttiness. Hop flavor is subtle, but it's there and leaves a woodsy-herbal impression. Moderate carbonation and light bodied for the color. The finish is dry, crisp, and refined.

Czech dark lagers are fairly hard to find in North America, but those who seek them out will be richly rewarded. Budvar B Dark is widely distributed and about as sessionable a dark lager as one could ask for. Far from the proverbial meal in a glass, this is a sheep in wolf's clothing well worth your time.

Morana, Devil's Backbone Brewing Company, Roseland, Va., USA

Flekovský tmavý ležák, U Fleků Pivovar, Prague, Czech Republic

Staropramen Černý, Pivovary Staropramen, Prague, Czech Republic

Žatec Dark Lager, Žatecký Pivovar, Žatec, Czech Republic

MUNICH DUNKEL

Munich dunkel may very well be the world's oldest continuously brewed major beer style. It is the classic lager of Bavaria, and even in today's pale lager-dominated marketplace, Munich dunkel remains popular. It is a rich, malty beer that showcases highly kilned Munich malt, kind of the lager equivalent of a Scottish 80/–.

Dunkel, which means "dark" in German, has approximately the same level of bitterness as märzen but much richer malt character. That richness, however, does not preclude drinkability, and a good dunkel is never cloyingly sweet.

TYPICAL COMPOSITION

ORIGINAL EXTRACT: 11.5–14°P (1.046–1.057 SG)

ALCOHOL: 4.5–5.5% by volume

BITTERNESS: 15–30 IBU

COLOR: 15–25 SRM

SENSORY PROFILE

Dunkel pours with a reddish-brown body that can exhibit varying levels of translucence. In most cases, you can still see through the beer despite its relatively dark color. An ivory head with good retention is typical. Aroma and flavor are malt-forward with a fresh, toasty character and little to no hop presence. There can be some cocoa-like notes, but these are typically subdued. The finish is long and malty, but with a firm hop bitterness that provides balance. Munich dunkel is full bodied and rich but not viscous, and creamy medium carbonation supplies enough prickle on the tongue to complement the substantial malt foundation.

SERVING SUGGESTION

Serve by the half liter in a dimpled mug or Willi becher, at 45 to 50°F (7 to 10°C).

OUTSTANDING EXAMPLES

Augustiner Bräu Dunkel, Augustiner-Bräu, Munich, Germany

Ayinger Altbairisch Dunkel, Brauerei Aying Franz Inselkammer KG, Aying, Germany

Mild dark fruit (plums and raisins), chocolate, and bread crust. No hop aroma. Deep russet body with red highlights. Off-white head dissipates to a thin layer of bubbles with very little lacing. A very beautiful beer! Rich malts evoke dried fruit and dark bread. Hints of caramel, chocolate, and slight roast character. Very low hop flavor. Despite the powerful malt, the finish is dry and immensely drinkable. Bitterness is mild. Medium bodied, crisp, and exceptionally refreshing. The richness of the dark malts in this dunkel leave one with the impression of a beer that's much heavier than it is. A great thirst-quenching dark beer. If you enjoy English brown ale, this is your lager.

Chuckanut Dunkel, Chuckanut Brewery and Kitchen, Bellingham, Wash., USA

Fearless Youth, Grimm Brothers Brewhouse, Loveland, Colo., USA

Toasted bread crust, light toffee, light floral notes. Moderate amber, very slightly hazy body; moderate head that dissipates quickly and leaves a thin raft of bubbles. Very low lacing. Toasted bread carries over from the aroma into the flavor, but aromatic suggestions of caramel aren't present. A straightforward expression of highly kilned (by today's standards) malt with just the faintest suggestion of hop flavor. Firm but restrained bitterness to balance. Creamy and slightly viscous with a pleasant weight on the tongue. Moderate carbonation with very slight astringency. Hopheads need not apply, but those who appreciate exploring the malty depths will relish this true expression of the term "liquid bread." Fearless Youth would pair well with Emmenthaler or triple-cream Brie, and, of course, a hearty Bavarian-style pretzel.

Hacker-Pschorr Münchner Dunkel, Hacker-Pschorr Bräu, Munich, Germany

I Dunkeled in My Pants, Figueroa Mountain Brewing Company, Buellton, Calif., USA

Knight Ryder Munich Dunkel, Equinox Brewing Company, Fort Collins, Colo., USA

Prost Dunkel, Prost Brewing Company, Denver, Colo., USA

Toasted bread and light toffee on the nose. Body is a deep reddish mahogany; thick, off-white head dissipates quickly. Deep toasty, bready malt supported by just enough bitterness to keep it in check. Virtually no hop flavor, but what there is has a floral component. Flavor really opens up as it warms. Recommend drinking it a little warmer than it's served. Good weight on the tongue—weighty without being heavy. Bitterness is fleeting but just the right amount to balance the malt. A slight astringency in the finish. Medium carbonation. A great lager for those who enjoy brown ale, amber ale, and the lighter Scottish-style ales. A good first foray into dark beer for those who have been afraid to try dark beer.

SCHWARZBIER

Schwarzbier, which means "black beer," is a beautiful style whose roasty, coffee-like notes will please fans of porter and stout, but because it's a smooth lager, pilsner aficionados will also feel right at home. Schwarzbier's color derives from a generous dose of roasted malts in the grist, but the types of roasted malts used tend to confer more of a "clean" roast character with none of the bitter and burned flavors that sometimes accompany dark beers.

The beer style's name lends itself to endless *Spaceballs* references, but there's nothing corny about a good schwarzbier. The best examples offer a rich, coffee-like roast profile with impossible smoothness that makes them very easy to drink. Germany's Köstritzer is arguably the most famous schwarzbier, and it is said that Goethe and Otto von Bismarck were both fans of the stuff. In North America, Devil's Backbone's Schwartz Bier (they spell it with an extra *t*) has won several prestigious international awards, while Smoke & Dagger from Jack's Abby introduces a bit of smoked malt into the mix.

TYPICAL COMPOSITION
ORIGINAL EXTRACT: 11–13.5°P (1.044–1.055 SG)

ALCOHOL: 4–5.5% by volume

BITTERNESS: 20–30 IBU

COLOR: 20–30 SRM

SENSORY PROFILE
Schwarzbier can span a range of colors, from very dark brown with ruby highlights to almost completely black. Like Irish stout, the head is usually off-white to khaki. The aroma delivers a mild malty profile, usually with a suggestion of coffee-like roast, though this need not be as heavy as the dark color might imply. On the palate, schwarzbier delivers a malty, rich, roasted flavor with perhaps more coffee and bittersweet chocolate notes than are apparent on the nose. Both the aroma and the flavor are typically very low in hop character, though hop bitterness is moderate and complements roast bitterness into a surprisingly dry finish. Expect a medium- to full-bodied beer with creamy carbonation.

SERVING SUGGESTION
Serve by the third liter or half liter in a dimpled mug or Willi becher, at 50 to 55°F (10 to 13°C).

OUTSTANDING EXAMPLES
Einbecker Schwarzbier, Einbecker Brauhaus, Einbeck, Germany

Köstritzer Schwarzbier, Köstritzer Schwarzbierbrauerei, Bad Köstritz, Germany
Looks like cola as it pours from the bottle, but a glass of the stuff looks almost identical to stout. Closer inspection reveals the beer to be not completely opaque, with beautiful garnet accents. The khaki head is fluffy and persistent and leaves

behind excellent lacing as the glass empties. The nose offers a delightful malt profile that combines the sweetness of light Continental malts with pleasant hints of roast and just the lightest touch of floral hops. On the tongue, one discovers an impossibly smooth roast that offers some coffee-like notes but no roast bitterness. There's a lovely sweetness that offers an impression of milk chocolate, and the mild bitterness is sufficient but not at all over the top. The beer has a silky texture and leaves a finish that is at once satisfying and refreshing.

If you enjoy milk stout, this might be your lager. This schwarzbier doesn't have the same kind of sugary sweetness, but there's enough malt sweetness to offer an impression of richness. Please, if you typically avoid dark beer, just try one of these. Close your eyes if it helps. Köstritzer is a classic.

Mönchshof Schwarzbier, Kulmbacher Brauerei, Kulmbach, Germany

Schwartz Bier, Devil's Backbone Brewing Company, Roseland, Va., USA

Smoke & Dagger, Jack's Abby Brewing, Framingham, Mass., USA
Chocolate, light smoke, very dark caramel, hints of coffee. Very dark brown, bordering on black, with faint coffee-colored highlights. Moderate tan head dissipates quickly and leaves behind adequate lacing. Initial impressions of dark chocolate and coffee give way to a light smokiness mid-palate. Moderately long finish is balanced between bitter and sweet, with a faint suggestion of a burnt note in the back of the throat. A little thinner in body than the appearance might initially suggest. More carbonic than creamy. Lingering sweetness nicely balances the roast and smoke to make this a dangerously drinkable smoked lager. Would pair as well with grilled game as it would the s'mores to follow. If you enjoy New Belgium 1554, give this one a try.

BOCK

For all its ubiquity, bock can be a hard style to describe to the uninitiated. A running joke in my house involves my unwavering inability to adequately describe to my wife what, exactly, bock is. She's far more knowledgeable about beer than most of us, and I suspect the dissonance between what I say and what she tastes must be unbearable. I'll do my best here.

Fundamentally, bock is a strong, dark, malt-forward German lager, but mechanical descriptions alone don't tell the whole story. In his style guide, *Bock*, Darryl Richman writes that bock and doppelbock "provide the extra Gemütlichkeit needed to endure cold, short, gray days." This is a fitting description, for *Gemütlichkeit* is as untranslatable as the beer that evokes it.

Bock is not one beer, but a family of beers. What we discuss here is what some call traditional bock, standard bock, or dunkles bock. By German law, it's beer of at least 16°P (1.066 SG) original gravity, which means that with typical yeast strains, it's going to come in at around 6.5 percent ABV or more. Obviously that law doesn't hold beyond Deutschland, but even bock brewed elsewhere tends to follow this convention.

Bock and winter go together beautifully, in part because of the aforementioned *Gemütlichkeit* that the elevated alcohol and dark, malty character offer. But bock also tends to pair quite well with seasonal winter treats. Even though traditional bocks are not spiced (which would be verboten under the Reinheitsgebot), bock's dark malts can evoke plums, figs, and other dried fruits, a natural complement to holiday cookies. Breweries in Iceland have a

OPPOSITE: Classic Bock (see recipe page 215).

tradition of brewing special Christmas beers (*Jólabjórinn*), which frequently take the form of bock or doppelbock.

If your taste in ales leans toward Belgian-style dubbel and English-style brown ale, bock may be your new favorite lager.

TYPICAL COMPOSITION
ORIGINAL EXTRACT: 16–18°P (1.066–1.075 SG)
ALCOHOL: 6–7.5% by volume
BITTERNESS: 20–30 IBU
COLOR: 15–30 SRM

SENSORY PROFILE
Standard bocks showcase a gorgeous, deep garnet color in the glass, with a robust ivory-colored head that might stick around or might not (alcohol tends to suppress head retention). Some describe these beers as brown, but that's not quite right. The best examples have luscious red highlights. On the nose and in the flavor, dark German malts dominate, with nary a hop in sight other than to supply enough bitterness to lend balance to the substantially malty body. Traditional examples will have undergone a decoction mash and an extended boil, both of which encourage the development of deeper flavors than malt alone can provide. The body, while dense and full, is simultaneously creamy and light on the tongue. It's an interesting dichotomy. Look for a long, malty finish with a bit of alcoholic warmth in the higher-octane examples.

SERVING SUGGESTION
Serve by the third liter or half liter in a dimpled mug or Willi becher, at 50 to 55°F (10 to 13°C).

OUTSTANDING EXAMPLES
Ayinger Winterbock, Brauerei Aying Franz Inselkammer KG, Aying, Germany

Colorado Native Winterfest, AC Golden Brewing Company, Golden, Colo., USA
Medium toffee and caramel. A relatively light nose for a beer of this color and strength. Deep bronze to ruby, with an off-white head that is initially quite robust before falling to a couple of millimeters of foam and then to nothing. Exquisite lacing that goes on for days. Rich toffee-like malt with a slight nuttiness. Toasted bread and just a kiss of hops. Bitterness is sufficient but not overwhelming. Slightly sweet finish. Medium bodied with a moderate, smooth, creamy carbonation. Slight alcoholic warmth. No astringency. This isn't the old AC Golden Winterfest Vienna lager of 5.5 percent ABV. This is a full-fledged bock with all of the chewy malt and warming alcohol that come along with it. It can be hard to find a good standard bock these days. Winterfest is one of them.

Einbecker Ur-Bock Dunkel, Einbecker Brauhaus, Einbeck, Germany

Samuel Adams Winter Lager, Boston Beer Company, Boston, Mass., USA

Schell's Bock, August Schell Brewing Company, New Ulm, Minn., USA

Uff-da, New Glarus Brewing Company, New Glarus, Wis., USA
Aroma is nutty, bready, and rich. Uff-da pours a deep russet with an initially moderate head that drops to a thin layer of bubbles. A sip reveals a deeply bready malt backbone with suggestions of light dried fruit and caramel. The balance is tilted toward malt, for sure, but there's enough hop

bitterness to make this beer immensely drinkable. Carbonation is light and spritzy and offers additional complexity. The finish is slightly sweet and remains well past the last sip.

Uff-da! This is a delightful bock that is only available in Wisconsin. If you hadn't been planning a trip to Wisconsin, now's the time. Standard bock can be elusive, and this one is worth finding.

Viking Íslenskur Úrvals Jóla Bock, Viking Ölgerd, Akureyri, Iceland

DOPPELBOCK

Doppelbock is the richest and strongest of the German lager styles, with the notable exception of eisbock, which itself begins life as a doppelbock before undergoing freeze-concentration. Although doppelbock literally means "double bock," the appellation was bestowed upon the style ex post facto. Bock has its origins in Einbeck, Lower Saxony, but doppelbock is a Munich beer through and through.

Traditionally, this strong beer style would have been brewed in late autumn, lagered all winter, and consumed during Lent, when the fasting pious eschewed solid bread in favor of the liquid variety. One can only guess at how festive the cloisters must have been when doppelbock was the only permissible foodstuff. (I have never entertained the idea of living a monastic existence, but were I to consider it, a doppelbock fast is definitely the way I'd go.)

Doppelbock is traditionally brewed using a labor- and energy-intensive triple decoction mash, which develops a rich malt character that is difficult to produce otherwise. The earliest hop addition offers just enough bitterness to balance the substantial malt backbone without overpowering it. Late kettle additions are minimal at best.

A particularly lovely take on the style is the smoked doppelbock, which makes use of generous quantities of smoked malt to deliver a doppelbock of unparalleled complexity. Aecht Schlenkerla Eiche from Bamberg, Germany, is perhaps the best known such example and is worth seeking out if you enjoy smoked beer (see Rauchbier on page 145).

TYPICAL COMPOSITION
ORIGINAL EXTRACT: 18–20°P (1.074–1.083 SG)
ALCOHOL: 7–9% by volume
BITTERNESS: 15–25 IBU
COLOR: 15–30 SRM

SENSORY PROFILE
Deep ruby to dark brown with brilliant clarity and a persistent, ivory to beige head. Head retention decreases with increasing alcoholic strength. This lager delivers a strong, malty first impression that may suggest toast, caramel, chocolate, or even hints of dried fruit. Roasted notes are rare and usually considered out of style. Hop aromas are subdued, if present at all, and stronger examples may have a discernable alcoholic warmth. Doppelbock is a celebration of highly kilned malts, so look for rich, malty depth. A decoction mash protocol, an extended boil, or use of certain specialty malts may deliver melanoidins that can come across as toasted and caramel-like on the low end to almost (but not quite) umami-like on the high end. Hop flavors are minimal at most, while bitterness is just enough to balance the substantial malt character. Look for a smooth alcoholic warmth to round out a finish that's surprisingly dry for such a hefty beer.

SERVING SUGGESTION

Serve by the third liter in a Willi becher or tulip at 55 to 60°F (13 to 16°C).

OUTSTANDING EXAMPLES

Ayinger Celebrator, Brauerei Aying Franz Inselkammer KG, Aying, Germany

Frelser, Mikkeller, Copenhagen, Denmark

Paulaner Salvator, Paulaner Brauerei, Munich, Germany

St. Victorious, Victory Brewing Company, Downingtown, Pa., USA

Samichlaus, Brauerei Schloss Eggenberg, Vorchdorf, Austria

Dark toffee with hints of cocoa, hazelnuts, cinnamon, and cloves. No hop aroma. Deep chestnut body with a very thin head and only token lace. The rich dark fruit promised in the aroma continues into the flavor. Plums and dates marry with moderately dark toffee, rum, and honey. Finish is sweeter than is typical for a doppelbock, but Samichlaus has twice the alcohol as most of them! Bitterness is just enough to back up the substantial malt. Alcohol is very apparent but offers a comforting warmth as the beer glides down the throat. Full bodied and syrupy. Alcohol leaves a slightly slick impression as it goes down. Just what you want on a cold winter's night. This example was barely a year old and could stand up to many years of aging. If your ale choices tend toward wee heavy and Belgian dark strong ales, or if you're into sack meads, Samichlaus is worth a try.

Samuel Adams Double Bock, Boston Beer Co., Boston, Mass., USA

Saxonator, Jack's Abby Brewing, Framingham, Mass., USA

Spaten Optimator, Spaten-Franziskaner-Bräu, Munich, Germany

Deep, dark malt. Figs and plums and raisins—oh my. Alcohol impression. Very dark brown body with faint russet highlights. Off-white head with remarkably good retention and excellent lacing. Big chewy malts evoking dark bread and dark fruit. Moderate melanoidin character. Finish is off-dry and just balanced by hop bitterness. A touch of alcoholic warmth, but it's subtle and less than suggested by the aroma. No astringency. A classic Bavarian doppelbock and one that most of us should be able to find. There are more interesting takes on the style, and the green bottle is a major ding, but Optimator remains a stalwart of the doppelbock category.

Troegenator, Tröegs Brewing Company, Hershey, Pa., USA

Rich dark fruit; deep caramel; intense malt; no hops. Deep, deep amber with a thin tan head. Intense malt with notes of plums, black cherry, and a bit of leather. Rich melanoidin character. Hints of chocolate. Malty-sweet but not cloying. No hop flavor. Bitterness is just enough to supply balance to the substantial malt. Chewy and viscous, but attenuation is high enough to keep it from feeling heavy. Creamy. A truly outstanding doppelbock, this is the ideal lager for those who gravitate toward wee heavy, Belgian-style dubbel, and old ale. If you like your beer big and malty, look no further.

Weihenstephaner Korbinian, Munich, Germany

Initial aroma offers hazelnuts and hints of spice, followed by dark toffee, dark fruit, dark bread, and dark chocolate. Did I mention dark? Pours a deep, deep, deep red, almost brown in

OPPOSITE: Tröegs Brewing Company Troegenator doppelbock (see recipe page 216).

the glass, with a beige head that falls immediately and doesn't offer much lacing. Rich dark malts on the tongue continue the festival of dark fruits promised on the nose. Dark caramel and a slight roast character. Finish is slightly sweet but not cloying. A full-bodied beer with creamy carbonation. There's a subtle hint of alcoholic warmth, but it's oh so smooth. Korbinian is a dangerous, dangerous sipper that's all too easy to throw back with abandon. The very definition of liquid bread, this epitomizes the triumph of the Bavarian doppelbock.

EISBOCK

Legend has it that eisbock was invented by accident when an apprentice brewer accidentally left casks of bock out in the freezing cold after a long brew day, but I don't buy it. Humans have a long track record of exploiting every available resource in pursuit of ever-stronger alcoholic beverages, so my guess is it was intentional.

To create eisbock, first a brewery brews a strong bock like doppelbock. Then the beer is cooled down to sub-freezing temperatures. Water has a higher melting point (32°F or 0°C) than does ethanol (–173°F or –144°C), so ice crystals form, pulling liquid water out of solution. Removing these crystals of pure water leaves behind a beer that has the same volume of alcohol as the original, but less water in which to dilute it. The resulting concentrate can lose up to a third of its original volume and enjoy a proportional increase in ABV.

TYPICAL COMPOSITION
ORIGINAL EXTRACT: 18–28°P (1.075–1.121 SG)
ALCOHOL: 9–15% by volume
BITTERNESS: 25–35 IBU
COLOR: 20–40 SRM

SENSORY PROFILE
Eisbock is to bock as espresso is to filter coffee. Look for an intensely malty aroma with strong dark fruit notes, a remarkable alcohol presence, and virtually no hops. The body is usually very dark brown with some hints of garnet, and what little tan head appears upon pouring is likely to go away rather quickly thanks to the alcohol. The flavor of these *über-bocks*, like the nose, is all about intense dark malt. Think plums, figs, chocolate, and dark toffee. There will be alcohol, but if the beer is brewed well, it offers warmth, not harshness. Bitterness is firm and just enough to balance out the malt sweetness. A good eisbock feels

weighty in the mouth but goes down far more easily than one might initially suppose, given its alcoholic heft.

SERVING SUGGESTION
Serve by the third liter in a tulip or Teku glass at 55 to 60°F (13 to 16°C).

OUTSTANDING EXAMPLES
Eisbock, Kulmbacher Brauerei, Kulmbach, Germany
Kulmbacher Eisbock is deep, deep mahogany with a tan head that doesn't stick around. The aroma is of intensely bready malt, raisins, figs, and toffee. There are also some lovely milk chocolate notes and very light ethanol. The flavor fully delivers on all the promises made in the aroma, with caramel and dark bread dominating the palate, along with a pleasant and not at all harsh alcoholic warmth. The texture is thick and viscous and offers moderate carbonation that, along with the supporting bitterness, helps hold up the substantial weight and sweetness. The finish is nicely balanced between malt and hop bitterness and lasts a long, long time.

This one's for the imperial lovers. It's a classic strong lager whose surprising drinkability belies its strength. If you normally go for Belgian dark strong ales and barleywines, give Kulmbacher Eisbock a go.

Double Ice Bock, Southampton Publick House, Southampton, N.Y., USA

RAUCHBIER

Rauchbier—German for "smoke beer"—takes us back to a time when all beer exhibited smoke character to some degree, thanks to the drying of malt using wood smoke. With the development of the coke-fired indirect kiln, malts could be dried simply using hot air, but prior to that, drying and roasting malt would have imparted some level of smoke.

With today's modern malting technologies, smoked malt has to be made deliberately, and several malting companies do just that. Many breweries incorporate small amounts of smoked malt to accent specialty recipes like smoked porter, but rauchbier is something altogether different. It's a deeply smoked beer that leaves no doubt as to its birth in fire. The rauchbiers of Bamberg, Germany, in particular, are deservedly famous. Two Bamberger breweries—Schlenkerla and Spezial—dry malt over beechwood flames to this day, and their beers are highly regarded by those who enjoy this unique style.

If you just can't get past the campfire notes in smoked lager, try sipping on one while you eat foods that also have strong smoky flavors: ham, barbecue, smoked gouda, and so on. The smoked aspects of the food will actually change how you perceive the beer, making it seem less smoky than it does when consumed on its own. You may start to pick apart the beer underneath the smoke, and when that happens, the smoke itself becomes just another flavor component and not as much a defining feature. But, be careful—rauchbier does polarize. Those who dislike it *really* dislike it, but those who enjoy it tend to become fanatics. You've been warned.

TYPICAL COMPOSITION

Original extract, alcohol content, bitterness, and color are all governed by the base style, which is typically märzen, bock, or doppelbock.

SENSORY PROFILE

Imagine drinking near a roaring campfire. That's the sort of language some use to describe rauchbier. Rauchbier isn't so much a single style as a collection of styles that include smoke. So the sensory description beyond the smoke begins with that of the base style that's often an amber or dark lager like märzen or bock, but could just as easily be helles or dortmunder.

SERVING SUGGESTION

Serve by the third liter in a Willi becher or in a tulip, at 50 to 60°F (10 to 16°C), depending upon the base style. Lighter styles can sit at the lower end of the temperature range, but don't go too cold, or the smoke character can become one-dimensional. When in doubt, serve smoked beer warmer than you might otherwise guess.

OUTSTANDING EXAMPLES

Aecht Schlenkerla Rauchbier Märzen, Brauerei Heller-Trum, Bamberg, Germany

Aecht Schlenkerla Rauchbier Urbock, Brauerei Heller-Trum, Bamberg, Germany

A powerfully smoky aroma greets the nose. It's hard to find much else beneath the thick veil of intense *Rauch*, but if you try hard, you'll detect some bready dark malt. The body is dark brown, borderline black, with hints of ruby. The khaki-colored head falls quickly to a thin layer of foam but leaves behind lacing that just won't quit. Everything you hope for from the aroma is there in the glass: smoke, smoke, and more smoke, backed up by a medium- to full-bodied malt foundation that delivers sufficient dark malt sweetness to provide contrast. There's even a bit of umami character in the back that hints at beef broth, the impression of which is no doubt enhanced by the aggressive smoke. The finish is balanced between dry and sweet, the substantial carbonation offers lightness on the tongue, and the bitterness supports but doesn't get in the way.

This is not a beer for the faint of heart, and if you're new to smoked beer and feeling timid, this might not be the best first choice. But if smoke is your thing, you'd be hard pressed to do better than Aecht Schlenkerla Rauchbier Urbock. Pair this bad boy with a turkey leg at your favorite Renaissance fair.

Aecht Schlenkerla Eiche, Brauerei Heller-Trum, Bamberg, Germany

Campfire, smoked ham, bacon, and everything that is good and holy in this world. There may be some malt and hops under there, but smoke dominates. Hazy deep amber. Fluffy white head that dissipates quickly, leaving behind bubbles of varying size. Beautiful smoke on top of a base of bready malt with hints of caramel. Lovely bitterness balances without overpowering. Creamy and smooth. Goes down dangerously easily. Truly one of the most powerful and memorable drinking experiences to be found in a lager—or in any beer, for that matter. You owe it to yourself to try this beer at least once in your life. It's not for everyone, but if it's for you, you'll find yourself longing for it. The perfect campfire beer and a natural accompaniment to barbecue.

Fire in the Ham, Jack's Abby Brewing, Framingham, Mass., USA

Rauch Ür Bock, Caldera Brewing Company, Astoria, Ore., USA

The aroma is of smoky dark malt, as if raisins had been toasted over a campfire. Look for a deep ruby body with a moderate ivory head that leaves behind exemplary lacing. The first sip is of smoked ham, but this is quickly mellowed by a rich melanoidin malt character evocative of plums, raisins, and toffee. The smoke isn't as intense as it is in some rauchbier examples, but there's more than enough to surprise those unfamiliar with the style. The palate is rich and creamy, with a slightly viscous feel on the tongue but enough carbonic bite to balance it perfectly. Finish is skewed toward sweetness, but the bitterness and smoke are enough to keep it in check.

Some rauchbiers offer a love-it-or-hate-it proposition in the smoke department, but Caldera's Rauch Ür Bock occupies a comfortable position in the middle. Yes, you will definitely taste the smoke, and if you're new to this, it may take some getting used to. But that's okay because you'll also find a lovely doppelbock in there. This is a beautifully executed smoked doppelbock, and it's worth seeking out.

Spezial Rauchbier Lager, Brauerei Spezial, Bamberg, Germany

BALTIC PORTER

Baltic porter is one of those fascinating outlier beer styles. There's nothing quite like it in the world of lager, which is why it gets its own section. Its history actually lies firmly in that of ale, specifically the strong porters and stouts that the royal court of Russia found so delightful at the end of the eighteenth century.

By the time lager techniques reached the Baltic states, brewers there had figured out how to brew strong dark ales to satisfy the domestic thirst. Adapting these strong beers to lager techniques gave us the beautiful Baltic porter style, one that craft brewers have thankfully started brewing with some regularity again. It's the perfect lager for those who normally gravitate toward Russian imperial stouts.

TYPICAL COMPOSITION

ORIGINAL EXTRACT: 15–22°P (1.061–1.092 SG)

ALCOHOL: 7–10% by volume

BITTERNESS: 20–40 IBU

COLOR: 20–30 SRM

SENSORY PROFILE

Baltic porter usually pours a very dark brown, but strong examples can be as black as any stout. The head is usually tan to chestnut brown and may not stick around for long, especially in the higher-alcohol versions. The aroma highlights a rich blend of malts that can suggest chocolate, caramel, plums, and raisins with nary a hop to be seen. When it hits the tongue, expect an intensely malty experience that evokes those same plums, raisins, and chocolate, with a moderate bitterness. Baltic porter is always smooth and may be quite viscous. Strong examples may offer some warmth from the elevated level of alcohol. The finish is usually on the sweet side, but bitterness is sufficient to keep it from seeming cloying.

SERVING SUGGESTION

Serve at 50 to 60°F (10 to 16°C) in a snifter, tulip, or Teku glass.

OUTSTANDING EXAMPLES

Gonzo Imperial Porter, Flying Dog Brewery, Baltimore, Md., USA

Danzig, Devil's Backbone Brewing Company, Roseland, Va., USA

Bourbon Barrel-Aged Framinghammer Baltic Porter, Jack's Abby Craft Lagers, Framingham, Mass., USA

Pours a deep, deep brown that becomes opaque black in the glass. Dense, rocky tan head dissipates quickly and leaves good lacing. Legs in the glass promise alcohol, but that promise only barely carries through to the nose, which offers only faint ethanol. The aroma is of vanilla and dark chocolate with coconut and a light whiskey character. A sip reveals a much stronger whiskey profile, though by no means overwhelming. Dark cocoa powder and vanilla dominate the palate, along with some subtle suggestions of dark dried fruit and brown sugar. Silky smooth mouthfeel feels downright luxurious, with a velvety texture and soft carbonation. The finish offers pleasant malt sweetness but is drier than expected for a beer of this heft. A long, smooth bitterness rounds out the finish.

Baltic porter is a fun lager style to begin with, and this barrel-aged version ups the ante by cramming in all of the goodness of a Bourbon barrel. Because it's a lager, there's not a lot of yeast character to get in the way, so one is left with a complex beer in which one can readily identify the individual contributions of malt, hops, and wood.

Framinghammer Baltic Porter, Jack's Abby Craft Lagers, Framingham, Mass., USA

Smuttynose Baltic Porter, Smuttynose Brewing Company, Hampton, N.H., USA

Black as night with a small tan head that disappears almost immediately. No lacing. A celebration of dark malts. Coffee and chocolate, blackstrap molasses, and a bit of licorice. Bitterness is subdued and leaves a long, semi-sweet finish. Silky, creamy, and smooth. No astringency. Full bodied.

The "I don't drink lager" contingent needs to drink this. The lager equivalent of a Russian imperial stout, this dark lager is phenomenal. Luscious and silky, it's like drinking a milk chocolate covered espresso bean.

Fear and Trembling, Hill Farmstead Brewery, Greensboro Bend, Vt., USA

OPPOSITE: With a powerful malt backbone and elevated alcohol, Baltic porter is lager's answer to dark, strong ales.

NORTH AMERICAN LAGERS, FOR BETTER AND FOR WORSE

As lager traveled beyond its native Europe, brewers adapted their recipes to take advantage of local ingredients and satisfy consumer preferences. At first, American lagers mirrored those of the lands from which brewers emigrated. But those immigrant brewers had to learn to work with the ingredients and brewing conditions available to them, which resulted in American lager's inevitable split from the traditional styles of Europe.

Classic American pilsner developed as a New World interpretation of the light lager that had taken Europe by storm. It was at one time a robust and flavorful beer. But following Prohibition, American variations almost universally became lighter in body, alcohol, and color, and it's these light, fizzy yellow beers that small and independent brewers reacted against in the earliest days of craft. Brewing ale was a way to differentiate microbreweries and brewpubs from the mass-market lagers of the midwestern behemoths.

Steaming Rancor California common (see recipe page 217).

Today's craft aficionados still enjoy big, barrel-aged, hyper-hopped ales, of course, but a nascent craft lager revolution has turned attention back to American lager as it used to be. We're learning to appreciate what German immigrants did with New World ingredients and circumstances, and we're finding that American lagers can, and should, stand on their own, not merely as alternatives to the European originals but as beautiful, interesting styles.

"American lager" no longer has to mean thin, watery shells of bygone glorious styles. It can mean a distinctively American craft take on a traditional style. It can mean imperial this and barrel-aged that. And, increasingly, our insatiable thirst for hops has brought forth a new style of American lager all its own: India pale lager (IPL).

CALIFORNIA COMMON

California common is a beautiful lager that too often goes unnoticed. Bill Howell offers the following description in *Alaska Beer: Liquid Gold in the Land of the Midnight Sun*:

> During the early days of the California gold rush in the mid-nineteenth century, brewers in San Francisco were forced to improvise a way to use lager yeast at higher temperatures than normal. The result of their efforts was what came to be known as "steam beer," though exactly why it was given that name remains a matter of debate. . . . Steam beer was (and still is) brewed using a lager yeast but at much higher than normal lager temperatures, resulting in beer that has some of the flavor characteristics of ale.[1]

Anchor Brewing Company in San Francisco, California, brews the definitive example of California common: Anchor Steam. The brewery trademarked the word *steam* long before craft beer hit its stride, so the rest of us have to use the uninspired name "California common" when discussing this uniquely American beer style that's anything but common. If you've not had Anchor Steam before, I urge you to prioritize doing so at your earliest convenience. It's an American classic and as full-flavored and satisfying a drink as one could ask for.

The result of brewing with a lager yeast at elevated temperatures, ste—I mean, California common, is a delightful style sometimes called a hybrid beer because of its neither-here-nor-there nature. But it's fermented with *S. pastorianus* and, thus, is a lager through and through. The higher than normal fermentation temperature permits a bit more yeast expression than is typical for, say, your typical Continental lager, but much, much less than that of most English, American, and Belgian ale strains.

Homebrewers who have exclusively made ale may find that California common offers a convenient springboard from which to explore the world of lager. This style is *supposed* to ferment in the lower 60s °F (upper teens °C), so a brewer with limited equipment can get into lager brewing without necessarily purchasing new gear. Furthermore, California common yeast strains like White Labs WLP810 San Francisco Lager and Wyeast 2112 California Lager can be used to ferment other lager styles, thus opening up a whole new family of beer styles to the ale brewer.[2]

TYPICAL COMPOSITION
ORIGINAL EXTRACT: 12–14°P (1.048–1.057 SG)
ALCOHOL: 4.5–6% by volume

BITTERNESS: 30–45 IBU

COLOR: 10–15 SRM

SENSORY PROFILE

California common is a rich copper color with an off-white head. The nose typically showcases the unmistakable woody, minty character of Northern Brewer hops, though craft brewers have begun to diversify in this arena. A clean malt backbone with elements of toast and light toffee round out the aroma. That caramel-like aspect comes through in the flavor and dominates the malt character. Hop bitterness is fairly assertive and serves to balance the malt. Look for a refreshingly dry finish and a full body. These beers can stand up to a lot of carbonation, and it's common (ha!) for them to feature up to 3 volumes (6 grams per liter) of carbon dioxide.

SERVING SUGGESTION

Serve at 50 to 55°F (10 to 13°C) in a tulip, Willi becher, or Stange.

OUTSTANDING EXAMPLES

Anchor Steam, Anchor Brewing Company, San Francisco, Calif., USA

A bit of pine and mint, light caramel, and some light esters. Deep copper; brilliant clarity; fluffy off-white head with a wide range of bubble sizes, great lacing, decent retention. Piney, a little citrusy, moderate caramel. Lingering bitterness just asks for another sip. Combination of caramel and pine is distinctive and delicious. Spritzy and lively on the palate. Great carbonation. A beer that's simultaneously complex and refreshing. There's a lot going on, and yet it's tremendously drinkable. It really does ask you to keep drinking it.

There's really no other beer like this. A true American classic, and one that's all too easily overlooked in favor of newer, sexier beers. If you've never had Anchor Steam, or if it's been a while, pick some up today.

Coastal, Heater Allen Brewing, McMinnville, Ore., USA

Toffee, biscuits, and hints of grapefruit. Some fruitiness that presents as more yeast-derived than hop-derived. Very hazy deep copper with red overtones. Short-lived head is off-white, bordering on tan. Leaves behind decent lace. Initial impression of caramel and toffee with a bracing bitterness. Hints of golden raisins and brown sugar throughout the middle, followed by grapefruit-like and herbal hops. Bitterness is long lasting and sticks with you well into the off-dry finish. You'll taste this one for days! Bitterness comes off as much more aggressive than the indicated 36 IBUs. Medium bodied with moderate carbonation with a creamy, pillowy aspect. Slight astringency.

Heater Allen says Coastal started life as a California common style beer with a Pacific Northwest twist, and that lineage is evident in the caramel and herbal character of this amber lager, another characterful beer to win over the lager deniers. If you normally gravitate toward hoppy American red ales, you should definitely give Coastal a try.

Skjálfti, Ölvisholt Brugghús, Selfoss, Iceland

Steam Engine Lager, Steamworks Brewing Company, Durango, Colo., USA

CLASSIC AMERICAN PILSNER

Classic American pilsner (CAP) is a true American original, a pale lager that adapts local ingredients to a New World pilsner that's more akin to the European original than to the mass-market adjunct lagers that eventually came to dominate American beer. It's what German immigrants brewed when they wanted pilsner but had to make do with what was available to them. Traditionally, that included American 6-row malt and maize in the grist, plus Cluster hops in the kettle, but CAP is an adaptable style, and modern craft brewers are experimenting with fun hop formulations.

It's next to impossible to find this beer style commercially today. Fortunately, the three examples listed here are wonderful and well worth seeking out when you find yourself inside their small distribution areas.

TYPICAL COMPOSITION
ORIGINAL EXTRACT: 11–15°P (1.044–1.061 SG)

ALCOHOL: 4.5–6% by volume

BITTERNESS: 30–40 IBU

COLOR: 3–5 SRM

SENSORY PROFILE

Classic American pilsner typically pours crystal-clear yellow with a fluffy white head that lasts, thanks in part to the higher protein levels of American 6-row barley. A whiff of the aroma should tell you that this is not your run-of-the-mill, mass-market American adjunct lager. You'll typically get some corn-like and grainy notes; a kick of floral, herbal, or woodsy hops; and maybe a bit of sulfur. The flavor is similar, with corresponding grainy, corn-like malt and herbal or spicy hops. But it's the bitterness that sets this beer style apart, a firm bitterness that isn't afraid to assert itself. The body should be spritzy with carbonic bite but somewhat creamy from the corn and malt. Expect a long, bitter, off-dry finish.

SERVING SUGGESTION

Serve at 45 to 50°F (7 to 10°C) in a pilsner glass.

OUTSTANDING EXAMPLES

1811 Pre-Prohibition Lager, Fort George Brewing Company, Astoria, Ore., USA

Soft bready malt, fresh corn, a hint of caramel, very subtle floral hop aroma, and a faint whiff of sulfur. Golden body; slightly turbid with beautiful effervescence; thick, fluffy white head that lasts and lasts; good lacing. Corn-like sweetness from both pale malt and maize itself, more than balanced by a substantial hop bitterness. Dry finish. Firm bitterness lingers well after the beer is gone. Crisp, clean, and spritzy. Fun on the tongue. Lingering bitterness after you swallow reminds you that this isn't your modern standard American lager.

A fun example of what American lager might have been before the temperance movement screwed things up. The carbonation in this example is especially enjoyable. Head retention is impeccable and continues delivering the lovely soft aroma as you drain the glass.

Colorado Native Olathe, AC Golden Brewing Company (a division of MillerCoors), Golden, Colo., USA

Initial aroma is of sweet corn and herbal, floral hops. A pleasant light malt character rounds out the nose. Deep gold body with virtually no head, but despite poor head retention, lacing is remarkably good. Flavor combines soft corn sweetness with a light grainy, doughy malt backbone. Moderate hop flavor suggests light pine and fresh hay. Soft, round body with moderately high carbonation. Finish leans malty, with enough bitterness to keep residual sweetness in check.

A beautiful classic American pilsner that's refreshing enough to drink all day. But at 6 percent ABV, drinking this all day could get you in trouble. The brewers over at AC Golden are cranking out some delightful lagers through their Colorado Native brand, and this one is no exception.

Pontius Road Pilsner, Short's Brewing Company, Bellaire, Mich., USA

Lemony, minty, floral, and pine-like hop aromas atop a grainy malt sweetness with hints of corn. Hazy, straw-blonde body. Initially robust white head fades to a faint raft of bubbles. Very little lacing clings to the glass. Lemon, pineapple, grass, mint, and herbs; light bready malt sweetness with sweet corn overtones; firm bitterness lingers into the finish. Straddles a line between creamy and spritzy. No astringency. Medium bodied. A very American take on the pilsner style. The use of corn is apparent but more subdued than in many other classic American pilsner examples. Hop flavors are more modern American than classically European, making this an enjoyable and refreshing riff on pilsner.

AMERICAN ALL-MALT PALE LAGER

This style is a natural follow-on to the classic American pilsner, and in some cases, the only difference between these beers and their CAP relatives is the use of 100 percent barley malt instead of a blend of malt and maize. This is a broad category that can include everything from light, sessionable, all-malt backyard pounders to relatively strong, assertive pilsner-inspired lagers with an American twist.[3]

American all-malt pale lagers are usually, but not always, a step down in bitterness from CAP. These session-strength beers are reclaiming American lager's rightful place as a full-flavored beer that can hold its own next to European imports.

TYPICAL COMPOSITION
ORIGINAL EXTRACT: 10–12.5°P (1.040–1.050 SG)
ALCOHOL: 4.5–5.5% by volume
BITTERNESS: 20–25 IBU
COLOR: 2–4 SRM

SENSORY PROFILE
Like its cousin the classic American pilsner, all-malt American lagers showcase a crystal-clear yellow body and a pillowy, persistent white head. The nose may offer some corn-like sweetness from pils malt or American 2-row malt, but not from corn itself. Hop character is often more subdued than in classic American pilsner, but more present than in most mass-market American lagers. The flavor is dominated by malt sweetness that is usually a little less grainy than adjunct lagers, owing to the use of 2-row, but as in the aroma, there is a mild hop flavor to lend complexity. The beer should be moderately to highly carbonated with a smooth finish that toes the line between malt sweetness and hop bitterness.

SERVING SUGGESTION

Serve at 45 to 50°F (7 to 10°C) in a pilsner glass.

OUTSTANDING EXAMPLES

American Flyer Craft Lager, Joseph James Brewing Company, Las Vegas, Nev., USA

Grainy pils malt, slight floral hop character, and a whiff of corn-like DMS. Brilliantly clear, straw-blonde body. Fluffy white head with good lacing and retention. Luscious, round pilsner malt backbone is nicely balanced by a firm but completely appropriate hop bitterness. Hop flavor is floral, slightly spicy, and reminiscent of noble lineage. Lovely bitterness on the back of the tongue. Dry finish. Creamier than you might expect for this style of beer. Good carbonic bite and lingering bitterness accentuate the impression of dryness.

A fine, well-crafted example of what American lager can (and should) be. This light lager easily stands shoulder to shoulder with European greats, and because it comes in a can, it goes anywhere without the risk of skunk. A real gem.

Brooklyn Pilsner, Brooklyn Brewery, Brooklyn, N.Y., USA

Crisp, spicy noble-like hop character; dry, cracker-like pils malt with a hint of creamed corn. Gold, crystal-clear body with festive bubbles and a frothy white head that dissipates to about 2 millimeters but leaves behind beautiful lacing on the sides of the glass. Spicy, noble-like hop bite up front, followed by a malt character that straddles a line between round and crisp. A touch of pine-like flavor. Enticing bitterness that goes down easily. A little heavier on the palate than a typical northern German pils, but lighter and spritzier than classic Czech examples of the style. A very light citric astringency and good creamy carbonation.

This is a great American-brewed pilsner that takes the classic European archetypes and gives them a refreshing New World twist. If you live where Brooklyn Brewery distributes, this will likely be a fresher, more flavorful choice than European imports of unknown age and shipping treatment conditions.

California Lager, Anchor Brewing Company, San Francisco, Calif., USA

Colorado Native Golden Lager, AC Golden Brewing Company (a division of MillerCoors), Golden, Colo., USA

Spicy hops with a lemony aspect. Cracker-like grainy malt. Hazy, straw-blonde body. Thick, fluffy white head with excellent retention and lacing. Intense, spicy hop flavor up front, with notes of grass, hay, and lemon peel. Cracker-like malt backbone plays a supporting role and gives the hops a place to call home. Firm bitterness lasts well into the dry finish. Moderately high carbonation; light to medium bodied; just a slight touch of astringency.

Chalk up another win for the brewers at AC Golden. This is a wonderful American riff on the Continental pilsner that leans more German than Czech but can proudly stand among the best examples of both. This beer never leaves the Centennial State, so Colorado residents are better off choosing this over any green-bottle import.

Craft Lager, Upslope Brewing Company, Boulder, Colo., USA

Jabby Brau, Jack's Abby Craft Lagers, Framingham, Mass., USA

Joe's Premium American Pilsner, Avery Brewing Company, Boulder, Colo., USA

Local's Light, Short's Brewing Company, Bellaire, Mich., USA

Sweet corn, grainy malt, a suggestion of hops. Slightly hazy pale straw, thin white head with poor retention. Malt and corn, a touch of hop flavor, and very low bitterness. Finish is malty and slightly sweet. Moderately carbonated. A little more viscous on the tongue than is typical for this kind of beer. American light lager is almost by definition meant to be inoffensive, and Short's did a great job of brewing a light lager that's right on the edge. Newcomers to craft will find enough familiarity not to be scared off, but there's enough of a flavor boost to remind them that this is more than your standard American lager. The subdued carbonation, which seems lower than is typical for this style, accentuates the grainy, corn-like malt flavor. Open-minded craft veterans in search of a thirst-quenching summer pounder need look no further. On a hot afternoon, you could throw back several of these. And at just north of 5 percent ABV, you can do just that. Kudos to the brewers for pulling a lot of flavor out of a challenging style.

Point Special, Stevens Point Brewery, Stevens Point, Wis., USA

Sweet, grainy light malt. Light fruity, slightly grassy hops. A bit of green apple. Crystal-clear blonde, between straw and gold. Initially dense white head falls to a thin raft of bubbles. Sweet pale malt with some light caramel overtones. Hop flavor is light with a grassy, hay-like character. Finish is balanced. Light bodied, moderately carbonated, no astringency.

A classic American pale lager that is a good step above the generic adjunct brands. This one makes good use of a blend of American 2-row and 6-row with no adjuncts, giving it a fuller flavor and weight on the palate than your typical ballpark beer. It would go great with just about anything you can think of on the grill.

Session Premium Lager, Full Sail Brewing Company, Hood River, Ore., USA

Vunderbar Pilsner, Smuttynose Brewing Company, Hampton, N.H., USA

Grainy pils malt, sweet corn, a touch of sulfur, faint floral hops. As the beer warms, hops emerge and acquire a spicy, grassy, hay-like character. Hazy, straw-blonde body. Fluffy white head. Great retention and lacing. Lemony citrus, grapefruit, orange peel, some resinous evergreen notes. Cracker-like pils malt, a little creamed corn. Grassy character comes out as beer warms. Assertive bitterness, off-dry finish. Crisp and clean; high carbonation; a little astringency on the tongue.

An American interpretation of German pilsner, this one is likely to appeal to IPA drinkers. The hop character is much stronger than is typical for the style and has a qualitatively "rougher" character. That's not a criticism by any means—in fact this beer strikes me as straddling a line between German pils and American India pale lager. A great pilsner for hopheads.

NORTH AMERICAN ADJUNCT LAGER

The North American adjunct lager represents another step down in bitterness. I call it North American because it's essentially the same style whether you're talking Mexico, the United

States, or Canada. It uses a large quantity of maize or rice in the grist and low levels of hops. The best examples are light and refreshing. The worst are thin and insipid. I've highlighted some of the best examples here.

Note: *If you require something lighter than the standard American adjunct lager, a sensory profile and statistics are neither necessary nor helpful. There's football on TV. Go for it.*

TYPICAL COMPOSITION
ORIGINAL EXTRACT: 10–12.5°P (1.040–1.050 SG)
ALCOHOL: 4.5–5.5% by volume
BITTERNESS: 20–25 IBU
COLOR: 2–4 SRM

SENSORY PROFILE
American adjunct lagers are brilliantly clear, straw blonde, and effervescent. A tall white head typically lasts throughout the pint and leaves excellent lace. Corn-like sweetness is common in maize-based versions, while rice-based examples are more neutral. Hop character is low and leans toward relatively neutral hop aromas and flavors. Expect a finish that leans on malt sweetness, with just enough hop bitterness to supply balance. Despite the malt-focused finish, these beers are meant to be refreshing and should finish dry.

SERVING SUGGESTION
Serve at 45 to 50°F (7 to 10°C) in a pilsner glass.

OUTSTANDING EXAMPLES
El Sully, 21st Amendment Brewery, San Francisco, Calif., USA

Hamm's, MillerCoors, Milwaukee, Wis., USA
Grainy malt with a sweet corn character and a faint husky note. Virtually no hops. Brilliantly clear gold with a big, fluffy white head. Head dissipates quickly and leaves behind a bit of lace. Corn-like malt sweetness carries over from the aroma. No discernable hop flavor. Very subtle bitterness. Soft grainy body with a creamy mouthfeel. No astringency.

Yes, Hamm's is owned by MillerCoors. Yes, it's an American adjunct light lager. And yes, if you need the enamel stripped off your teeth, this ain't your beer. But, if you want a light lager to knock back on a hot day, you could do worse than this—much worse. Unlike many of the large adjunct lagers, Hamm's still tastes of beer (and boasts four Great American Beer Festival awards). Have a Hamm's. You know you want to.

Schlitz Classic 1960s Formula, Pabst Brewing Company, Woodridge, Ill., USA

Pabst Blue Ribbon, Pabst Brewing Company, Woodridge, Ill., USA

Narragansett Brewing Company, Providence, R.I., USA
Grainy malt with some corn sweetness. A faint whiff of herbal hops and a touch of sulfur. Gold with brilliant clarity and a big fluffy white head that drops a little but remains robust. Great lacing. Smooth malt with a pleasant

OPPOSITE: Una Más Mexican lager (see recipe page 218).

sweetness. Faint herbal/spicy hop flavor; low to medium bitterness. Smooth finish. Creamy on the palate with good, spritzy carbonation.

A fine American lager for the patio, pool, or porch swing. Your dad would like this. Your mom would like this. Your grandparents would like this. You'll like it too. Your snobby beer friends might say they don't like it, but trust me: they pound this beer when you're not looking.

HOPPY PILSNER

The modern hoppy pilsner is one of the great achievements of the craft lager renaissance. Brewers have taken the classic pilsner—typically German pils—and amped up the hops to American West Coast standards. Refreshing, dry, and oh-so drinkable, the hoppy pilsner offers much more flavor per ounce (or milliliter) than most American pale lagers. They're pilsner through and through, but with a New World twist that will satisfy taste buds that have become accustomed to heaps of hops.

TYPICAL COMPOSITION
ORIGINAL EXTRACT: 11–14°P (1.044–1.057 SG)

ALCOHOL: 4.5–6% by volume

BITTERNESS: 20–50 IBU

COLOR: 2–6 SRM

SENSORY PROFILE
Straw-blonde to golden and brilliantly clear body, with a dense, white, long-lasting head. Hop aroma is strong and typically noble or noble-like in character—herbal, floral, and spicy. Citrusy and fruity American hops aren't typical, but that may well have changed by the time this book goes to press! Crisp, malty-sweet pilsner malt supplies the foundation, and bitterness is firm.

SERVING SUGGESTION
Serve at 45 to 50°F (7 to 10°C) in a pilsner glass.

OUTSTANDING EXAMPLES
Prima Pils, Victory Brewing Company, Downingtown, Pa., USA
Crisp pils malt, spicy noble-like hops with some citrus notes, a faint hint of sulfur. Brilliantly clear blonde; fluffy snow-white head that falls to a couple of millimeters of foam and leaves excellent lacing. Spicy, floral noble-like hops dominate the palate up front, along with some citrus elements that have an American hop character, followed by a crisp, clean, cracker-like malt foundation. A touch of sulfur. Finish is firmly bitter and thirst-quenchingly dry. Spritzy, effervescent, light-medium body, no astringency.

Not as hop-forward as some newer American craft pilsners, but still miles ahead of most so-called pilsners in terms of pure hoppy goodness. This can stand next to the freshest German imports, and if you're a hophead, you'll probably like this one better.

Pivo Pils, Firestone Walker Brewing Company, Paso Robles, Calif., USA

Noble-like spicy hop aroma atop a cracker-like pils malt base. Brilliantly clear straw-blonde body topped by a small white head that quickly fades. Good lacing. Spicy, lemony, bracing noble-like hop flavor up front—this pilsner does not apologize. Crisp, cracker-like malt in the middle. Substantial bitterness lingers well into a crisp, bone-dry finish. Light bodied, aggressively carbonated, no astringency.

Among the finest domestic pilsners you'll come across. The intense dry hop character lets you know this is an American beer, one that could very easily cross into IPL territory. Outstanding.

Samuel Adams Noble Pils, Boston Beer Company, Boston, Mass., USA

STS Pils, Russian River Brewing Company, Santa Rosa, Calif., USA

Assertive spicy hop aroma dominates, with notes of lemon and some grass. Bready pils malt offers support, but the focus here is clearly on the hops. Turbid gold, leaning into very light bronze territory, probably due to the suspended yeast. Fluffy white head with great retention leaves excellent lacing. Bright, citrusy, grassy hop flavor dominates, delivering a very American take on the classic German pilsner. Beautiful pils malt backbone holds everything together with just a very slight hint of corn. Finish is dry. Medium bodied. The beer feels soft on the palate, but the carbonation and assertive hop bitterness leave a sharper, lasting impression.

Go for the Pliny. Stay for the STS.

Tipopils, Birrificio Italiano, Lurago Marinone, Italy

INDIA PALE LAGER

Given our continued adoration of the American IPA, it was only a matter of time until someone applied the tenets of India pale ale to lager. India pale lager (IPL) hasn't yet achieved style status in the guidelines that govern beer competitions, but it's qualitatively different enough that it doesn't really fit into the IPA or American pale lager categories. Look for this exciting style to gain more prominence as our appreciation for lager increases alongside our perennial thirst for *Humulus lupulus*.

TYPICAL COMPOSITION
ORIGINAL EXTRACT: 10–21°P (1.040–1.088 SG)
ALCOHOL: 4.5–10% by volume
BITTERNESS: 50–100+ IBU
COLOR: 5–15 SRM

SENSORY PROFILE
Everything you love about IPA in lager form. A big explosion of hop aromatics greet the nose, with perhaps some toasty malt in the background, but little to no yeast character. There may be a whiff of sulfur, but the focus is on malt and hops—period. Clarity can range from crystal clear to hazy. The flavor serves up what is promised in the aroma, with a huge charge of hop flavor supported by a malty backbone. A long, off-dry, bitter finish rounds out these fun and innovative lagers.

SERVING SUGGESTION

Serve at 45 to 50°F (7 to 10°C) in a Willi becher or your favorite IPA glass.

OUTSTANDING EXAMPLES

Airwaves, Flying Dog Brewery, Frederick, Md., USA

Calyptra, Jack's Abby, Framingham, Mass., USA

Honeydew melon, pineapple, and light hints of lemon zest and grapefruit, some dry grassy notes. Crystal clear, gold body. Moderate white head with large bubbles dissipates quickly but leaves behind good lacing. Fruity aspects of the aroma carry over into the flavor. Malt structure is sound and slightly sweet but mostly stays out of the way and allows hops to shine. Off-dry finish with respectable bitterness that lingers. Light and spritzy, with a weight and carbonation reminiscent of keller-style kölsch. Slight astringency.

A challenge with session IPA, and by extension session IPL, is achieving enough elevated hop aroma and flavor to warrant the "India pale" appellation without leaving the beer watery and thin. Calyptra does this better than most and is a sessionable light lager that will appeal to devoted hopheads and IPA fiends. Another great counterargument to your friends who say they don't drink lager.

Fathom, Ballast Point Brewing Company, San Diego, Calif., USA

Hoponius Union, Jack's Abby, Framingham, Mass., USA

An explosion of hop aroma! Grapefruit-like citrus; evergreen; dank, earthy hops; plenty of mango and pineapple. Hazy gold; robust, persistent white head with great lacing. Intense tropical and citrus fruit hop flavor supported by a soft, bready malt backbone. Clean fermentation. Creamy with high carbonation and no astringency.

Proof that lagers can be just as hop-forward as ales. Everything we love about IPA is in this beer. Hopheads can rejoice in Hoponius Union.

Excess, Jack's Abby, Framingham, Mass., USA

An explosion of tropical fruit: mango, pineapple, banana, grapefruit, and tangerine. Fruit salad in a glass. Hazy orange body with an off-white head that drops to a light film of foam. Very good lacing. The tropical celebration continues, and hints of evergreen join the party. Big, fruity flavors deliver everything the nose promises. Malt base has a slightly grainy aspect with a touch of caramel sweetness—it supports the big hop character but doesn't get in the way. Bitterness is substantial but not unbalanced in a lager this boisterous. Finish is decidedly bitter and nicely balanced between dry drinkability and malt sweetness. Full bodied but not chewy. There's a viscous, almost oily aspect suggestive of layer upon layer of hop oils painting your tongue.

The perfect lager for New England IPA fangirls and fanboys. Every bit as satisfying as those famous 16-ounce cans from Vermont and considerably easier to obtain (and easier on the wallet to boot). Jack's Abby Excess raises the bar for what to expect from hoppy lager.

Hoppy Lager, Sierra Nevada Brewing Company, Chico, Calif., USA

Samuel Adams Double Agent IPL, Boston Beer Company, Boston, Mass., USA

Samuel Adams Ella Blanc IPL, Boston Beer Company, Boston, Mass., USA

OPPOSITE: India pale lager pairs the hoppy punch of IPA with the smooth finish of a well-crafted lager.

IMPERIAL LAGERS

Imperial lager isn't as much a style as it is a frame of mind. As craft brewers increasingly explore the possibilities of lager, expect this broad category of extra-strong beers to grow ever larger. This small but growing category is where American craft brewers can do what they do best: pack more flavor into a seemingly familiar beer.[4]

TYPICAL COMPOSITION
ORIGINAL EXTRACT: High
ALCOHOL: High
BITTERNESS: Varies
COLOR: Varies

SENSORY PROFILE
These hefty lagers can be all over the place! It's impossible to pin down a single sensory profile. Instead, look to the base style and amplify it.

SERVING SUGGESTION
Serve at 50 to 55°F (10 to 13°C) in a pilsner glass.

OUTSTANDING EXAMPLES
Brandy Barrel-Aged Cherry Lager, Lakefront Brewery, Milwaukee, Wis., USA
Strong notes of English toffee, vanilla, dried cherries, and almonds. Hazy red body with a small white head that falls quickly. Lacing is nonexistent, which definitely is not a fault in a beer of this strength. Initial flavor is of toffee, toffee, and more toffee. Vanilla bean with hints of butterscotch and coconut. Dried tart cherries round out the middle and deliver balancing acidity well into a finish that's surprisingly dry for a beer of this heft. Bitterness is subdued but sufficient. Medium body with high carbonation and a bit of puckering astringency. Very slight ethanol warmth from a beer with more than 10 percent alcohol by volume.

A great lager for those who normally gravitate toward Kriek and Belgian dark strong ales. I guarantee you've never had a lager like this before. The brewery's suggested pairings would all be winning combinations, or consider enjoying a glass of this alongside an oversized slice of Dresdner Stollen on Christmas morning. And then take a nap.

Spruce Pilsner, Short's Brewing Company, Bellaire, Mich., USA
Bright and citrusy with an evergreen burst of aroma. Delicate grainy malt underneath, but the focus here is on hops and spruce. Beautiful, brilliantly clear, deep yellow. Thin head that leaves surprisingly good lace for a beer of this strength. Some alcoholic legs on the glass. A resinous punch of evergreen flavor, backed up by citrusy, slightly grassy notes. Malt backbone is substantial enough to support the bright pop of botanical flavor but remains comparatively subdued. The 85 IBUs are evident but not overpowering. Deceptively light bodied, with a lively, spritzy carbonation that complements the resinous notes nicely. Some astringency, but it works well.

Short's has outdone itself with this unique strong lager. If you enjoy Duvel, and you like the forest, you're likely to enjoy this.

OPPOSITE: Short's Brewing Company Spruce Pilsner (see recipe page 219).

LAGER WORT PRODUCTION

Strictly speaking, the choice to ferment wort with lager yeast instead of an ale strain needn't influence the manner in which a brewer creates said wort. Wort is wort prior to fermentation, which is one reason the Reinheitsgebot never mentioned yeast—Bavarian brewers simply made wort and allowed nature's course to turn it into beer. That said, certain wort production techniques are associated with lager brewing for a number of reasons.

First off, there's history. Why do a third of the world's motorists drive on the left side of the road and two-thirds on the right? Why do 120-volt outlets dominate in the Americas and Japan, while the rest of the world gets twice that? There may or may not have been a compelling reason to choose a particular way of doing things at a given point in history, but these conventions have a way of sticking with us even in light of technological developments.[1]

Fresh, high-quality malted barley is essential when brewing lager.

The same is true when it comes to preparing lager wort: certain practices became standard in breweries that historically produced lagers. The classic example is decoction mashing, which is a technique we primarily associate with Continental European brewers. But British brewers have an enviable brewing heritage and have never needed to resort to such methods. The historical association between decoction and lager is more a function of simultaneity than cause and effect. But there are also practical matters at work.

For example, pale lagers make use of very lightly kilned malt that is so intimately associated with a style that we give it the same name: pilsner malt. And with such light malt comes certain brewhouse considerations needed to overcome its peculiarities. Highly kilned malts lose certain volatile compounds during the long, hot kilning process. Conversely, pilsner malt enjoys no such treatment and thus retains certain compounds that must be dealt with during wort production.

But perhaps the most significant wort production consideration for lagers is the most fundamental. We expect that ales will exhibit some yeast-derived elements: fruit, spice, perhaps a bit of diacetyl in certain styles. There's no room for such things in lager beer and consequently no curtain behind which to hide, should things go a little less perfectly in the malt and hops department. Lager beer demands precision, and that precision starts in the brewhouse.

FUNDAMENTALS OF WORT PRODUCTION

Wort production is the process of transforming malt, hops, and water into the sugary soup that yeast further transforms into ethanol and carbon dioxide. There are five basic steps.

1. Mashing

2. Lautering

3. Sparging

4. Boiling

5. Chilling

We consider each of these in turn here, though not comprehensively. The details of how to conduct these operations are already more than adequately covered in a number of excellent texts, so this overview is for completeness and reference. Readers who desire a more thorough treatment of the fundamentals of wort production are encouraged to refer to the sources listed in the bibliography in the back of this book.

Mashing

Mashing is the most fundamental step in brewing, for it is here that kernels of malted grain give up the sugars locked within, the sugars that will ultimately form the foundation of any beer, lager or otherwise. Beer is built on malt sugars, just as wine is built on grape sugars, mead on honey sugars, and cider on apple sugars.

Mashing consists of holding a porridge-like mixture of malt and water at one or more temperatures for a specified length of time. Holding a mash at a single temperature for a certain length of time is called a *rest*, and each rest is designed to favor the activity of specific mash enzymes that affect certain biochemical reactions. Some enzymes convert starches to sugars. Others transform complex proteins into simpler structures. Still others increase the acidity of the mash, thus creating more favorable conditions for other enzymes.

Mashing is covered in greater detail later in this chapter.

Lautering

At the end of the mash program, the brewer is left with a mix of spent malt (solid) and sugar-rich wort (liquid). Lautering is the name for separating and collecting the sugar-rich liquid from the grain solids. Most craft brewers and homebrewers let the wort percolate through the grain bed itself, using the grain husks as a mash filter, but some larger breweries rely on a mechanical mash filter press to physically separate the wort instead.

In either case, the goal of lautering is physical separation. Large production breweries will pump mash out of the mash tun and into a separate lauter tun, while homebrewers and most small commercial brewers use a combination mash-lauter tun equipped with a mesh filter of some kind at the base (commonly a false bottom). The advantage of maintaining a separate lauter tun is that a new beer may be mashed-in in the mash tun during lautering, but homebrewers and small craft brewers rarely pack the brewing schedule tightly enough to justify the cost and operating expense of a separate lauter tun.

Homebrewing setups most commonly feature a combination mash-lauter tun equipped with a false bottom, a stainless-steel braid, a slotted manifold, or some other device that allows liquid to flow while keeping solid materials out. The principle is not unlike that of the filter in a French press coffee beaker. Under the influence of gravity, wort flows out of the grain bed, through the filter device, and out a valve, from which it is transferred to the boil kettle.

A growing trend in homebrewing involves so-called brew-in-a-bag methods. Rather than use a dedicated mash-lauter tun, the brewer places the grist within a large mesh bag, usually made from nylon. The grain bag is lowered into the boil kettle and infused with a large volume of hot water, the temperature of which has been calculated to result in the desired mash temperature when combined with the grain. After the mash is complete, the bag is lifted out of the kettle, leaving behind the full batch volume, which is then boiled.

Sparging

Simply draining wort from the grain bed can leave behind an appreciable quantity of malt sugars. Sparging is the process by which the grain bed is rinsed of these sugars so that maximum yield is obtained from the grain. In principle, this is similar to subsequently infusing tealeaves to obtain a second, weaker cup of tea. And, like reusing tealeaves, over-sparging can lead to some undesirable flavors, so restraint is always advised.

In commercial craft breweries, sparging usually involves sprinkling hot water on top of the grain bed, allowing it to filter through the grain bed to pick up sugars, and collecting it at the bottom. Homebrewers may follow a similar method by using gravity to introduce sparge water from a hot liquor tank as wort flows out the bottom of the lauter tun and into the boil kettle. This is the basis for the common three-tiered system popular among homebrewers. An alternative approach uses a pump to push hot water up and into the top of the lauter tun, making for easier reach at the expense of greater mechanical complexity.

Batch sparging is a popular alternative to continuous sparging, in which the brewer calculates in advance the volume of sparge water needed to make up the difference between the initial runoff and the desired pre-boil volume. If, say, the initial runoff yields one gallon (3.8 liters) of wort, and the brewer desires 6.5 gallons (24.6 liters) of wort prior to a 90-minute boil, then he or she needs 5.5 gallons of sparge water to make up the difference. This entire volume of "makeup" water is added in one or two batches rather than as a continuous sprinkling.

Experimentally minded homebrewers have found that the extract efficiency of batch-sparged beer can approach, and even match or exceed, the efficiency of a continuously sparged beer. Batch sparging also avoids issues related to tannin extraction because the runoff pH remains low. Tannin extraction is primarily associated with alkaline conditions (high pH), and continuous sparging continuously increases the pH of the runoff as it becomes ever more dilute. In the limit of infinite sparging, the pH of the runoff asymptotically rises toward the pH of the sparge water itself. Batch sparging obviates the need to worry about this.

Parti-gyle techniques, in which individual sets of wort are collected corresponding to first, second, and even third runnings, are interesting, but they're beyond the scope of this book. Thus, we assume that one grist equals one beer and that the brewer uses his or her preferred sparge technique to get there.

Boiling

The runoff is sometimes called sweet wort because it has not yet received hops' bitter kiss. That magic happens in the boil, which is, as the name suggests, the stage of wort production that involves boiling. It serves a few purposes.

1. **Boiling sterilizes the wort.** Except when brewing certain wild and sour beer styles, and certainly when brewing clean lagers, brewers only want a specific culture of brewer's yeast to ferment the wort into beer.

2. **Boiling promotes clarity.** Proteins coagulate during the boil, which encourages them to drop out of solution later.

3. **Boiling condenses wort.** A 5-gallon batch of beer might need to begin life with 6.5 gallons of wort to survive a 90-minute boil. That's a nearly 25 percent loss in volume. "But isn't that a chicken-and-egg proposition?" you ask. Well, in the case of high-gravity beer, not so much. A big barleywine or doppelbock might require a big pre-boil volume to get all of those wort sugars out of the tun and into the kettle. Increasing the boil time is one way to achieve high original gravities.

4. **Boiling darkens wort.** Some wort darkening may be desirable, especially in darker styles like Munich dunkel and bock. In such cases, an extended boil can help tease additional color out of the dark malts already used.

5. **Boiling isomerizes hop alpha acids.** Now we're talking. This, more than any other reason, is why we boil wort. In order to get bitterness out of hops, the internal bittering compounds called alpha acids need to be converted to what are called iso-alpha acids. And this requires the moisture and heat of a rolling boil.

6. **Boiling extracts hop flavor and aroma.** Similarly, the boil is necessary to getting at the organoleptic goodness that hops have to offer. Yes, dry hopping is another way to do it, but the quality is fundamentally different from what one obtains from kettle hops.

7. **Boiling drives away unwanted flavors and aromas.** The complement to extracting positive qualities from hops is getting rid of negative qualities from other sources. The most vilified is dimethyl sulfide, which is produced when a compound called S-methyl-methionine (SMM) is heated. SMM is a natural byproduct of the malting process and is especially abundant in very lightly kilned malts like pilsner. SMM converts to DMS at elevated temperatures. The key to getting rid of it is, perhaps counterintuitively, to boil harder and longer.

The boil may be followed by a hot kettle whirlpool to encourage trub precipitation. During this time, additional hops can be added to the wort, which extracts additional flavor, aroma, and bitterness.

Chilling

When the boil is complete, the hopped wort is cooled down to fermentation temperature. In a professional brewery, this usually means pumping the wort through a plate heat exchanger that uses cold propylene glycol as a working fluid. Homebrewers rarely have access to glycol systems, so for most of us, cold tap water has to suffice.

Counterflow chillers, plate chillers, and immersion chillers are all popular options, and each comes with its own particular set of advantages and disadvantages. Regardless of the method used, though, cooling the wort to fermentation temperature in as short an amount of time as possible is important for all kinds of beer, but the logistics involved with doing so can be particularly challenging for lager brewers. It's simply more work to take boiling liquid from 212°F (100°C) down to 46°F (8°C) than it is to take it down to 64°F (18°C), especially in summer and in warm climates, when tap water might even have trouble taking wort down to ale temperatures.

One way to start solving the problem is to employ a pre-chiller. A pre-chiller is a device that chills tap water to a temperature below that at which it emerges from the faucet. The simplest approach is to use a standard immersion wort chiller (either stainless steel or copper) that is immersed into an ice bath and inserted in-line between the faucet and a second chiller (immersion, counterflow, or otherwise) that does the actual job of removing heat from wort. Water, then, exits the faucet and is then cooled even further in the pre-chiller before it is tasked with cooling wort.

As an alternative to the pre-chiller, some brewers fill a large bucket or cooler with ice water and use a submersible pump to force cold water through the wort chiller. This is the method I use, for the simple reason that a pond pump was an inexpensive purchase. Whether you use a pre-chiller or you pump cold water, you'll get the greatest cooling bang for your ice buck if you first cool the wort as much as you can with straight tap water before switching to a method involving ice.

Even with a good chiller and very cold water, it's possible—likely, even—that your wort won't quite make it down to fermentation temperature. In such cases, there's very little risk in simply placing the fermenter in a temperature-controlled environment and waiting for the temperature to fall. Spoiling organisms are relatively sluggish in the cold (which is why refrigeration is so darn effective), and if your sanitation practices are up to par, then it doesn't hurt to wait to pitch yeast.

INGREDIENTS

As with process, there's nothing inherently unique about ingredients (except for yeast) that warrants a different treatment for lager versus ale. But, certain malts, hops, and water profiles have become so intimately associated with lager styles that they necessitate some discussion here.

Malt

Malt is sometimes called the soul of beer, and that's not just lip service to the supernatural. It's malt that makes beer beer. Sure, the other big three ingredients play a role, but beer as we know it depends on sugars derived from cereal grains: barley, wheat, rye, oats, corn, rice, and so on. Grains provide sugars to beer the same way that grapes provide sugars to wine.

Technically, Japanese sake is a kind of unhopped beer, though we more commonly refer to it as rice wine. Chicha, the South American corn drink famously made via collective chewing is also a beer. As are kvass (Slavic rye bread beer), sahti (Finnish juniper beer), and pombe (African millet beer). These bear little resemblance to what we think of as beer in the everyday sense of the word, but they're certainly soulmates.

Two-row barley is preferred for most lagers, but some American lagers make good use of six-row varieties.

Because lagers were born and perfected in Europe, we naturally tend to lean on Continental European malts when brewing them; that means Pilsner, Munich, and Vienna base malts and the countless caramel and roasted malts derived from them. European malts are built on European barley, and Continental malts enjoy a well-deserved reputation for refinement and high quality. Experience and personal taste should, as always, be your guide, but it's hard to go wrong by selecting malts that hail from the region of origin of the style you're brewing. That means Continental malt for German and Czech lagers and American malt for American lagers.

Now, I'm not for a minute suggesting that European malts are superior to American ones. But just as butter from Normandy has a certain quality that can't be exactly replicated elsewhere, so, too, does barley exhibit its own peculiarities of *terroir* and production methods. It's entirely possible to brew a very good German-style pilsner using American-grown barley, but it won't be the same as one brewed from German malt. All other aspects being equal, American pilsner malt tends to lend a grainier quality to light beer styles than do European pilsner malts, which are more doughy, bready, and cracker-like in quality. It's not about one being better than the other. It's about knowing the characteristics you want and selecting the malts that will deliver them.

Just as I prefer German malts for German-style beers, I prefer American malts for New World lagers. American 6-row malt, which was long shunned by small brewers who rightfully rebelled against its use in mass-produced macro-lager, is the malt of choice for classic American pilsner. Its rich enzymatic content and grainy, almost rustic profile makes it the perfect companion for maize, the flavor of which can overpower more delicate European malts.

Hops on the bine are ready to harvest in the autumn.

Choosing the right malt has less to do with brewing a lager than it does with brewing a style that hails from a particular geographic region. Of course, anything goes when it comes to craft brewing and homebrewing, so experimentation should be the rule, not an exception.

Hops

Hops offer a great deal of leeway, and not just because innovative new styles like India pale lager have pushed the boundaries of what's acceptable in a lager. Hops are successfully grown in Europe, North America, New Zealand, and Australia, and the range of aromas and flavors they deliver can range from subtle and spicy to boisterous and bombastic.

The noble hops—Hallertauer Mittelfrüh, Tettnanger, Spalt, and Saaz—are excellent options for all European lagers, and you really can't go wrong using any of them in any style. Saaz is the classic choice for Czech lagers, but saying that Saaz is preferred over Tettnanger is a bit like saying that black truffles are preferred over white varieties. Both are excellent and memorable. But a number of North American hop cultivars like Mt. Hood, Crystal, and Sterling are sufficiently "noble-like" in quality that they may be effectively substituted for classic European varieties.

So what *is* up with noble hops? Why are they special? Well, partly it's that they have low levels of cohumulone, which is one of three alpha acids found in hops (the other two being humulone and adhumulone). Brewers have historically preferred hops with low cohumulone levels thanks to a 1972 study that suggested a correlation between elevated cohumulone and perceived harshness. In the years since, other experiments have failed to validate this claim, and the jury is still out on whether or not cohumulone is responsible for what tasters perceive as harsh.

Other unifying qualities of the noble and noble-like hops include relatively low alpha acid concentrations, relatively high levels of humulene, poor storage qualities, and low beta acid levels. Such hops also display a certain Continental character in their flavor and aroma profiles that's hard to describe, but unmistakably European. Interestingly, these hops don't usually do so well when they're grown outside their regions of origin.[2]

Lager's delicacy and historical association with the noble hops means that selecting noble and noble-like varieties will almost always turn out a good beer with refined character. But, as with malt, experimentation is half the fun. Firestone Walker's Pivo Pils makes use of a relatively new German hop called Sapphir, while Russian River's STS Pils relies on a legacy French variety called Aramis. Both hops work exceedingly well in these beers.

You can really have some fun when it comes to India pale lager. Whatever you might normally put in an IPA can go right into your IPL: Amarillo, Centennial, Citra, Columbus, Mosaic, Simcoe, you name it. The sky is the limit. Jack's Abby's excellent Excess IPL includes heaps of Citra, Chinook, Ekuanot, Calypso, and Simcoe hops, which deliver a mélange of flavors ranging from passion fruit and peach to lime and pine.

Hop cones supply bitterness, flavor, and aroma to the finished beer.

Water

It's impossible to do justice to the importance of water in this book. It merits a book of its own, and that's just what you'll find in *Water: A Comprehensive Guide for Brewers* by Colin Kaminski and John Palmer. I cannot recommend this reference enough.

Nonetheless, we can consider a few aspects of water at a basic level. After all, through differences in water composition pale lager evolved from its origins in Plzeň to places like Munich and Dortmund. The water in Plzeň is extraordinarily soft, meaning it has very low concentrations of dissolved ions. This sort of water was key to Josef Groll's being able to pack in large amounts of hops without making for an overly bitter beer.

WATER PROFILES FOR IMPORTANT LAGER BREWING CITIES, PARTS PER MILLION (PPM)[3]

City	Calcium	Magnesium	Bicarbonate	Sodium	Chloride	Sulfate
Pilsen	7	2	16	2	6	8
Dortmund	230	15	235	40	130	330
Vienna	75	15	225	10	15	60
Munich	77	17	295	4	8	18

The table above illustrates how water profiles vary in cities important for lager brewing, including Plzeň and Munich. When brewers attempted to recreate pilsner in Munich, they found that they had to back off on the hopping levels in order to make the beer palatable. Thus, we have helles, whose soft, round, malt character is unmistakably different from snappy, hop-forward pilsner.

But it is mash pH that ultimately drives a brewer's concern about water chemistry. Mash enzymes are most effective when the pH of the mash (not of the water) falls within the range of 5.2 to 5.5. Crystal and roasted malts bring enough acidity to the game that including them is usually sufficient to bring mash pH into the desired range, but pale malts—pilsner malt, especially—might not be enough. In these cases, it's up to the brewer to introduce additional acidity.

In the old days, brewers would introduce an acid rest into the mash schedule, a short rest at around 100°F (38°C) that would activate the enzyme phytase, which breaks down phytin to create phytic acid. This acid lowered the mash pH. Today's brewers have more convenient choices. The simplest solution is to add pure acid, usually in the form of 88 percent lactic acid, directly to the brewing liquor. Another approach is to substitute a portion of the grist with acidulated malt—*Sauermalz* in German—which is a kind of pilsner malt that has been naturally soured using the *Lactobacillus* bacteria that already inhabit the malt husks. German brewers use acidulated malt as a sort of loophole for getting around the inconvenient fact that the Reinheitsgebot forbids adding lactic acid.

Again, water is simply too complex a topic to treat in any depth in this book, and as it's just as relevant to ale brewing as to lager brewing, readers are directed to more authoritative texts like *Water* to gain insight on this important aspect of wort production.

MASHING FOR LAGER BREWING

The simplest mash regimens involve a single rest: one temperature for one length of time. Since achieving the desired temperature involves infusing a measure of hot water into the grain, such a mash is commonly referred to as a single-infusion mash. This is the method favored in British brewing, and American craft breweries are well equipped to perform this kind of mash. Indeed, the single-infusion mash is the workhorse of American craft brewers and homebrewers alike.

The single temperature chosen for such a mash represents a compromise between the optimal working temperature for the beta amylase and alpha amylase enzymes. Beta amylase is most active between 140 and 150°F (60 to 66°C) and works on the ends of sugars, snipping off two glucose molecules at a time. These pairs of glucose molecules are called maltose, a sign of their intimate association with brewer's wort.

Beta amylase can only work so far down a chain of sugars before encountering a junction between branches of the sugar. The enzyme's structure, however, prevents it from getting close to those junctions, which is where alpha amylase comes in. Alpha amylase has an optimal working temperature range of approximately 155 to 165°F (68 to 74°C). However, it is still active outside this range, especially on the low end, just as beta amylase continues to work, albeit with less efficacy, outside its preferred range of 140 and 150°F (60 to 66°C). In employing a single-infusion mash, the brewer chooses one mash rest temperature, usually between 150 and 155°F (66 to 68°C), that represents a compromise between the relative activities of the two enzymes.

"Mashing low," which is to say around 150°F (66°C), or even a few degrees cooler, favors beta amylase and encourages fermentability, and thus dryness, in the finished beer. "Mashing high," or around 155°F (68°C) or a touch warmer, promotes alpha amylase activity, which leaves residual unfermentable sugars in the finished beer, corresponding to body and sweetness. The vast majority of American craft ales are mashed within a couple of degrees of 152 to 154°F (67 to 68°C).

In most cases, a single-infusion mash will turn out great beer. However, many lagers can benefit from the extra effort of performing a stepped mash, which is to say a mash protocol that stops at two or more mash rests along the way. Stepped mashes take advantage of the temperature optima of each mash enzyme as they climb the temperature scale toward mash-out. The most commonly used temperature rests today are:

Protein rest at 113–138°F (44–59°C)

Beta amylase rest at 140–150°F (60–66°C)

Alpha amylase rest at 155–165°F (68–74°C)

Mash out at 168–172°F (76–78°C)

The protein rest is used less and less these days, owing to the high degree of modification of modern malts. It simply isn't needed as much. However, it still comes in handy when using intentionally under-modified malts (such as some Bohemian pilsner varieties) and when using large amounts of unmalted adjuncts (such as the flaked maize in a classic American pilsner).

OPPOSITE: Malt starches are converted to fermentable sugars in the mash.

The most straightforward way to move a mash from temperature A to temperature B is to heat it directly. This may be accomplished with a direct flame, but doing so runs the risk of scorching the mash. A better approach is to use a modern HERMS (heat exchanger recirculating mash system) or RIMS (recirculating infusion mash system), both of which apply gentler heat to wort as it recirculates through the grain bed. An added bonus of such systems is the ultra-clear wort that results from continuous recirculation.

Another method for raising the temperature of the mash is to use hot water infusions. This is the approach best suited to homebrewers who mash in a plastic cooler. Brewing software like BeerSmith can predict the temperature and volume of water required to raise the temperature of a mash. A challenge with such methods is that each step introduces additional water volume, which makes it harder to move to the next mash step (water has a high specific heat) and also pushes the capacity limits of the mash tun.

The most traditional—and most energy- and time-consuming—method for raising mash temperature is the decoction mash. In a decoction mash, a portion of the mash is removed from the mash tun and placed in a separate cooker. It is then boiled for a length of time and returned to the main mash, raising the temperature in the process. The act of boiling a portion of the mash improves extract efficiency somewhat and was once a way to squeeze every last bit of sugar out of under-modified malt. Today, the decoction mash mostly exists as a historic relic, though the extended boiling does create certain aroma and flavor compounds that can be difficult to otherwise achieve.

The Hochkurz Mash Profile

All of this brings us to a mash profile that is widely used in German breweries: the *Hochkurz* mash. Derived from the German words for high and short (*hoch* and *kurz*, respectively), the

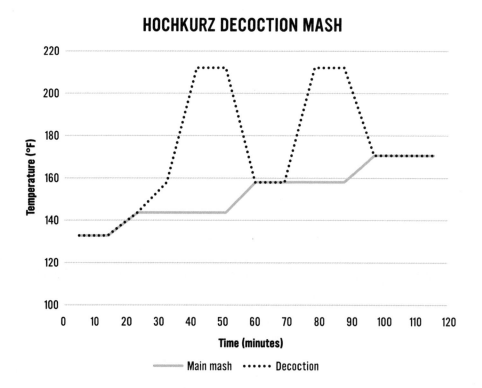

Hochkurz mash's name comes from the fact that it mashes in at a temperature above the protein rest (high) and takes much less time than traditional protocols (short). It's a fairly simple approach:

- Mash in at the beta amylase—or *maltose*—rest temperature of 140 to 150°F (60 to 66°C) and hold for 30 to 45 minutes. A good maltose rest temperature is 144°F (62°C) if you have no reason to choose otherwise.

- Raise the mash temperature to 155 to 165°F (68 to 74°C) for an alpha amylase—or *saccharification*—rest and hold for 30 to 45 minutes. A good all-purpose temperature here is 160°F (71°C).

- Raise the mash temperature to mash out and hold for 10 to 15 minutes. This is typically around 170°F (77°C).

That's it. If you're accustomed to single-temperature mashes, the Hochkurz protocol requires only one extra step (two if you don't currently perform a mash out). How you achieve those temperature changes is up to you: direct heat, hot water infusions, or decoctions—it's your call.

When the mash is complete, you can lauter, sparge, and collect wort just as you always would. The resulting wort will deliver a full-bodied but crisp and well-attenuated lager.

BOILING LAGER WORT

Boiling lager wort is just like brewing ale wort, but there is one thing that deserves special attention, though it's unrelated to the fact that you're going to ferment cold with *S. pastorianus*. Instead, it has to do with the association between lager and lightly kilned pilsner malt.

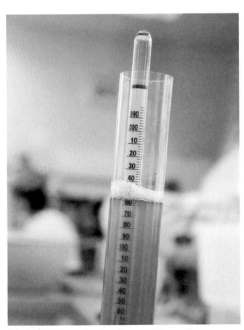

A hydrometer reads a beer's specific gravity (density).

The act of malting barley creates a compound called S-methyl-methionine (SMM) in every malt under the sun. When exposed to heat, SMM converts to dimethyl sulfide (DMS), which, in high concentrations, can lend a corn-like, or even cabbage-like, character to beer. Now for all but the very lightest of malts, the heat of kilning is sufficient to volatize and drive away SMM and DMS. Very gentle kilning, however, allows more SMM to remain in pilsner malt when it heads out the door of the malt house. Six-row contains even more SMM than 2-row, and when combined with flaked maize in a classic American pilsner, it can become cornier than Dad's jokes.

In the boil kettle, SMM converts to DMS, but because DMS is rather volatile, it is quickly driven away. For this reason, styles that include a large percentage of pilsner malt can benefit from an extended boil of 90 to 120 minutes. I recommend 90 minutes for lighter styles like helles and 120 minutes for darker ones like bock.

When the boil is complete, avoid covering the kettle, as condensation may develop and fall back into the wort—condensation that contains appreciable amounts of DMS.

Despite all your best efforts, lager yeast strains naturally produce more sulfur during fermentation than do ale strains, and all the boiling in the world won't stop the rotten-egg aroma of a lager fermentation. But a healthy fermentation scrubs most of that sulfur character away, and a small amount of residual sulfur character is acceptable, even desirable, in the very lightest of lager styles.

The end of the boil brings us to the end of wort production. Wort production for lagers and ales follow roughly the same path with just a few small potential differences along the way. But, after the boil, things become very different indeed.

Hops are added to sweet wort during the boil, which takes place in giant copper kettles at the Pilsner Urquell brewery.

FERMENTATION, CONDITIONING, AND PACKAGING

Wort production for lagers may proceed according to any number of mash and lauter protocols, all of which are just as applicable to ale as they are to lager. As we have seen, there is some historical precedent for choosing the decoction mash in lager brewing, but it's entirely possible to brew an excellent lager using the humble single-infusion mash with a batch-sparge (or even no-sparge) technique. It is after the boil, however, that the gap widens between beers made with *S. cerevisiae* and those fermented with *S. pastorianus*.

It is this part of the beer production process that is most likely to mystify newcomers to lager brewing. When do I pitch the yeast? How much yeast do I pitch? How long does fermentation last? Do I lager in the primary fermenter or in another vessel? Can I lager in bottles? These are all questions I had when I first started brewing lager, and I ran across a fair amount of conflicting information. The most reliable information is locked away in professional brewing texts, but even these have limitations because what works best in a commercial brewhouse may or may not be best practice in a small-scale home, or even nanobrewery or microbrewery, setup.

Lagers were traditionally fermented in open vessels.

The cold temperatures at which lager fermentation occurs present the brewer with a number of unique considerations that are of little to no concern for most ales. Recognizing these considerations and understanding how best to deal with them are the keys to successfully taking your beer into the cold. My goal with this chapter is to give homebrewers (and even very small craft brewers) the confidence to ferment, condition, and package their own lagers.

YEAST STRAIN SELECTION

We begin, necessarily, with the yeast, for it is yeast that transforms our carefully produced wort into delicious (we hope) lager beer. The Germans have an expression, "Wer die Wahl hat, hat die Qual," which literally means, "Whoever has a choice has agony." A related expression, "die Qual der Wahl," refers to the stress one experiences when faced with too many choices. It's a beautiful language, German.

Today's homebrewers and professional brewers are faced with a selection of yeast strains that would have been baffling even three decades ago, not to mention all the way back in 1553! Yeast determines beer character every bit as much as do malts, hops, and water, and, in most cases, even more. In fact the only difference between some beer styles comes down to the yeast strains with which they are fermented.

Take classic Bavarian hefeweizen (an ale, yes, but I'm trying to make a point, so bear with me). The grist couldn't be simpler: about two-thirds wheat malt and one-third pilsner malt. Some brewers adjust those percentages north or south or include small amounts of specialty malts, but Pils and wheat dominate. Hops in hefeweizen are only there for bitterness, and there's not much of that. So, a small dose of bittering hops at the beginning of the boil usually suffices.

At this point, we could very well have just as easily described American wheat beer as German weissbier. Sure, most American wheats go a little easier on the wheat and use American 2-row pale malt instead of pilsner, but they're fundamentally the same thing. Americans might throw in some late kettle hops (we can't resist the urge), but that's completely optional. At the most basic level, American and German wheat beers begin their lives the same.

If you taste these two styles side by side, you witness firsthand the difference that yeast makes. American wheat beers are usually fermented with a strain of yeast variously described as "clean" or "neutral." It's a yeast that allows malt and hops to shine, and, let's face it, we're talking wheat beer, so that essentially just means malt. Bavarian wheat beer, on the other hand, explodes with notes of bananas, cloves, and even bubblegum, all of which are attributable to the strain of yeast selected for the job.

In fact, brewers of German wheat beer will sometimes manipulate the mash with what's called a ferulic acid rest because the yeast used to ferment hefeweizen has a proclivity for converting ferulic acid into 4-vinyl-guaiacol, the phenol we associate with cloves. Producers of American wheat beer would never consider bothering with a ferulic acid rest. There's no need to since the clove character can't be teased out of their yeast.

So yeast makes a difference—a great difference, indeed—and in this admittedly extreme example, it creates two completely different beer styles. "Die Qual der Wahl." But here's an area where lager brewing is actually a little simpler than ale brewing. If you're accustomed to brewing ales, where yeast can mean the difference between a fruity New England–style IPA and a clean West Coast IPA, or between an American wheat and German wheat, you will be pleasantly surprised at how easy it is to select a lager yeast strain.

There's simply not as much diversity within *S. pastorianus*, at least not as much diversity that directly translates into the organoleptic experience, and virtually all commercially available strains, fermented properly, will turn out a crisp, clean lager. Differences exist, but they're far less dramatic than those found between members of *S. cerevisiae*. Because lagers ferment cold, many of the byproducts of fermentation, the compounds that define ale styles, simply aren't there. Or at least they're not there in appreciable amounts.

In a well-made lager, there are no fruity esters—no apples, no bananas, no peaches. In a well-made lager there are no phenols—no cloves, no pepper, and certainly no horse blanket funk. A well-made lager is mostly about malt and hops. So don't stress about choosing a strain.

All of that said, it's not true that yeast stays completely out of the way, and lager yeast selection does matter, just in different ways than you might be used to. Here are some of the key lager yeast properties to look out for.

1. **Sulfur production.** Lager yeast naturally produces more sulfur than ale yeast, and some strains are worse offenders than others. Your basement, fermentation closet, garage, or chest freezer will at some point smell as if your child has graced it with a stink bomb. In fact, the offending odor—hydrogen sulfide—is identical to that of a stink bomb. Fortunately, in most cases, little of it remains in the finished beer, so let your inner twelve-year-old be free.

2. **Diacetyl production.** All yeasts create diacetyl as part of the fermentation process, but ale fermentation is sufficiently vigorous that carbon dioxide carries away diacetyl on its way out of the fermenter. Lagers ferment more slowly and allow more diacetyl to remain in solution. That lager is cold only compounds this issue, but we shall discuss effective mitigation strategies shortly.

3. **Relative expression of malt and hops.** Some yeast strains accentuate malt more than hops and vice versa. This is no different than ale yeast, some strains of which are known to favor malt, and some of which tend to highlight hops. When in doubt, think about the beer style for which the yeast strain is named. A yeast strain given the name of a town in the Czech Republic will, in all likelihood, accentuate hops a bit more than one named for the capital of Bavaria.

4. **Fermentation temperature.** All lager yeasts—scratch that—*most* lager yeasts work best in the cold, but the question is "How cold is cold?" If, despite your best efforts, you simply cannot create or find a space that you can cool to less than 55°F (13°C), then you might need to stick with a temperature-tolerant lager strain like San Francisco lager, or even with a cold-tolerant ale strain like kölsch or alt.

When choosing a strain, all of the above considerations merit thought, but the difference between choosing a Czech pilsner strain over a Munich lager strain is going to be much less than, say, the difference between choosing a German hefeweizen yeast instead of an American ale yeast. So what yeast should you choose?

Well, as with many things, it depends, but I'm going to let you in on a secret, so listen up: When in doubt, use Weihenstephan 34/70.

Weihenstephan 34/70 is to lager as Chico is to American ale, the all-purpose workhorse of the lager brewery. It's said to be the most widely used lager yeast in the world, and you can find it everywhere. White Labs sells it as WLP830 German Lager, Wyeast markets it as 2124

Bohemian Lager, and Fermentis brands it in dry form as Saflager W-34/70 (how about that?). The yeast bank at Weihenstephan banks it as W 34/70, and the Brewing Science Institute (BSI) northwest of Colorado Springs keeps it going as 3470 German Lager.

Especially if you're new to lager brewing, it's much better to get to know *one* yeast strain well than it is to use a yeast for this and a yeast for that. With ale brewing, choosing the right yeast can be the difference between an American-style pale ale and a pale ale with characteristically Belgian esters and phenols. It's easier with lager. Just use W-34/70 until you know it like the back of your hand, and then branch out to other strains. And there are a few worth mentioning.

The Augustiner lager strain isn't readily available to homebrewers (BSI sells it to pro brewers), but it's a reliable strain that is especially appreciated for its low diacetyl and sulfur production. If you know someone who works at a brewery, you could ask them to special order it for you, but you're going to get a *lot* of yeast, so be ready to split it with your friends. Or, your club can order a 1-barrel pitch and share it. Anecdotally, Wyeast 2352 Munich Lager II shares many of the same characteristics as Augustiner lager yeast, and Wyeast notes that it comes from "a famous brewery in Munich," so read into that what you will.

Another fantastic lager yeast is Swiss lager 189, originally sourced from the now-defunct Hürlimann brewery, whose claim to fame was the extra-strong Samichlaus doppelbock (Samichlaus is now brewed by Schloss Eggenberg in Austria). Most lager yeasts are only moderately flocculent, but S-189 is an exception, making it an

Modern cylindroconical vessels are preferred by most brewers today for their sanitation advantages.

excellent choice for getting very clear beer without fining or filtration. Of course, given lager's cold temperament, most yeast won't require fining or filtration if you leave it long enough, but it's worth keeping in mind. S-189 is available from White Labs as WLP885 Zurich Lager and in dry form from Fermentis as Saflager S-189.

White Labs German Lager X was originally a seasonal strain, but it has recently been revived through the Yeast Vault program. Said to have originated from the Kloster Andechs brewery (the description says it comes "from a famous Bavarian monastery," plus Lager X rhymes with Andechs), this is one of my favorite strains. Like Augustiner, it generates less sulfur than some of the other options.

There are countless others that have names like Urquell, Budejovice, Munich this, German that, Pilsner, Budvar, Copenhagen, Danish lager, Rocky Mountain lager, and Mexican lager. Don't get me wrong: each of these strains is unique, but the differences are much less pronounced than they are in ale territory.

Again, if you only ever work with Weihenstephan 34/70, you're still going to turn out excellent lager, so don't get too caught up on selecting a specific yeast at first. After all, in lager land, it's less about the type of yeast you use than it is about how you use it. Which brings us to fermentation.

FERMENTATION

The transformation of wort sugars into ethanol and carbon dioxide is fundamentally the same process whether one brews ale or lager. The major difference between the two comes down to the temperature at which that metabolic process takes place, and it's largely the manipulation of temperature that makes lager fermentation a study unto itself.

Gases are more soluble in cold liquids than they are in warmer ones, especially carbon dioxide. It's this propensity for CO_2 to remain in solution that the lager brewer must recognize, for carbon dioxide is an excellent solvent for the flavor and aroma compounds that we desire in beer.

Hop aromas in particular are readily absorbed in carbon dioxide. It's one of the reasons that hop-forward ales rely on dry hops to deliver their aromatic punch. Late kettle hops contribute their share, of course, but the vigorous nature of ale fermentation forces volatile aromatics aloft on rising bubbles of CO_2.

Lagers, therefore, offer two advantages over ales when it comes to preserving hop aroma. First, the subdued nature of lager fermentation itself reduces the degree to which carbon dioxide drives hop aromas out of our beer. Second, because lager beer remains cold throughout its life, more carbon dioxide remains in suspension within the liquid, and along with it, more precious flavors and aromas. It's an aromatic twofer.

The reverse is also true—off-flavors linger in finished beer just as easily as desirable compounds do. And since many lagers rely on lightly kilned pilsner malt, the end effect is all the more noticeable since there's so little behind which flaws may hide. Pilsner malt brings its own issues in the form of dimethyl sulfide (DMS), as we have seen.

Speaking of sulfuric compounds, sulfur is a product of every beer fermentation, ale and lager alike. But lager yeasts produce it in abundance. A homebrewer's first lager fermentation is always a memorable experience thanks to the aromatic characteristics that pervade the space in which it takes place, customarily a repurposed refrigerator or chest freezer. Such enclosures

Lagering (cold storage) gives lager beer its name.

have the added benefit of allowing odors to accumulate and concentrate until the door is opened, at which point the brewer's olfactory glands (or, in the most unfortunate cases, those of the brewer's spouse) become flooded with the aroma of recently liberated rotten eggs.

Diacetyl, which offers the taster the artificial butter notes of cinema popcorn, remains similarly soluble in fermenting lager beer. Again, all yeast strains produce diacetyl in some amounts, but ales ferment warm enough that a natural cleanup of sorts occurs as fermentation draws to a close. Yeast, as it happens, is a rather tidy microbe that likes to pick up after itself and will readily do so if given the opportunity. That opportunity comes in the form of an elevated temperature, which ale fermentation supplies by its very definition.

Lager fermentation, on the other hand, is cold enough that diacetyl produced during fermentation is likely to remain in the finished beer unless preventive measures are taken. One such measure is the so-called *diacetyl rest*, which is nothing more than a brief warming of the fermenting beer as yeast activity begins to slow. The diacetyl rest is commonly initiated when a hydrometer indicates that fermentation is about two-thirds complete.

The actual temperature at which the rest occurs may vary from one brewer to the next, but most seem to aim for a sweet spot somewhere between 54 and 62°F (12 to 17°C). Conducting a diacetyl rest is as simple as holding your lager at its ideal fermentation temperature until the hydrometer indicates that fermentation is two-thirds through, usually about seven to ten days. At that point, you can raise the temperature of your fermentation chamber to the desired rest temperature and allow the yeast to work its way through the remaining fermentable sugars.

The goal of the diacetyl rest is simply to boost yeast metabolism as fermentation winds down so that the yeast does not slow down before it has an opportunity to clean up its own buttery mess. However, following good pitching and fermentation practices in the first place can diminish the need for such a rest.

Many well-intentioned brewers and yeast manufacturers recommend pitching lager yeast warm, say between 65 and 70°F (18 to 21°C), and then cooling the wort to the desired temperature when visible signs of fermentation are present. However, this practice is not optimal and is likely to enhance diacetyl production in the best of cases and add substantial fruity esters in the worst. Fermentation may proceed more quickly in the beginning using such a method, but additional conditioning will likely be needed to smooth out the inevitable coarse notes—if they can be smoothed out at all.

A better and more elegant approach is to follow the lager fermentation schedule endorsed by Prof. Ludwig Narziß of the Technical University of Munich at Weihenstephan. In Narziß's method, yeast is pitched into cold wort, which is then allowed to gradually warm a few degrees to the desired fermentation temperature. So, if one wishes to ferment at 48°F (9°C), then one might pitch yeast into 7°C (45°F) wort and then allow it to free-rise as fermentation commences.

An advantage of this approach is that it obviates the need for a diacetyl rest, though many brewers perform one anyway. It is cheap insurance, after all. On the flip side, though, pitching yeast into cold wort means that one's culture must be in tiptop shape and ready to begin work immediately. There's not much time for a long growth phase.

Dr. Narziß is also well known for a particular fermentation schedule that is regularly attributed to him. It's an approach that starts with a cold ferment (46 to 50°F or 8 to 10°C) and remains at that temperature until the specific gravity of the beer falls about half way from the measured original gravity to the expected final gravity. Then, the temperature is raised to 54°F (12°C) and held until the beer reaches terminal gravity, after which time it is gradually cooled by about 2°F (1°C) per day to a lagering temperature near 32°F (0°C) and conditioned for several weeks or months.

Industrious homebrewers have pushed this schedule even further, most notably in the method advocated by Mike "Tasty" McDole. Tasty's method uses four temperatures: a low temperature until the specific gravity falls by half, a slightly warmer temperature for another quarter, a third at the 15 percent mark, and finally an even warmer temperature until fermentation is complete. A typical "Tasty" schedule might be as follows:

- 48°F (9°C) from original gravity until 50 percent apparent attenuation
- 52°F (11°C) from 50 to 75 percent apparent attenuation
- 57°F (14°C) from 75 to 90 percent apparent attenuation
- 62°F (17°C) from 90 percent apparent attenuation to final gravity

The eponymous lager phase is the long, cold period during which lager beer matures, mellows, and smooths out around the edges. An important aspect of the process is that it takes place on the yeast. This is crucial, as lager yeast continues to remain active even at temperatures near freezing.

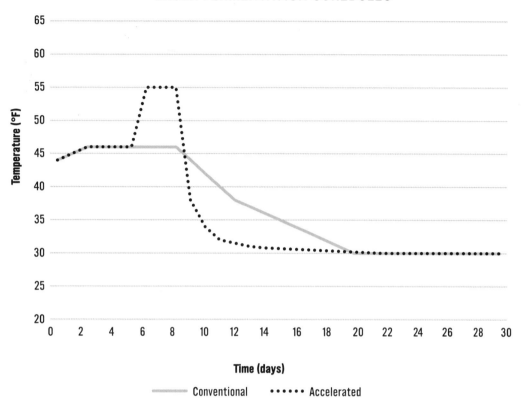

LAGER FERMENTATION SCHEDULES

Time (days)

——— Conventional   • • • • • Accelerated

Lagering is best performed in bulk, which is to say in a single vessel. The largest breweries blend batches from multiple brews to achieve consistency, a testament to the law of averages. While it may be tempting as a homebrewer to bottle first and lager second, doing so negates some of the "averaging" that takes place when a beer is aged in bulk. An exception, of course, is to lager in a serving keg, which brings us to packaging.

PACKAGING

When the lagering phase is complete, the finished beer is ready to be packaged in bottles or kegs. Packaging in kegs is the simplest approach, especially if you don't mind violating the Reinheitsgebot and force carbonating from a cylinder of compressed carbon dioxide (I don't mind). In addition to saving time, racking to a keg instead of packaging in bottles offers a couple of real advantages to lager brewers:

1. Applying CO_2 at a given pressure to a keg at a known temperature guarantees a predictable carbonation level. There's none of the guesswork associated with bottle priming.

2. Beer served from a keg almost always emerges from the faucet clearer than bottle-conditioned homebrew poured from a bottle. Perhaps not the first pint, but certainly the last. Everything in between is a matter of degree.

Now the latter of these two may be purely aesthetic, perhaps even a bit perfectionist. But part of the appeal of a well-crafted Czech-style pilsner is its brilliant clarity, so it's a

point worth considering on aesthetic merits alone. There is, however, a practical impetus at work as well.

The very aspects of a well-crafted lager that make it such a delight for the senses also conspire to make it difficult to bottle condition with priming sugar using methods that work perfectly well for ale. The long, cold lagering period encourages yeast cells to collect on the bottom of the aging vessel, and when the beer is racked off that yeast for bulk priming and bottling, fewer yeast cells are transferred over in the process.

Furthermore, those yeast cells that do transfer over have been sitting in the cold for a rather long time, and they may not be in the best of shape to ferment priming sugar for carbonation purposes. The higher the original gravity of the beer, the bigger a problem this becomes. Stressed yeast does not make for predictable carbonation. If you are bottle conditioning with priming sugar, I recommend dosing your finished beer with some fresh yeast. You don't need a lot, but a sachet of dry lager yeast like—wait for it—Weihenstephan 34/70 is relatively cheap insurance. No need to rehydrate—simply sprinkle the contents atop your beer alongside the priming sugar and stir *gently* to incorporate.

An excellent, though somewhat cumbersome, alternative solution to this little conundrum is the traditional German practice of kräusening. This is a process in which a small portion of actively fermenting beer is added to the finished beer at packaging, thus introducing just enough residual sugar and healthy, active yeast cells to carbonate the bottled beer. An added advantage is that actively fermenting yeast can help scavenge oxygen and clean up possible byproducts of fermentation that may have stuck around after the main event. The trick to kräusening is knowing just how much young beer to add, and at what stage of fermentation.

Large breweries have a definite advantage here because most will have the same beer in process at various stages of completion. It's easy enough for them to siphon off a portion of one at the desired level of attenuation to add to beer that's ready to be packaged. Homebrewers rarely have this luxury, but if you think ahead, you can reserve a little wort on brew day for this express purpose.

After knockout, transfer a portion of wort, typically a few quarts (liters) for a homebrew-sized batch, into a separate, sterile container that can be frozen. How much to siphon off depends on the wort's original gravity and the terminal gravity you expect it to reach. Rather than go into the math here, I would recommend that readers consult one of the many great online calculators.[1] Freeze the reserved wort on brew day and hold it until a day or two before you wish to bottle.

When you're ready to kräusen, remove the reserved wort from the freezer and bring it to a boil for sanitation purposes. Chill it down to fermentation temperature and add a small amount of yeast to get it going.[2] Now you have to wait and watch. When the kräusen beer starts to show signs of vigorous activity, add it to your main batch and then bottle as usual. After a week or two, you'll have carbonated beer.

Again, the process is a little cumbersome, but for homebrewers who want to be as authentically German as possible, and adhere to the Reinheitsgebot in the process, kräusening is a good tool to keep in one's belt.[3]

OPPOSITE: *Kräusen* is the name of the murky foam that develops atop fermenting beer.

CHAPTER 13
RECIPES

The recipes I have chosen for this book exemplify the diversity of styles that comprise the lager family. From the lightest of light American lagers to the darkest of Baltic porters, there's something here for every taste and proclivity.

If you're new to lager brewing or you can't get the temperature control just right with your current equipment, I recommend starting with a forgiving recipe, such as the California common. Once you are confident in your fermentation temperature control, the amber and dark styles like Prague after Dark offer an opportunity to brew lager with some leeway in case things don't go perfectly. The lightest styles here, from Annie Johnson's Mow the Damn Lawn to pFriem Pilsner, are the most challenging. Looks can be deceiving!

Have fun with these recipes. They're here for you to enjoy, interpret, and modify. Don't stress if your homebrew shop doesn't stock the exact ingredients listed. Ask your retailer about good substitutions, and you'll turn out an excellent lager.

NOTES ON THE RECIPES

When an established brewery opens a new location—Oskar Blues, New Belgium, and Sierra Nevada, for example, have all opened second breweries in North Carolina—brewers, equipment manufacturers, and process engineers spend countless hours tweaking and refining the new systems to faithfully reproduce flagship beers in the new facility. In brewing, it's not enough to simply have a recipe. Process variables are just as important as ingredient specifications.

Brewing methods and equipment are as diverse as the brewers who use them, and it's impossible to account for every possible variation in mash tun, fermenter, and packaging regimen. This book has lots of recipes—twenty, if you're counting—which I have standardized using a few basic assumptions. Those assumptions are detailed in these notes so that readers may adjust the recipes to fit their own brewing systems and practices.

I cannot recommend brewing software strongly enough for recipe conversion. In BeerSmith, for example, you can create an equipment profile that corresponds to the assumptions described in these notes. Then, with a few clicks of the mouse, you can convert a recipe to suit your own brewery, assuming you have a profile that accurately captures your equipment and process.

Batch Size and Volume Losses

The batch size for all recipes in *Lager* is **5 US gallons**, which is **18.9 liters** or **4.2 imperial (UK) gallons**. If you wish to brew more or less than this volume at once, you'll need to scale the recipe up or down.

In developing and adapting these recipes, I have not accounted for volume losses during fermentation, transfer, and packaging: The volume of beer packaged in kegs or bottles is assumed equal to the volume of wort transferred into the fermenter on brew day. Of course, this notion of zero post-boil loss never happens in practice. But using this idealized model makes it much easier for you to adapt these recipes to your own brewing system.

For example, I might lose half a gallon to trub in a flat-bottomed brew bucket, but you might lose just a quart in a cylindroconical vessel. Dry hops that soak up precious beer in the India pale lager recipes complicate the matter even more. It's up to you to add this fermenter loss to the batch and adjust the recipe accordingly.

Many homebrewers find that increasing a recipe's batch volume by 5 to 10 percent is enough to offset fermentation, transfer, and packaging losses. Anecdotally speaking, I usually aim for a pre-fermentation volume of 5.5 gallons, which virtually guarantees at least 5 full gallons of finished beer to rack into bottles or kegs. If I have a little extra, that's okay—and much better than coming up short!

TOTAL EFFICIENCY

A different but related concept is efficiency, which is a complex answer to a simple question: What fraction of the grain's potential fermentable sugars makes it into the wort? Stated another way: What fraction of the available sugars is lost along the way from grain to fermenter?

The total efficiency, sometimes called brewhouse efficiency, of the recipes in this book is **70 percent**. *Total efficiency* is based on collecting a desired volume of wort at a desired original gravity at the end of brew day. *Extract efficiency*, which I do not specify here, is based on how effectively your mash methods coax sugars out of malted grain. It's an important number, but not as important to recipe design as total efficiency.

Extract efficiency has to do with mash chemistry, but total efficiency has to do with the whole brew system. You can have the best mash efficiency in the world, but if half the batch volume is lost to the lauter tun, total efficiency suffers. Most homebrew recipes you'll find published in magazines, in books, and on the Internet assume a total efficiency of around 70 to 75 percent.

Wort Production

When a mash schedule is indicated in a recipe, the brewer who submitted that recipe has provided the schedule. Recipes that do not describe a specific mash schedule follow the **Hochkurz mash** protocol (*Hochkurzmaischverfahren*) detailed by Ludwig Narziß and Werner Back in *Die Bierbrauerei: Band 2: Die Technologie der Würzebereitung.* The same mash protocol is described in English as a "two-mash method" by Martin Krottenthaler, Werner Back, and Martin Zarnkow in *Handbook of Brewing*, edited by Hans Michael Eßlinger.

The Hochkurz mash skips the protein rest, owing to the well-modified quality of today's malts, and mashes in directly at the maltose rest (140 to 147°F or 60 to 64°C). The brewer then uses his or her choice of decoctions, infusions, or direct heat to raise the mash to the dextrin rest (158 to 162°F or 70 to 72°C) and mash out (169 to 172°F or 76 to 78°C).

Lautering may proceed according to the brewer's preferred approach. Most beer styles of low to moderate gravity will do just fine using a continuous-sparge, a batch-sparge, or even a no-sparge method. The handful of high-gravity beers (above, say, an original extract of 16°P or 1.065 SG) may benefit from slight efficiency gains to be had from continuous-sparge methods, but most homebrewers today find that a batch-sparge approach on an optimized system is as good as a traditional continuous sparge.

Boiling

Unless otherwise indicated, all recipes use a 90-minute boil. Most recipes in *Lager* are built upon a foundation of pilsner malt, and a longer boil may help reduce S-methylmethionine (SMM), which is the precursor to the dreaded dimethyl sulfide (DMS). A very small hint of DMS is appropriate, even expected, in some of the lighter German lager styles, but most brewers need not encourage DMS production. A long boil also adds stability, aids in protein coagulation, and slightly darkens wort.

I assume an evaporation rate of **1 gallon (3.8 liters) per hour** during the boil. Again, this will vary from one brewer to another. At my home in Colorado, where humidity is often quite low, I can boil off as much as twice that on a cold, dry day. I also use BeerSmith's standard shrinkage rate of **4 percent**, which is the volumetric difference between boiling wort and room-temperature wort.

Thus, for a 5-gallon (18.9 liter) batch—again, that's 5 gallons going into the fermenter—pre-boil volumes should be approximately 6 gallons (22.7 liters), 7 gallons (24.6 liters), and 7 gallons (26.5 liters) for 60-, 90-, and 120-minute boils, respectively. You'll need to adjust accordingly for the peculiarities of your system, as well as weather, boil vigor, and so on.

Unless otherwise specified, wort should be chilled as rapidly as possible from boiling to fermentation temperature and pitched immediately.

Pitch Rate

In beer lingo, *pitch rate* measures how much yeast a brewer adds to a given volume of wort. A review of classic German brewing texts by Heyse (*Handbuch der Brauerei-Praxis*), Narziß (*Abriss der Bierbrauerei*), Eßlinger (*Handbook of Brewing*), and Kunze (*Technology Brewing and Malting*) suggests that a pitch rate of 15 to 20 million yeast cells per milliliter of wort is advised for most commercial brewers of lager beer. Noonan (*New Brewing Lager Beer*) recommends a lower concentration of 12 to 15 million cells per milliliter, while Lewis and Young (*Brewing*) are at the low end with just 10 million cells per milliliter of wort.

In this book, I use a lager pitch rate of **1.5 million yeast cells per milliliter per degree Plato (°P) of wort** as suggested in *Yeast: The Practical Guide to Beer Fermentation* by White and Zainasheff (the Plato scale is a measure of wort or beer density in which every 1°P represents 1 percent sugar by weight). This is a widely used, all-purpose lager pitch rate that should suit most homebrewers quite well. Adjusting the pitch rate for original extract (Plato) ensures that high-gravity doppelbocks are given enough yeast to do the job without requiring that the casual brewer propagate or purchase an onerously large pitch for a low-gravity helles.

You may prefer to adjust this figure according to your own experience and practices. Lots of oxygen and yeast nutrient might let you get away with a lower number, while a larger quantity might be advised if your yeast culture isn't in tiptop shape.

Fermentation and Lagering

Unless indicated otherwise, all recipes in this book are fermented using cold fermentation and slightly warmer maturation. The details of this schedule are outlined in Chapter 12 and are based on the schedules described in various texts as:

- "Kalte Führung mit anschließender Warmreifung" in Ludwig Narziß's *Abriss der Bierbraurerei.*
- "Cold Fermentation with Integrated Maturation at 12°C" in Hans Michael Eßlinger's *Handbook of Brewing.*
- "Kalte Hauptgärung mit integrierter Reifung bei 12°C" in Karl Ulrich Heyse's *Handbuch der Brauerei-Praxis.*

This protocol entails fermenting cold (46 to 50°F or 8 to 10°C) until a gravity reading indicates that fermentation has proceeded about halfway from original to final gravity. At this point, the temperature is raised to 54°F (12°C) and held until the beer reaches final gravity. Then the beer is gradually cooled to a lagering temperature near freezing and conditioned for a period of weeks or months.

Yeast is *always* pitched into cold wort. None of this pitching at room temperature and waiting until signs of life appear before dropping the temperature. You don't pitch your ale yeast warm and then cool it down. Why would you do this to your lagers? Warm pitching has its advantages (lower cell requirements and a shorter lag time), but it does so at the expense of increased fermentation byproducts.

When fermentation is complete—that is to say, when the beer reaches terminal gravity—then it is gradually cooled by about 2°F (1°C) per day until it reaches approximately the freezing point of water. Lagering times vary, but a good rule of thumb is to lager for 1 week per every 10 points of original gravity. Thus, a 1.040 helles might lager for 4 weeks, while a 1.080 doppelbock would need at least 8.

Note: *Several commercial breweries have been kind enough to offer scaled-down versions of popular lagers for this book. In most cases, I have adjusted these recipes to match the assumptions described herein. Any errors or misrepresentations of the commercial recipes are mine.*

OPPOSITE: A long, cold aging period yields smooth, crisp lagers of incomparable clarity.

GRUIT BEER

This recipe is not intended to offer an authentic taste of gruit beer, as it was brewed in the old days. We don't know exactly what those old beers would have tasted like. The ingredients (malts especially) that were used in medieval beer would have been quite different from what we have available today. And even if we could faithfully recreate gruit beer from seven hundred years ago, there's a very good chance our modern palates would find it revolting.

Instead, this recipe combines a few things we know about gruit beer into an approachable ale. Vienna malt and a little bit of brown malt combine to simulate the dark malts that were the only thing available until the nineteenth century. A touch of peat-smoked malt introduces the inevitable smokiness that would have come from drying malt with fire. And a relatively high mash temperature leaves some residual body. (Murkiness, floating pieces of grain, political instability, and gangrenous ergotism are optional.)

The gruit herbs are introduced at two different stages in the boil to supply bitterness, flavor, and aroma. A relatively clean German ale (kölsch/alt) is used, but for additional "authenticity," there's an option to introduce a blend of *Brettanomyces* and souring bacteria that will change the finished product over time. If you go that route, know that your results may vary.

Vital Stats

BATCH SIZE: 5 gallons (18.9 liters)
BOIL TIME: 90 min.
ORIGINAL EXTRACT: 11.4°P (1.046 SG)
APPARENT EXTRACT: 2.3°P (1.009 SG)
ALCOHOL: 4.8% by volume
BITTERNESS: 0 IBU
COLOR: 8 SRM

Malts

8 LB. (3.63 kg) Vienna malt (3–4°L)
4 OZ. (113 g) Crisp brown malt (60–70°L)
4 OZ. (113 g) Peat-smoked malt (2–3°L)

Botanicals*

2 OZ. (57 g) yarrow leaves and flowers at 60 min.
1 OZ. (28 g) heather tips at 60 min.
1 OZ. (28 g) yarrow leaves and flowers at 10 min.
1 OZ. (28 g) heather tips at 10 min.
0.25 OZ. (7 g) bog myrtle at 5 min.
1 OZ. (28 g) juniper berries at 5 min.

Yeasts

Wyeast 1007 German Ale
OPTIONAL: Wyeast 3763 Roeselare Ale Blend

Brewing Notes

Mash at 155°F for 60 minutes and collect enough wort to yield 5 gallons (18.9 liters) after a vigorous 90-minute boil, about 6.5 gallons (24.6 liters). Boil for 90 minutes, adding botanicals per the schedule above. After knockout, chill wort to room temperature or pour into a shallow pan or vessel and allow to naturally cool. Pitch German Ale yeast and ferment until specific gravity stabilizes near 2.3°P (1.009 SG). If desired, add Roeselare blend and allow to continue fermenting until specific gravity falls to approximately 1°P (1.004 SG).

If you are bottle conditioning, note that the Roeselare version may continue fermenting for months. Use caution, and refrigerate bottles if you get gushers.

Gruit fell out of favor in the Middle Ages as brewers switched from herbs to hops for bitterness, flavor, and aroma. But the craft beer renaissance has made gruit fashionable again, and botanical beer is increasingly easy to find. Williams Bros. Brewing Co. in Alloa, Scotland, produces a full lineup of ales that feature heather, pine, and even seaweed. Scratch Brewing Company in Ava, Illinois, brews with homegrown and foraged ingredients such as lemongrass, basil, fennel, dandelion, nettle, and more. And many brewers have discovered the simple joys of adding spruce tips to otherwise "normal" beer styles (see Short's Spruce Pilsner on page 219).

International Gruit Day is celebrated annually on February 1, so keep your eyes open. Virtually all commercially brewed gruits have been ales, so we can only hope that gruit lagers are the next big thing!

Variation: Hopped Gruit Beer Hybrid

Early brewers didn't switch over from gruit to hops in one move; the transition would have been gradual. This transitional recipe is identical to the gruit beer also in this chapter, except a portion of the gruit blend has been replaced with hops. It makes use of a single bittering charge of Saaz hops to deliver 15 IBUs, with the flavor and aroma still coming from gruit herbs. The recipe is identical to the preceding Gruit Beer recipe, except for the hops and botanicals:

1 OZ. (28 g) Saaz hops [3.75% A.A.] at 60 min.

1 OZ. (28 g) yarrow leaves and flowers at 10 min.

1 OZ. (28 g) heather tips at 10 min.

0.25 OZ. (7 g) bog myrtle at 5 min.

1 OZ. (28 g) juniper berries at 5 min.

* These botanicals should be safe for most readers when used at the indicated concentrations, but always exercise caution when consuming unfamiliar plants. If you have reason to believe that consumption of yarrow, heather, bog myrtle, or juniper may cause a physiological reaction, consult your physician before brewing this beer! Pregnant women are especially advised to avoid such botanicals, as well as alcohol in general.

PRAGUE AFTER DARK

Prague after Dark is inspired by the famous Flekovský Tmavý Ležák, served at Prague's U Fleků brewpub, which claims to have been brewing continuously since 1499. This homebrew formulation is adapted from a recipe published by Horst Dornbusch in the Nov/Dec 2010 issue of *The New Brewer*, with a few modifications.

Vital Stats

BATCH SIZE: 5 gallons (18.9 liters)

BOIL TIME: 90 min.

ORIGINAL EXTRACT: 12.8°P (1.052 SG)

APPARENT EXTRACT: 3.3°P (1.013 SG)

ALCOHOL: 5.1% by volume

BITTERNESS: 30 IBU

COLOR: 27 SRM

Malts

4 LB. (1.81 kg) Weyermann Floor-Malted Bohemian Dark malt (6.5°L)

4 LB. (1.81 kg) Weyermann Floor-Malted Bohemian pilsner malt (1.7°L)

1 LB. 8 OZ. (680 g) Weyermann CaraBohemian malt (73°L)

7 OZ. (198 g) Weyermann Carafa Special III malt (470°L)

Hops

1 OZ. (28 g) Saaz [3.75% A.A.] at 110 min.

1 OZ. (28 g) Saaz [3.75% A.A.] at 100 min.

1 OZ. (28 g) Saaz [3.75% A.A.] at 5 min.

Yeast

Wyeast 2124 Bohemian Lager

Mash Schedule

MASH IN AT 100°F (38°C) and hold for 30 min.

30 MINUTES AT 126°F (52°C)

20 MINUTES AT 147°F (64°C)

20 MINUTES AT 162°F (72°C)

MASH OUT AT 171°F (77°C)

Brewing Notes

Mash per the indicated schedule, using decoctions to move from one temperature rest to the next, and collect enough wort to yield 5 gallons (19 liters) after a vigorous 120-minute boil, about 7 gallons. Boil for 120 minutes, adding hops per the schedule above. After knockout, cool wort as rapidly as possible to 50°F (10°C) and transfer to primary fermenter.

Pitch 363 billion healthy yeast cells and ferment at 50 to 55°F (10 to 13°C) for 2 weeks. Lager at 32°F (0°C) for 2 to 4 weeks.

WEYERMANN BOHEMIAN PILSNER, JOSEF GROLL 1842

Recipe courtesy Weyermann® Specialty Malts, Bamberg-Germany

From the brewer (author's translation): "This light gold pilsner gains its delicate light fruit and floral notes on the nose, with hints of citrus fruit, geraniums, and lilac, from the exclusive use of Saaz hops, which also deliver a pleasant bitterness to the palate. In addition to its refreshing mouthfeel, this beer offers a fine malt body thanks to the finest Weyermann® Bohemian malt. Using floor-malted barley gives this beer a pleasing graininess, while the dry bitterness in the aftertaste invites another sip."

Vital Stats

BATCH SIZE: 5 gallons (18.9 liters)

BOIL TIME: 90 min.

ORIGINAL EXTRACT: 11.6°P (1.047 SG)

APPARENT EXTRACT: 2.6°P (1.010 SG)

ALCOHOL: 4.8% by volume

BITTERNESS: 38 IBU

COLOR: 5 SRM

Malts

8 LB. 8 OZ. (3.9 kg) Weyermann® pilsner malt

3 OZ. (85 g) Weyermann® acidulated malt

3 OZ. (85 g) Weyermann® Carabohemian® malt

Hops

1 OZ. (28 g) Saaz [3.75% A.A.] at 60 min.

1 OZ. (28 g) Saaz [3.75% A.A.] at 30 min.

1 OZ. (28 g) Saaz [3.75% A.A.] at 15 min.

1 OZ. (28 g) Saaz [3.75% A.A.] at 5 min.

Yeast

Weihenstephan 34/70

Water

SOFT WATER with very low mineral content.

Mash Schedule

MASH IN AT 122°F (50°C) and hold for 20 min.

40 MINUTES AT 145°F (63°C)

5 MINUTES AT 154°F (68°C)

20 MINUTES AT 162°F (72°C)

MASH OUT AT 169°F (76°C)

Brewing Notes

Mash per the indicated schedule and collect enough wort to yield 5 gallons (19 liters) after a vigorous 90-minute boil, about 6.5 gallons. Boil for 90 minutes, adding hops per the schedule above. After knockout, cool wort as rapidly as possible to 46°F (8°C) and transfer to primary fermenter.

Pitch 329 billion healthy yeast cells and ferment per the Narziß schedule in the recipe notes on page 190. Keg or bottle with 2.6 volumes (5.2 grams per liter) of CO_2.

DEVIL'S BACKBONE VIENNA LAGER

Recipe courtesy Devil's Backbone Brewing Company, Roseland, Virginia

From the brewer: "With its amber chestnut-colored good looks and smooth malty finish, Vienna Lager was an obvious choice to put into package. It blends color and flavor without heaviness or bitterness. Just as Vienna lagers historically inspired Munich's oktoberfest beers to evolve, this amber lager has evolved since we opened in 2008 into the award-winning beer it is today. Experience the taste and tradition."

Awards

GOLD: Great American Beer Festival 2016, 2015, 2012, and World Beer Cup 2012

SILVER: Great American Beer Festival 2009 and World Beer Cup 2014

Vital Stats

BATCH SIZE: 5 gallons (18.9 liters)

BOIL TIME: 90 min.

ORIGINAL EXTRACT: 12.5°P (1.051 SG)

APPARENT EXTRACT: 2.8°P (1.011 SG)

ALCOHOL: 5.2% by volume

BITTERNESS: 18 IBU

COLOR: 9 SRM

Malts

3 LB. 10 OZ. (1.64 kg) pilsner (1.7°L)

3 LB. 10 OZ. (1.64 kg) Vienna malt (3°L)

1 LB. 3 OZ. (539 g) Dark Munich malt (8.5°L)

1 LB. 3 OZ. (539 g) Weyermann Caraamber malt (36°L)

Hops

0.45 OZ. (13 g) Northern Brewer [8.5% A.A.] at 90 min.

0.2 OZ. (6 g) Saaz [3.75% A.A.] at 20 min.

Yeast

Augustiner Lager

Mash Schedule

MASH IN AT 125°F (52°C)

147°F (64°C) for 30 min.

162°F (72°C) for 30 min.

MASH OUT AT 170°F (77°C)

Brewing Notes

Mash per the indicated schedule using a water-to-grist ratio of 3.2:1 by weight. Collect enough wort to yield 5 gallons (19 liters) after a vigorous 90-minute boil, usually about 6.5 gallons (24.6 liters). Boil for 90 minutes, adding hops per the schedule above. After knockout, cool wort as rapidly as possible to 51 to 53°F (10 to 12°C) and transfer to primary fermenter.

Pitch at least 355 billion healthy yeast cells into 51 to 53°F (10 to 12°C) wort, allow temperature to free rise to 54°F (12°C), and ferment until the apparent extract as read by a hydrometer falls to about 6°P (1.024 SG). Raise temperature to 57°F (14°C) for a diacetyl rest and hold until apparent extract as read by a hydrometer falls to approximately 2.8°P (1.011 SG) and stabilizes. Gradually lower temperature by 2°F (1°C) per day until it reaches 42 to 44°F (5 to 7°C), then rack to secondary vessel and crash cool to a lagering temperature of 28 to 34°F (–2 to 1°C) and lager at least 2 weeks (4 or more is better) before kegging or bottling.

YAMANOTE-SEN

Recipe courtesy of the author

Yamanote-sen is inspired by the "premium" lagers of Japan, which rely on rice to lighten body. Rice lends a crispness to this style of beer and helps dry out the finish. Unlike big macro-lagers, though, you'll find plenty of hop flavor and aroma here, including the characteristically lemony contributions of Sorachi Ace, a hop variety originally developed for Japan's Sapporo brewery.

The Yamanote-sen is one of the busiest rail lines in Tokyo. It's also the name of a Japanese drinking game.

Vital Stats

BATCH SIZE: 5 gallons (18.9 liters)

BOIL TIME: 90 min.

ORIGINAL EXTRACT: 12.3°P (1.051 SG)

APPARENT EXTRACT: 2.3°P (1.009 SG)

ALCOHOL: 5.6% by volume

BITTERNESS: 22 IBU

COLOR: 3 SRM

Malts

8 LB. (3.63 kg) pilsner malt

2 LB. (907 g) Flaked rice

Hops

0.25 OZ. (7 g) Sorachi Ace [13% A.A.] at 60 min.

0.5 OZ. (14 g) Strisselspalt [4% A.A.] at 10 min.

0.25 OZ. (7 g) Sorachi Ace [13% A.A.] at 10 min.

0.5 OZ. (14 g) Strisselspalt [4% A.A.] at 0 min.

0.5 OZ. (14 g) Sorachi Ace [13% A.A.] at 0 min.

Yeast

Weihenstephan 34/70

Mash Schedule

45 MINUTES AT 144°F (62°C)

45 MINUTES AT 162°F (72°C)

10 MINUTES AT 170°F (77°C)

Brewing Notes

Mash per the indicated schedule and collect enough wort to yield 5 gallons (19 liters) after a vigorous 90-minute boil, about 6.5 gallons. Boil for 90 minutes, adding hops per the schedule above. After knockout, cool wort as rapidly as possible to 46°F (8°C) and transfer to primary fermenter.

Pitch 350 billion healthy yeast cells and ferment per the Narziß schedule in the recipe notes on page 190. Lager for 3 weeks before kegging or bottling with 2.7 volumes (5.4 grams per liter) of CO_2.

GENERIC GREEN BOTTLE

Recipe courtesy of the author

This recipe is for a classic generic European "premium" pale lager that comes in a green bottle. It's not a clone of Stella Artois, Heineken, Grolsch, Kronenburg 1664, Beck's, Amstel, Carlsberg, or any of the other countless international pale lagers out there. But it's definitely inspired by them, minus the potential light-struck skunky character that can come from travel in a green bottle. For extra authenticity, serve this beer with skinny jeans, a cigarette, good public transit, and relaxed social mores.

Vital Stats

BATCH SIZE: 5 gallons (18.9 liters)

BOIL TIME: 90 min.

ORIGINAL EXTRACT: 12.1°P (1.049 SG)

APPARENT EXTRACT: 2.6°P (1.010 SG)

ALCOHOL: 5.1% by volume

BITTERNESS: 22 IBU

COLOR: 4 SRM

Malts

9 LB. (4.08 kg) Weyermann pilsner malt

4 OZ. (113 g) Weyermann CaraHell malt

Hops

0.25 OZ. (7 g) Magnum [14% A.A.] at 60 min.

0.5 OZ. (14 g) Hallertauer Mittelfrüh [4% A.A.] at 15 min.

1 OZ. (28 g) Saaz [3.75% A.A.] at 5 min.

Yeast

Wyeast 2042 Danish Lager

Mash Schedule

147°F (64°C) for 30 min.

162°F (72°C) for 30 min.

170°F (77°C) for 5 min.

Brewing Notes

Mash according to the indicated schedule and collect enough wort to yield 5 gallons (19 liters) after a vigorous 90-minute boil, about 6.5 gallons (24.6 liters). Boil for 90 minutes, adding hops per the schedule above.

Chill wort, pitch yeast at 48°F (9°C), and ferment according to the Narziß schedule given on page 190. Lager for 4 weeks before packaging.

1811 PRE-PROHIBITION LAGER

Recipe courtesy of Fort George Brewery, Astoria, Oregon

Two centuries ago, on the site of what is now the Fort George Brewery block, fur magnate John Jacob Astor's expedition boldly built a trading post they called Astoria—the first US settlement west of the Rocky Mountains. Today, we're proud to craft the Official Bicentennial Beer of Astoria.

Many West Coast brewers in the nineteenth century had no ice, so they improvised an effervescent beer by brewing lager yeasts at higher-than-normal temperatures. Described as a "refreshing drink, much consumed by the laboring classes," it's the inspiration for 1811 lager. More flavorful than most modern lagers, and fermented at warmer temperatures, 1811 is lovingly concocted from 2-row malted barley and cracked maize; corn was a popular beer ingredient in pre-Prohibition days. 1811's hop character gives it a distinctive Northwest style worthy of Astoria's two-hundred-year history.

Vital Stats

BATCH SIZE: 5 gallons (18.9 liters)

BOIL TIME: 90 min.

ORIGINAL EXTRACT: 12.1°P (1.049 SG)

APPARENT EXTRACT: 2.6°P (1.010 SG)

ALCOHOL: 5.1% by volume

BITTERNESS: 25 IBU

COLOR: 4 SRM

Malts

7 LB. 11 OZ. (3.49 kg) Pale 2-row malt

1 LB. 5 OZ. (595 g) Vienna malt

11 OZ. (312 g) Flaked maize

Hops

0.6 OZ. (17 g) Saaz [3.75% A.A.] at 80 min.

0.45 OZ. (13 g) Saaz [3.75% A.A.] at 20 min.

0.25 OZ. (7 g) Nugget [12.6% A.A.] at 20 min.

0.85 OZ. (24 g) Saaz [3.75% A.A.] whirlpool 10 min.

0.25 OZ. (7 g) Nugget [12.60% A.A.] whirlpool 10 min.

Yeast

American Lager

Brewing Notes

Mash per the indicated schedule and collect enough wort to yield 5 gallons (19 liters) after a vigorous 90-minute boil, about 6.5 gallons. Boil for 90 minutes, adding hops per the schedule above. After knockout, cool wort as rapidly as possible to 50°F (10°C) and transfer to primary fermenter.

Pitch 345 billion healthy yeast cells and ferment at 50°F (10°C) until final gravity is reached. Transfer to secondary and lager for 4 weeks at 32°F (0°C) before kegging or bottling with 2.6 volumes (5.2 grams per liter) of CO_2.

MOW THE DAMN LAWN

Recipe courtesy Annie Johnson, 2013 NHC Homebrewer of the Year

The coveted NHC Homebrewer of the Year award goes to the contestant whose beer is judged as best of show out of all the gold medal winners in all twenty-six beer categories of the National Homebrew Competition. When Annie Johnson won the honor in 2013 with this light American lager, homebrewers' jaws dropped from sea to shining sea. Winning with a lager is rare enough. Wining with a light American lager is unheard of.

But Annie knows her stuff, and this is her award-winning recipe. Even if you don't normally drink light American lager, you owe it to yourself to brew this, if not for you, then for your curmudgeonly grandfather who doesn't understand why youngins today have to drink such fancy beer.

Vital Stats

BATCH SIZE: 5 gallons (18.9 liters)

BOIL TIME: 90 min.

ORIGINAL EXTRACT: 11.9°P (1.048 SG)

APPARENT EXTRACT: 2°P (1.008 SG)

ALCOHOL: 5.3% by volume

BITTERNESS: 14 IBU

COLOR: 2 SRM

Malts

7 LB. 11 OZ. (3.49 kg) American 2-row pale malt

1 LB. 14 OZ. (850 g) Flaked rice

Hops

0.7 OZ. (20 g) Hallertau [4.5% A.A.] at 60 min.

Yeast

WHITE Labs WLP840 American Lager (4 liter starter)

Mash Schedule

149°F (65°C) for 60 min.

Brewing Notes

Mash according to the indicated schedule and collect enough wort to yield 5 gallons (19 liters) after a vigorous 90-minute boil, about 6.5 gallons (24.6 liters). Boil for 90 minutes, adding hops per the schedule above.

Chill wort, pitch yeast at 48°F (9°C), and ferment for 21 days. Lower temperature to 32°F (0°C) and lager for 30 days before force carbonating to 2.6 volumes (5.2 g/L) of CO_2.

"STS-INSPIRED" HOPPY PILSNER

Recipe courtesy Russian River Brewing Company, Santa Rosa, California

Vinnie Cilurzo is famously generous when it comes to sharing his recipes with homebrewers. What homebrewer hasn't seen the scaled-down version of cult-classic double IPA Pliny the Elder? This isn't an exact clone recipe for STS—you'll have to figure out water and yeast on your own—but it's close.

Vital Stats

BATCH SIZE: 5 gallons (18.9 liters)

BOIL TIME: 90 min.

ORIGINAL EXTRACT: 12°P (1.049 SG)

APPARENT EXTRACT: 2°P (1.008 SG)

ALCOHOL: 5.3% by volume

BITTERNESS: 40 IBU

COLOR: 3 SRM

Malts

9 LB. 3 OZ. (4.17 kg) Weyermann Pilsner*

Hops

0.6 OZ. (17 g) Aramis [8% A.A.] at 60 min.

0.5 OZ. (14 g) Aramis [8% A.A.] at 30 min.

0.5 OZ. (14 g) Aramis [8% A.A.] at 10 min.

0.5 OZ. (14 g) Aramis [8% A.A.] whirlpool 10 min.

1 OZ. (28 g) Aramis [8% A.A.] dry hop 7 days

Yeast

Augustiner Lager

Mash Schedule

10 MINUTES AT 130°F (54°C)

30 MINUTES AT 140°F (60°C)

20 MINUTES AT 150°F (66°C)

10 MINUTES AT 170°F (77°C)

Brewing Notes

Mash per the indicated schedule and collect enough wort to yield 5 gallons (19 liters) after a vigorous 90-minute boil, usually about 6 gallons (24.6 liters). Boil for 90 minutes, adding hops per the schedule above.

Ferment with Augustiner lager or similar yeast at 48 to 52°F (9 to 11°C) to a gravity of 4 to 5°P (1.016 to 1.020), then raise to 60°F (16°C) until final gravity is reached. Lager at 32°F (0°C) for 4 to 6 weeks, adding the dry hops about a week before packaging. Carbonate with 2.6 volumes (5.2 g/L) CO_2.

Substitute a small portion of acidulated malt for pilsner malt as necessary to adjust mash pH to 5.3.

THE KAISER IMPERIAL OKTOBERFEST

Recipe courtesy Avery Brewing Company, Boulder, Colorado

From the brewery: "The Kaiser once said, 'Give me a woman who loves beer and I will conquer the world.' If the Kaiser and his significant other had tipped this bottle, we'd all be 'sprechenden Deutsch!' We took all that is good in a traditional oktoberfest—gorgeous, deep copper sheen, massive malty backbone and spicy, floral, pungent Noble hops—then intensified each into this, an imperial oktoberfest."

Vital Stats

BATCH SIZE: 5 gallons (18.9 liters)

BOIL TIME: 90 min.

ORIGINAL EXTRACT: 20.3°P (1.085 SG)

APPARENT EXTRACT: 3.8°P (1.015 SG)

ALCOHOL: 9.3% by volume

BITTERNESS: 24 IBU

COLOR: 8 SRM

Malts

10 LB. 9 OZ. (4.79 kg) Pale 2-row malt (1.8°L)

1 LB. 15 OZ. (879 g) Light Munich malt (7°L)

1 LB. 15 OZ. (879 g) Vienna malt (3°L)

1 LB. 5 OZ. (595 g) Dark Munich malt (8.5°L)

10 OZ. (283 g) Aromatic malt (19°L)

Hops

0.6 OZ. (17 g) Hallertauer [4.8% A.A.] at 60 min.

0.2 OZ. (6 g) Magnum [12% A.A.] at 60 min.

0.4 OZ. (11 g) Sterling [7.5% A.A.] at 30 min.

0.5 OZ. (14 g) Hallertauer Hersbrucker [4% A.A.] at knockout

0.5 OZ. (14 g) Tettnang [4.5% A.A.] at knockout

Yeast

Weihenstephan 34/70

Brewing Notes

Pitch yeast at 55°F (13°C) and lower temperature to 50°F (10°C) mid-fermentation. When specific gravity falls to 1.030 (7.5°P), raise temperature to 60°F (16°C) for a diacetyl rest.

FORT COLLINS BREWERY MAIBOCK

Recipe courtesy Fort Collins Brewery, Fort Collins, Colorado

A smooth, malty flavor attained from the richness of Munich malts that finishes with gentle warming sweetness. Toffee notes and understated hop bitterness round out the bock experience. Brewed in fall, aged in winter, celebrated in spring. Prost!

Vital Stats

BATCH SIZE: 5 gallons (18.9 liters)

BOIL TIME: 120 min.

ORIGINAL EXTRACT: 16.5°P (1.068 SG)

APPARENT EXTRACT: 5.1°P (1.020 SG)

ALCOHOL: 6.4% by volume

BITTERNESS: 25 IBU

COLOR: 11 SRM

Malts

5 LB. 3 OZ. (2.35 kg) Weyermann pilsner (1.7°L)

4 LB. 13 OZ. (2.18 kg) Weyermann Munich Type I (7°L)

1 LB. 8 OZ. (680 g) Melanoidin malt (30°L)

14 OZ. (397 g) Weyermann Carahell malt (13°L)

8 OZ. (227 g) Weyermann Caraamber malt (36°L)

Hops

0.35 OZ. (10 g) Hallertau Magnum [14% A.A.] at 75 min.

0.35 OZ. (10 g) Tettnang [4.5% A.A.] at 20 min.

0.25 OZ. (7 g) Tettnang [4.5% A.A.] at 10 min.

Yeast

White Labs WLP833 German Bock

Mash Schedule

154°F (68°C) for 45 min.

169°F (76°C), achieved via 10-min. decoction

Brewing Notes

Mash in at 154°F (68°C) at a water-to-grist ratio of 3.2:1 by weight, and rest for 45 minutes. Decoct one-third of the mash, boil for 10 minutes, and carefully mix back into the main mash to achieve a temperature of 169°F (76°C), adding heat if necessary. Sparge at 169°F (76°C). Boil for 120 minutes and add hops per the indicated schedule. Knockout at 52°F (11°C). Ferment at 52°F (11°C) until specific gravity reaches 1.022, then ramp temperature to 60°F (16°C) for diacetyl rest. Crash cool to 31°F (−0.5°C) and lager at that temperature for at least four months before packaging.

PFRIEM PILSNER

Recipe courtesy pFriem Family Brewers, Hood River, Oregon

The story of pilsner starts in nineteenth-century Bohemia, when a Bavarian monk smuggled a special yeast to a brewmaster in Pilsen. The story of pFriem Pilsner starts in the Pacific Northwest, where it acquires the aroma of fresh grass and flowers and a touch of honey. While there are no monks involved in this pilsner, there is still a crisp and spicy finish.

Shines brilliantly gold with fluffy white foam. Aromas of fresh grass, spring flowers, with a touch of lemon zest quaffs from the glass. The mouth fills with zesty spiciness, a touch of honey, and finishes crisp, snappy, and refreshing.

Awards

SILVER: Great American Beer Festival 2015

BRONZE: European Beer Star 2016

Vital Stats

BATCH SIZE: 5 gallons (18.9 liters)

BOIL TIME: 70 min.

ORIGINAL EXTRACT: 11.5°P (1.046 SG)

APPARENT EXTRACT: 1.9°P (1.007 SG)

ALCOHOL: 4.9% by volume

BITTERNESS: 38 IBU

COLOR: 3 SRM

Malts

8 LB. 6 OZ. (3.80 kg) German pilsner malt

5 OZ. (142 g) Weyermann CaraFoam malt

2 OZ. (57 g) Weyermann acidulated malt

Hops

0.5 OZ. (14 g) Perle [8% A.A.] at 60 min.

0.25 OZ. (7 g) Tettnang [4.50% A.A.] at 60 min.

0.75 OZ. (21 g) Tettnang [4.50% A.A.] at 10 min.

0.5 OZ. (14 g) Saphir [3.50% A.A.] at 10 min.

0.5 OZ. (14 g) Spalt [4.75% A.A.] at 10 min.

0.75 OZ. (21 g) Tettnang [4.50% A.A.] whirlpool 10 min.

0.5 OZ. (14 g) Saphir [3.50% A.A.] whirlpool 10 min.

0.5 OZ. (14 g) Spalt [4.75% A.A.] whirlpool 10 min.

Yeast

Weihenstephan 34/70

Water

HIGH-QUALITY GLACIER WATER (or the best you can get)

Mash Schedule

142°F (61°C) for 40 min.

156°F (69°C) for 40 min.

168°F (76°C) during transfer to lauter tun

Brewing Notes

Mash per the indicated schedule and collect enough wort to yield 5 gallons (19 liters) after a vigorous 70-minute boil, about 5.8 gallons (22 liters). Boil for 70 minutes, adding hops per the schedule above. After knockout, cool wort as rapidly as possible to 46°F (8°C) and transfer to primary fermenter.

Pitch 300 billion healthy yeast cells and ferment per the Narziß schedule in the recipe notes on page 190. Keg or bottle with 2.6 volumes (5.2 grams per liter) of CO_2.

CLASSIC FESTBIER

Recipe courtesy of the author

The beer served at Oktoberfest these days is more an export-strength helles than it is a traditional oktoberfest/märzen. This festbier offers more complexity and alcohol than your everyday quaffing helles but remains supremely drinkable.

Vital Stats

BATCH SIZE: 5 gallons (18.9 liters)

BOIL TIME: 90 min.

ORIGINAL EXTRACT: 14.7°P (1.060 SG)

APPARENT EXTRACT: 3.1°P (1.012 SG)

ALCOHOL: 6.3% by volume

BITTERNESS: 32 IBU

COLOR: 5 SRM

Malts

8 LB. (3.6 kg) German pilsner malt

3 LB. (1.4 kg) German Vienna malt

7 OZ. (198 g) Weyermann Carahell malt

Hops

1.75 OZ. (50 g) Hallertauer Mittelfrüh [4.3% A.A.] at 60 min.

0.5 OZ. (14 g) Hallertauer Mittelfrüh [4.3% A.A.] at 5 min.

Yeast

Wyeast 2308 Munich Lager

Miscellaneous Items

WHIRLFLOC or Irish moss, added 10 min. before end of boil

Mash Schedule

149°F (65°C) for 30 min.

162°F (72°C) for 30 min.

170°F (77°C) for 10 min.

Brewing Notes

Mash per the indicated schedule and collect enough wort to yield 5 gallons (19 liters) after a vigorous 90-minute boil, about 6.5 gallons (24.6 liters). Boil for 90 minutes, adding hops per the schedule above. Add Whirlfloc or Irish moss 10 minutes before end of boil to promote protein coagulation and precipitation. After knockout, cool wort as rapidly as possible to 46°F (8°C) and transfer to primary fermenter.

Pitch 417 billion healthy yeast cells into 46°F (8°C) wort, allow temperature to free rise to 50°F (10°C), and ferment for 10 days, or until the apparent extract as read by a hydrometer falls to about 8.9°P (1.035 SG). Raise temperature to 54°F (12°C) and hold until apparent extract as read by a hydrometer falls to approximately 3.1°P (1.012 SG) and stabilizes, usually 4 to 7 days. Rack to secondary vessel and lager at 32°F (0°C) for 6 weeks or longer before kegging or bottling. Carbonate to 2.6 volumes (5.2 grams per liter) of CO_2 and serve at 45°F (7°C).

SMUTTYNOSE
BALTIC PORTER

Recipe courtesy Smuttynose Brewing Company, Hampton, New Hampshire

Most porters are brewed as ales, but Baltic porter is actually a strong lager. The royal court of Russia was famously obsessed with English stout, and that obsession led to what we know today as Russian imperial stout. The Russians also fancied a bit of porter, and by the middle of the nineteenth century, several breweries located in the Baltic region had begun brewing their own versions of the English beer to a strength similar to that of imperial stout. Around the same time, lager techniques began supplanting ale brewing, and the Baltic porter transformed into the strong dark lager we enjoy today.

Smuttynose Brewing Company makes one of the top-rated Baltic porters in North America. The brewers at Smuttynose graciously provided the following homebrew recipe.

Vital Stats

BATCH SIZE: 5 gallons (18.9 liters)

BOIL TIME: 90 minutes

ORIGINAL EXTRACT: 23°P (1.098 SG)

APPARENT EXTRACT: 7°P (1.028 SG)

ALCOHOL: 9.2% by volume

BITTERNESS: 40 IBU

COLOR: 65 SRM

Malts

10 LB. 8 OZ. (4.76 kg) pilsner malt

4 LB. (1.81 kg) Munich malt

1 LB. (454 g) Weyermann CaraHell malt

1 LB. (454 g) Caramel 120°L malt

1 LB. (454 g) Carastan malt

12 OZ. (340 g) Black malt

12 OZ. (340 g) Chocolate malt

Hops

1.25 OZ. (35 g) Sterling [6.6% A.A.] at 60 min.

0.75 OZ. (21 g) Sterling [6.6% A.A.] at 20 min.

0.65 OZ. (18 g) Sterling [6.6% A.A.] whirlpool 20 min.

Yeast

Your favorite lager yeast

Mash Schedule

152°F (67°C) for 30 min.

162°F (72°C) for 15 min.

Brewing Notes

Mash per the indicated schedule and collect enough wort to yield 5 gallons (19 liters) after a vigorous 90-minute boil, about 6.5 gallons (24.6 liters). Boil for 90 minutes, adding hops per the schedule above. After knockout, cool wort as rapidly as possible to the fermentation temperature of your favorite lager yeast strain and transfer to primary fermenter. Ferment cool.

CLASSIC BOCK

Recipe courtesy of the author

Doppelbock has become a popular lager style for many American craft breweries, but it can still be somewhat hard to find a good standard bock. If you enjoy rich malt complexity with mild bitterness and a clean finish, this is the beer for you. For those who like to plan ahead, brew this bock in late summer or early autumn so that it's ready to drink when the snow starts to fall. Save the yeast and use it to brew a doppelbock for Lent.

Vital Stats

BATCH SIZE: 5 gallons (18.9 liters)

BOIL TIME: 90 min.

ORIGINAL EXTRACT: 17.3°P (1.071 SG)

APPARENT EXTRACT: 4°P (1.016 SG)

ALCOHOL: 7.3% by volume

BITTERNESS: 24 IBU

COLOR: 18 SRM

Malts

7 LB. 8 OZ. (3.40 kg) Weyermann Munich Type I malt

5 LB. (2.27 kg) German pilsner malt

8 OZ. (227 g) Weyermann Caraaroma malt

8 OZ. (227 g) Weyermann Caramunich II malt

Hops

0.8 OZ. (23 g) Perle [8% A.A.] at 60 min.

Yeast

White Labs WLP833 German Bock Lager

Mash Schedule

149°F (65°C) for 30 min.

162°F (72°C) for 30 min.

170°F (77°C) for 10 min.

Brewing Notes

Mash per the indicated schedule and collect enough wort to yield 5 gallons (19 liters) after a vigorous 90-minute boil, about 6.5 gallons (24.6 liters). Boil for 90 minutes, adding hops per the schedule above. Add Whirlfloc or Irish moss 10 minutes before end of boil to promote protein coagulation and precipitation. After knockout, cool wort as rapidly as possible to 46°F (8°C) and transfer to primary fermenter.

Pitch 491 billion healthy yeast cells into 46°F (8°C) wort, allow temperature to free rise to 50°F (10°C), and ferment for 10 days, or until the apparent extract as read by a hydrometer falls to about 8.4°P (1.033 SG). Raise temperature to 60°F (16°C) for a diacetyl rest and hold until apparent extract as read by a hydrometer falls to approximately 4°P (1.016 SG) and stabilizes, usually 4 to 7 days. Rack to secondary vessel and lager at 35°F (2°C) for 6 weeks or longer before kegging or bottling. Carbonate to 2.6 volumes (5.2 grams per liter) of CO_2 and serve at 45°F (7°C).

TRÖEGS TROEGENATOR

Recipe courtesy Tröegs Brewing Company, Hershey, Pennsylvania

Monks had fasting figured out. No food? No problem. Just drink a doppelbock. Thick and chewy with intense notes of caramel, chocolate, and dried stone fruit, 'Nator (as we call him) serves as a tribute to this liquid-bread style. Beer writer Lew Bryson called Troegenator "the best beer I had in 2004."

Awards

GOLD: Great American Beer Festival 2014, 2013, 2011, 2009, 2007, and World Beer Cup 2010

SILVER: Great American Beer Festival 2010, 2006

BRONZE: World Beer Cup 2012, 2008, 2006

Vital Stats

BATCH SIZE: 5 gallons (18.9 liters)

BOIL TIME: 90 min.

ORIGINAL EXTRACT: 19.9°P (1.083 SG)

APPARENT EXTRACT: 4.6°P (1.018 SG)

ALCOHOL: 8.7% by volume

BITTERNESS: 22 IBU

COLOR: 20 SRM

Malts

9 LB. 6 OZ. (4.25 kg) Cargill EuroPils (1.8°L)

4 LB. (1.81 kg) Cargill Munich malt (9.5°L)

1 LB. 10 OZ. (737 g) Gambrinus Munich dark malt (30°L)

13 OZ. (369 g) Briess caramel malt (80°L)

6 OZ. (170 g) Weyermann melanoidin malt (30°L)

1.5 OZ. (43 g) Special B malt (180°L)

1 OZ. (28 g) Chocolate malt (450°L)

Hops

0.25 OZ. (7 g) Bravo [14.70% A.A.] at 90 min.

0.5 OZ. (14 g) Northern Brewer [6% A.A.] at 60 min.

Yeast

3 packages White Labs WLP830 German Lager (or an equivalent starter culture)

Water

Treat brewing liquor with 0.4 g calcium chloride per gallon of water (0.1 g per liter)

Miscellaneous Items

1 Whirlfloc tablet, added 10 min. before end of boil

1 tbsp. Yeast nutrient, added 10 min. before end of boil

Mash Schedule

144°F (62°C) for 20 min.

149°F (65°C) for 20 min.

154°F (68°C) for 15 min.

162°F (72°C) for 15 min.

MASH OUT AT 172°F (78°C)

Brewing Notes

Mash per the indicated schedule and collect enough wort to yield 5 gallons (18.9 liters) after a vigorous 90-minute boil, about 6 gallons (22.7 liters). Boil for 90 minutes, adding hops per the schedule above. Add Whirlfloc 10 minutes before end of boil to promote protein coagulation and precipitation. After knockout, cool wort as rapidly as possible to 55°F (13°C) and transfer to primary fermenter.

Pitch yeast and ferment for 14 days at 55°F (13°C), rack to secondary, and hold for another 14 days at 55°F (13°C), or until the apparent extract as read by a hydrometer falls to about 4.6°P (1.018 SG). Keg and force carbonate to 2.6 volumes (5.2 grams per liter) of CO_2 and lager for an additional 14 days at 32°F (32°C). Serve at 45 to 50°F (7 to 10°C) in a lager glass.

STEAMING RANCOR

Recipe courtesy of the author

This isn't intended to be an exact Anchor Steam clone, just a highly drinkable California common that pays homage to the original. Feel free to substitute malts based on what you have on hand and your preference. The most important aspects of this beer are the Northern Brewer hops and the forgiving San Francisco lager yeast, which remains lager-like up to about 65°F (18°C). You'll get a few esters, to be sure, but that's part of the style.

This is an easy beer to brew! There's no need for strict temperature control (especially if you brew in winter or have a basement) and no extended lagering phase. Pair this one with Dungeness crab or Rice-A-Roni (hey, I eat everything).

Vital Stats

BATCH SIZE: 5 gallons (18.9 liters)

BOIL TIME: 90 min.

ORIGINAL EXTRACT: 13°P (1.053 SG)

APPARENT EXTRACT: 3.8°P (1.015 SG)

ALCOHOL: 5% by volume

BITTERNESS: 41 IBU

COLOR: 11 SRM

Malts

5 LB. (2.27 kg) Weyermann Munich Type II malt

4 LB. 4 OZ. (1.93 kg) American pale malt

1 LB. (454 g) Caramel 40 malt

Hops

0.5 OZ. (14 g) Northern Brewer [8.5% A.A.] at 60 min.

1 OZ. (28 g) Northern Brewer [8.5% A.A.] at 15 min.

1 OZ. (28 g) Northern Brewer [8.5% A.A.] at 5 min.

1 OZ. (28 g) Northern Brewer [8.5% A.A.] at 0 min.

Yeast

White Labs WLP810 San Francisco Lager

Mash Schedule

151°F (66°C) for 30 min.

Brewing Notes

Single-infusion mash per indicated schedule and collect enough wort to yield 5 gallons (19 liters) after a vigorous 90-minute boil, about 6.5 gallons (24.6 liters). Boil for 90 minutes, adding hops per the schedule above. After knockout, cool wort as rapidly as possible to 60°F (16°C) and transfer to primary fermenter.

Pitch 276 billion healthy yeast cells into 60°F (16°C) wort, allow temperature to free rise to 62°F (17°C), and ferment for 7 days, or until the apparent extract as read by a hydrometer falls to about 8.9°P (1.035 SG). Raise temperature to 54°F (12°C) and hold until apparent extract as read by a hydrometer falls to approximately 6.8°P (1.027 SG) and stabilizes. Carbonate to 2.8 volumes (5.6 grams per liter) of CO_2 and serve at 50°F (10°C).

UNA MÁS MEXICO-INSPIRED LAGER

Recipe courtesy of the author

A famous Mexican brewery packages its beer in clear bottles and has convinced tourists that Mexican beer should be served with a lime wedge. Some have argued that the lime is there to distract from the distinctively skunky flavor and aroma of light-struck beer, while others think it's just marketing.

As my tastes have evolved, I've come to appreciate a little bit of a hint of lime when that lime flavor is infused into the beer itself. For this beer, I have opted to use lime extract, which is sold at many gourmet and spice shops, because it's so easy to work with, and it offers intense lime flavor in a small package. I'm particularly fond of the Natural Key Lime Extract available through Savory Spice Shop (www.savoryspiceshop.com), which offers a small 2 fl. oz. bottle that's just the right size for this recipe. A little bit of salt gives the impression of a salty sea breeze, but don't waste your expensive sea salt on this beer. Kosher salt will do just fine.

If you enjoy drinking gose, give this one a try. You might just find yourself asking *for una más* Una Más!

Vital Stats

BATCH SIZE: 5 gallons (18.9 liters)

BOIL TIME: 90 min.

ORIGINAL EXTRACT: 12.3°P (1.051 SG)

APPARENT EXTRACT: 2.6°P (1.010 SG)

ALCOHOL: 5.3% by volume

BITTERNESS: 20 IBU

COLOR: 3 SRM

Malts

4 LB. (1.81 kg) German pilsner malt

3 LB. (1.36 kg) American 6-row pale malt

3 LB. (1.36 kg) Flaked maize

Hops

0.5 OZ. (14 g) Sterling [7.5% A.A.] at 60 min.

0.5 OZ. (14 g) Sterling [7.5% A.A.] at 5 min.

Yeast

White Labs WLP 940 Mexican Lager

Additional Items

0.5 OZ. (14 g) Kosher salt at 10 min.

2 FL. OZ. (60 ml) Key lime extract in secondary

Mash Schedule

40 MINUTES AT 145°F (63°C)

30 MINUTES AT 162°F (72°C)

MASH OUT AT 170°F (77°C)

Brewing Notes

Mash per the indicated schedule and collect enough wort to yield 5 gallons (19 liters) after a vigorous 90-minute boil, about 6.5 gallons. Boil for 90 minutes, adding hops per the schedule above. After knockout, cool wort as rapidly as possible to 46°F (8°C) and transfer to primary fermenter.

Pitch 329 billion healthy yeast cells and ferment per the Narziß schedule in the recipe notes on page 190. Transfer to secondary and add the key lime extract. Lager for 4 weeks at 32°F (0°C), then keg or bottle with 2.6 volumes (5.2 grams per liter) of CO_2. Serve cold with tacos al pastor or menudo.

SHORT'S SPRUCE PILSNER

Recipe courtesy Short's Brewing Company, Bellaire, Michigan

Of course, to really make an American lager worthy of the new craft sense of the word, it should be both hoppy and strong. And while we're at it, why not throw in some strange ingredients as well? That's what Short's Brewing Company of Bellaire, Michigan, has done with its Spruce Pilsner, an imperial pilsner that features locally sourced, handpicked spruce tips. An outstanding—and deceptively light—pilsner in its own right. The addition of spruce delivers an extra dimension of aroma and flavor that nicely complements the already aggressive hop presence.

Vital Stats

BATCH SIZE: 5 gallons (18.9 liters)

BOIL TIME: 90 min.

ORIGINAL EXTRACT: 18.5°P (1.077 SG)

APPARENT EXTRACT: 4.1°P (1.016 SG)

ALCOHOL: 8.1% by volume

BITTERNESS: 85 IBU

COLOR: 6 SRM

Malts

13 LB. 2 OZ. (5.95 kg) pilsner malt

1 LB. 10 OZ. (737 g) Flaked maize

Hops

0.65 OZ. (18 g) Summit [18.5% A.A.] at 60 min.

0.65 OZ. (18 g) Summit [18.5% A.A.] at 30 min.

0.65 OZ. (18 g) Summit [18.5% A.A.] at 10 min.

1 OZ. (28 g) Summit [18.5% A.A.] at flameout

Other Ingredients

1.6 OZ. (45 g) Freshly picked spruce needles, chopped

Yeast

American Lager

Mash Schedule

MASH AT 152°F (67°C) for 60 min.

Brewing Notes

Mash per the indicated schedule and collect enough wort to yield 5 gallons (19 liters) after a vigorous 90-minute boil, usually about 6 gallons (24.6 liters). Boil for 90 minutes, adding hops per the schedule above.

After the boil, draw a small portion of hot wort from the kettle to heat sanitize the chopped spruce needles while the remaining wort chills to 56°F (13°C). Add the spruce needles and their hot wort to the primary fermenter along with the chilled wort.

Pitch at least 525 billion healthy yeast cells, ferment at 56°F (13°C), then crash cool and allow spruce needles to settle. Rack finished beer into clean secondary and package.

FEARLESS YOUTH MUNICH DUNKEL

Recipe courtesy Grimm Brothers Brewhouse, Loveland, Colorado

Munich dunkel is one of the world's oldest continuously brewed beer styles. Before the development of pale malt, all beer was brown or black to some degree. Malting technology simply didn't allow for anything else.

This homebrew version of the brewery's award-winning Munich dunkel was graciously provided by Don Chapman, one of the founders of Grimm Brothers Brewhouse in Loveland, Colorado. They have won numerous awards for their German-style and German-inspired lagers and ales. Naturally they happen to brew one of the finest Munich dunkels in North America: Fearless Youth.

Awards

SILVER: Great American Beer Festival 2015

BRONZE: Great American Beer Festival 2013

Vital Stats

BATCH SIZE: 5 gallons (18.9 liters)

BOIL TIME: 90 min.

ORIGINAL EXTRACT: 12.9°P (1.052 SG)

APPARENT EXTRACT: 3°P (1.012 SG)

ALCOHOL: 5.2% by volume

BITTERNESS: 20 IBU

COLOR: 13 SRM

Malts

7 LB. 7 OZ. (3.37 kg) Dark Munich malt (8.5°L)

2 LB. 4 OZ. (1.02 kg) pilsner malt (1.7°L)

1.5 OZ. (43 g) dextrin malt (2°L)

1.5 OZ. (43 g) chocolate malt (450°L)

Hops

1.1 OZ. (31 g) Hallertauer [4.5% A.A.] at 75 min.

Yeast

Augustiner Lager or White Labs WLP830
German Lager

Mash Schedule

SINGLE INFUSION AT 153°F (67°C)

Brewing Notes

Mash per the indicated schedule and collect enough wort to yield 5 gallons (18.9 liters) after a vigorous 90-minute boil, about 6.5 gallons (24.6 liters). Boil for 90 minutes, adding hops per the schedule above.

Pitch at least 366 billion healthy yeast cells into 52°F (11°C) wort, allow temperature to free rise to 54°F (12°C), and ferment until the apparent extract as read by a hydrometer falls to about 7.9°P (1.031 SG). Raise temperature to 54°F (12°C) and hold until apparent extract as read by a hydrometer falls to approximately 3°P (1.012 SG) and stabilizes. Gradually lower temperature by 2°F (1°C) per day to 32°F (0°C), rack to a lagering vessel, and lager at least 3 weeks before kegging or bottling.

OPPOSITE: Munich dunkel is the perfect everyday session lager for those who enjoy the richness of Munich malt.

NOTES ON THE BEER EVALUATIONS

I have provided sensory descriptions of commercial examples of various lager beer styles to help you discover what you might enjoy. My goal with these evaluations is to offer objective descriptions to help you decide what to buy or brew, not to endorse or criticize specific products. I can't know what you like and don't like, so you won't find ratings, and only in a few cases will you find suggestions for improvement (e.g., in green-bottle imports that suffer from a light-struck skunky character).

Beer judges do their best to develop an objective vocabulary with which to describe what they taste, but sensory evaluation is fundamentally subjective. If you and I were to sit down together for a pint, we'd probably come up with quite different descriptions of the same beer. Indeed, when trained beer judges sit down to analyze and score beer in competitions, even they have different experiences. Our biology is partly to blame.

Take cilantro leaves, one of the most polarizing ingredients in the great cuisines of Mexico, India, and Thailand. Those who like cilantro describe a fresh, lemony, citrus-like herb. Those who can't stomach the stuff prefer words like *soapy* and *rotten*. As it happens, researchers have uncovered a genetic factor associated with cilantro that is tied to encoding in our organoleptic receptors. In one study, 80 percent of identical twins were found to agree on whether they liked or disliked the herb. In fraternal twins, however, agreement was only 50/50—as good as a coin flip.

Obviously, if I taste lemon and you taste soap, we're going to have rather different opinions about salsa, so it stands to reason that we'll also have different opinions about beer. We're all sensitive to various flavor and aroma compounds to different degrees. Diacetyl, a butter-like flavor that's so buttery manufacturers put it in movie theatre popcorn, reveals itself to my palate more as a slick textural sensation than as a flavor. Only in elevated concentrations do I perceive diacetyl as buttery, while other tasters pick up butter straight away.

Some tasters perceive certain hops as having an oniony or garlicky quality. Summit is the most famous such hop variety, but Columbus, Simcoe, and many others can also take on an allium character that varies with crop, lot, and usage in the brewery. I'm incredibly sensitive to these compounds and have dumped beer that others have raved about when all I could taste was onion and garlic.

I have done my best to use sensory vocabulary that should be widely understood, but I do take advantage of a few shortcuts in cases where experience is your best guide. For example, the best German pilsners have an aromatic character I describe as "noble-like," which is a reference to four cultivars traditionally called the noble hops: Hallertauer Mittelfrüh, Tettnanger, Spalt, and Saaz. Tasters variously describe noble hops as spicy, herbal, floral, woody, or any number of other descriptors, but it's hard to know what that means unless you smell and taste them.

Once again, biology is at fault—aromas and flavors (which are, themselves, mostly aromas) are processed in the hippocampus and amygdala, parts of the brain associated with memory and emotion respectively. Language skills, on the other hand, are concentrated in what are known as Broca's area and Wernicke's area. If you smell or taste something, but the words to describe it seem on the tip of your tongue and just out of reach, you can blame your anatomy.

I think it's more descriptive to simply say, "This smells like noble hops," and be done with it. The downside of such an approach is that you must know what noble hops are like before that sentence will mean anything to you. The upside, though, is that you can learn what it means by drinking a lot of beer that features noble hops. To learn what Saaz hops are like, drink some Pilsner Urquell, which is hopped exclusively with that variety. To discover Hallertauer Mittelfrüh and Tettnanger, taste Sam Adams Boston Lager.

Another such term is *melanoidin*. This is a specific flavor sensation associated with the Maillard reaction, which is the same phenomenon responsible for the browning of beef in a hot pan. When heat, sugars, and amino acids come together in the right way, they create flavors that in beer can be described as deeply malty, caramelly, or coffee-like. In extreme cases, melanoidins can even take on a roasted broth-like character, something that occasionally shows up in doppelbock.

Ultimately, the best way to choose the beer that's right for you is not to read descriptions but to taste a lot of beer. There's no way around this, and it's a chore most of us find rewarding. Especially important is sampling styles that might be outside your normal repertoire. If you tend to prefer dark, malty beers, then spring for a pilsner now and then. If hop bombs are your go-to, slip in a maibock here and there.

Above all, have fun. The world of lager is diverse and enjoyable. With styles that run the gamut from helles to IPL and dunkel to doppelbock, you should find plenty to keep you busy.

RECOMMENDED READING

I relied on a great number of sources in preparing this manuscript, all of which are indicated in the bibliography. The sources listed here were particularly helpful, and I highly recommend that interested readers seek them out.

Dornbusch, Horst D. *Prost! The Story of German Beer*. Boulder, CO: Brewers Publications, 1998.
This excellent volume discusses the history of German brewing from the beginning of time to present. Mr. Dornbusch draws from a great number of works in both English and German to deliver a comprehensive picture of the development of beer in Germany. Much of the material in the first three chapters of *Lager* was inspired by *Prost!* You'll also find detailed discussions of the history of German ale styles altbier, kölsch, and weißbier (hefeweizen).

Eßlinger, Hans Michael, ed. *Handbook of Brewing: Processes, Technology, Markets*. Weinheim, Germany: Wiley-VCH Verlag, 2009.
Handbook of Brewing is like having several brewing textbooks in one. Each chapter has been written by one or more experts in the field and covers one major aspect of beer brewing. If you don't read German, this is probably the most easily accessible English-language text that details standard practice in German lager breweries. There is also an excellent section on the history of beer, as well as tips on brewing alt, kölsch, Bavarian wheat beer, and Berliner Weiße.

Heyse, Karl-Ullrich. *Handbuch der Brauerei-Praxis*. Nürnberg: Verlag Hans Carl Getränke-Fachverlag, 1995.
A classic German brewing text, Heyse's *Hanbuch der Brauerei-Praxis* is hard to find in North America, but it's worth the effort if you can read German. More richly illustrated than some of the other standard texts, this tome is particularly noteworthy for the graphs of fermentation schedules that illustrate the diverse ways in which lagers can be fermented, matured, and cold-conditioned. Special thanks to the United States Department of Agriculture's Agricultural Library in Beltsville, Maryland, for making this volume available through interlibrary loan, and for the Poudre River Library District in Fort Collins, Colorado, for jumping through the hoops necessary for me to borrow it.

Jackson, Michael. The Beer Hunter website, www.beerhunter.com.
The late Michael Jackson's success as a beer writer has as much to do with his beautiful prose as with his technical and stylistic descriptions. Should I ever write with even one-hundredth the skill, finesse, eloquence, and grace that Mr. Jackson possessed, I will feel very accomplished indeed. If the only Michael Jackson you've known was as a pop star, I encourage you to seek out the Beer Hunter website, as well the classics, *Michael Jackson's Great Beers of Belgium, Michael Jackson's Beer Companion, and the World Guide to Beer.*

Knoedelseder, William. *Bitter Brew: The Rise and Fall of Anheuser-Busch and America's Kings of Beer.* **New York: HarperCollins, 2012.**

A fascinating narrative of the history of Anheuser-Busch, *Bitter Brew* traces the company's evolution from Eberhard Anheuser's fledgling concern—given new vigor with the buy-in of Adolphus Busch—all the way to the 2008 takeover by InBev, which created the world's largest brewer, Anheuser-Busch InBev. Whether you're a committed craft beer connoisseur or a mass-market lager lover, it's hard not to feel the ups and downs of this American company turned international behemoth.

Narziß, Ludwig. *Abriss der Bierbrauerei.* **Weinheim, Germany: Wiley-VCH Verlag, 2004.**

One of the most complete brewing texts available today, and written by a legend in the field, *Abriss der Bierbrauerei* is your one-stop shop for German brewing science. This book is not for the faint of heart—there's no English translation and no illustrations—but if it's authoritative, detailed, reliable lager brewing science you're after, you'd be hard pressed to find a better volume.

Narziß, Ludwig, and Werner Back. *Die Bierbrauerei: Band 2: Die Technologie der Würzebereitung.* **8th ed. Weinheim, Germany: Wiley-VCH Verlag, 2012.**

Even more formidable than *Abriss der Bierbrauerei* is Prof. Dr. Ludwig Narziß's and Prof. Dr. Werner Back's two-volume set, *Die Bierbrauerei*. Volume 1 has more than nine hundred pages and is devoted exclusively to malting technology. Volume 2, *Die Technologie der Würzebereitung*, is all about wort preparation. This book offers the advantage of numerous illustrations, graphs, and tables, so the more visually inclined may prefer this text to *Abriss der Bierbrauerei*.

Noonan, Gregory J. *New Brewing Lager Beer.* **Boulder, CO: Brewers Publications, 1996.**

Greg Noonan's *New Brewing Lager Beer* is a classic and remains very much the authoritative English-language text concerning the theory and practice of decoction mashing. The title is misleading, as the text is just as applicable to ale brewing as lager brewing. But it is Noonan's exhaustive and relatively accessible treatment of the many variations of the decoction mash that have made this book a must-have for craft brewers across North America and around the world.

Oliver, Garrett, ed. *The Oxford Companion to Beer.* **Oxford University Press, 2011.**

When I was a child, I loved to sit down with the encyclopedia—specifically any volume from a mid-1980s vintage *World Book Encyclopedia*—and open to a random page to read. The *Oxford Companion to Beer* brings that same joy to beer-loving adults. Comprehensive and imminently readable, this beer book is the one to buy if you love beer and want to learn a little bit about a lot of topics.

Strong, Gordon, and Kristen England, eds. "Beer Judge Certification Program 2015 Style Guidelines." BJCP, Inc., 2015. www.bjcp.org/docs/2015_Guidelines_Beer.pdf.
The Beer Judge Certification Program (BJCP) periodically updates this style guide, which serves as the reference standard for beer competitions around the world. Virtually all homebrew competitions are judged according to the stylistic criteria outlined in the BJCP standard. As with style guides for language, it's important to remember that the descriptions in the BJCP document are *descriptive*, not *prescriptive*. If you want to medal in a homebrew competition, then yes, your beer needs to adhere to the stylistic descriptions spelled out within. But if you just want to brew and enjoy great beer, consider the BJCP guide more a compass than a roadmap.

Unger, Richard W. *Beer in the Middle Ages and the Renaissance*. Philadelphia: University of Pennsylvania Press, 2004.
I relied heavily on this text in writing the first two chapters. The depth of information available here is without compare. Unger brings together a tremendous amount of research into this surprisingly accessible and entertaining book. It's a masterwork of brewing history and well worth the time of anyone who enjoys history, beer, or both.

White, Chris, and Jamil Zainasheff. *Yeast: The Practical Guide to Beer Fermentation*. Boulder, CO: Brewers Publications, 2010.
Chris White and Jamil Zainasheff need no introduction. Dr. White is the founder of White Labs, one of North America's largest suppliers of high-quality pure cultures of brewer's yeast. Mr. Zainasheff is an accomplished, award-winning homebrewer turned professional, who delights drinkers at Heretic Brewing Company. *Yeast* is a valuable resource for homebrewers and professionals alike and breaks down the complexities of yeast metabolism into relatively simple terms. There are also great tips on propagation, yeast health, and yeast banking.

BIBLIOGRAPHY

Abernathy, Jon. *Bend Beer: A History of Brewing in Central Oregon.* Charleston, SC: American Palate, 2014.

Acitelli, Tom. *The Audacity of Hops.* Chicago: Chicago Review Press, 2013.

Armon, Rick. *Ohio Breweries.* Mechanicsburg, PA: Stackpole Books, 2011.

Arnold, John P. *Origin and History of Beer and Brewing.* Reprint edition 2005. Cleveland, OH: BeerBooks.com, 2005.

Baron, Stanley. *Brewed in America: A History of Beer and Ale in the United States.* New York: Arno Press, 1972.

Bernstein, Joshua M. *Brewed Awakening: Behind the Beers and Brewers Leading the World's Craft Brewing Revolution.* New York: Sterling Epicure, 2011.

Black, J. A., G. Cunningham, E. Fluckiger-Hawker, E. Robson, and G. Zólyomi. "A hymn to Ninkasi." *The Electronic Text Corpus of Sumerian Literature.* Accessed September 9, 2016. www-etcsl.orient.ox.ac.uk.

Bostwick, William. *The Brewer's Tale: A History of the World According to Beer.* New York: W. W. Norton & Company, 2014.

Brewers Association. "Brewers Association Mid-Year Metrics Show Continued Growth for Craft." Accessed July 31, 2016. www.brewersassociation.org/press-releases/brewers-association-mid-year-metrics-show-continued-growth-craft.

———. "Number of Breweries and Brewpubs in US." Accessed August 21, 2016. www.brewersassociation.org/statistics/number-of-breweries.

CraftBeer.com. "Beer Styles." Accessed September 5, 2016. www.craftbeer.com/beer-styles.

Daniels, Ray. *Designing Great Beers: The Ultimate Guide to Brewing Classic Beer Styles.* Boulder, CO: Brewers Publications, 1996.

Deutscher Brauer-Bund e.V. "Rechtsentwicklung." Accessed April 10, 2016. www.brauer-bund.de/bier-ist-rein/reinheitsgebot/rechtsentwicklung.html.

Dornbusch, Horst D. *Bavarian Helles: History, Brewing Techniques, Recipes.* Boulder, CO: Brewers Publications, 2000.

———. *Prost! The Story of German Beer.* Boulder, CO: Brewers Publications, 1998.

———. "The Reinheitsgebot: Is It Still Relevant?" *Zymurgy* 39, no. 3 (May/June 2016): 50–58.

Eden, Karl. "History of German Brewing." *Zymurgy* 16, no. 4 (Special 1993): 6–8.

———. "History of German Oktoberfest." *Zymurgy* 16, no. 4 (Special 1993): 33–34.

Ensminger, Peter A. "The History and Brewing Methods of Pilsner Urquell." *BrewingTechniques* 5, no. 3 (May/June 1997).

Eßlinger, Hans Michael, ed. *Handbook of Brewing: Processes, Technology, Markets.* Weinheim, Germany: Wiley-VCH Verlag, 2009.

Fix, George. "Diacetyl: Formation, Reduction, and Control." *BrewingTechniques* 1, no. 2 (July August 1993): 20.

Fix, George, and Laurie Fix. *Oktoberfest, Vienna, Marzen*. Boulder, CO: Brewers Publications, 1998.

Garber, Megan. "Discovered: The Tomb of an Ancient Egyptian Beer Brewer." *The Atlantic*, January 3, 2014. www.theatlantic.com/international/archive/2014/01/discovered-the-tomb-of-an-ancient-egyptian-beer-brewer/282801/.

Gordon, Dan. "Lager Brewing the German Way." *Zymurgy* 34, no. 6 (2011): 32–37.

Hackel-Stehr, Karin. "Unser Bier: Entstehung und Entwicklung des Reinheitsgebotes." PhD diss., Technische Universität Berlin, 1987.

Haskell, Warren, and Jason Oliver. "Long Live Lagers." Presentation at the American Homebrewers Association National Homebrewers Conference, Grand Rapids, MI, June 12–14, 2014.

Heyse, Karl-Ullrich. *Handbuch der Brauerei-Praxis*. Nürnberg: Verlag Hans Carl Getränke-Fachverlag, 1995.

Hieronymus, Stan. *Brewing Local: American-Grown Beer*. Boulder, CO: Brewers Publications, 2016.

Hindy, Steve. *The Craft Beer Revolution: How a Band of Microbrewers Is Transforming the World's Favorite Drink*. New York: Palgrave Macmillan, 2014.

Howell, Bill. *Alaska Beer: Liquid Gold in the Land of the Midnight Sun*. Charleston, SC: American Palate, 2015.

Jackson, Michael. "Michael Jackson's Beer Hunter." Accessed September 18, 2016. www.beerhunter.com.

Klemp, K. Florian. "Stylistically Speaking: Märzen/Oktoberfest." *All About Beer Magazine* 29, no. 5, November 1, 2008. www.allaboutbeer.com/article/marzenoktoberfest.

———. "Stylistically Speaking: Märzen/Oktoberfest." *All About Beer Magazine* 34, no. 6, January 1, 2014. www.allaboutbeer.com/article/oktoberfest-style.

Knoedelseder, William. *Bitter Brew: The Rise and Fall of Anheuser-Busch and America's Kings of Beer*. New York: HarperCollins, 2012.

Koch, Jim. *Quench Your Own Thirst: Business Lessons Learned Over a Beer or Two*. New York: Flatiron Books, 2016.

Koehler, Wolfram. "Lager Beer—A Brief History." *Zymurgy* 16, no. 4 (Special 1993): 17–19.

Kunze, Wolfgang. *Technology Brewing and Malting*. 1st intl. ed. Berlin: VLB Berlin, 1996.

Labadie, Jeremy, and Argyle Wolf-Knapp. *New Orleans Beer: A Hoppy History of Big Easy Brewing*. Charleston, SC: American Palate, 2014.

Lewis, Michael J., and Tom W. Young. *Brewing*. 2nd ed. New York: Springer Science+Business Media, 2001.

Libkind, Diego, Chris Todd Hittinger, Elisabete Valério, Carla Gonçalves, Jim Dover, Mark Johnston, Paula Gonçalves, and José Paulo Sampaio. "Microbe Domestication and the Identification of the Wild Genetic Stock of Lager-Brewing Yeast." *Proceedings of the National Academy of Sciences* 108, no. 35 (August 30, 2011): 14539–44.

MacIntosh, Julie. *Dethroning the King: The Hostile Takeover of Anheuser-Busch, an American Icon.* Hoboken, NJ: John Wiley & Sons, 2011.

Mason, Betsy. "April 23, 1516: Bavaria Cracks Down on Beer Brewers." *WIRED*, April 23, 2010. www.wired.com/2010/04/0423deutsche-reinheitsgebot-german-beer-purity-law.

McDole, Mike. "Fast Lager Yeast Fermentations." Presentation at the American Homebrewers Association National Homebrewers Conference, Baltimore, MD, June 9–11, 2016.

Merrill, Ellen. *Germans of Louisiana.* Gretna, LA: Pelican, 2004.

Miller, David. *Continental Pilsener.* Boulder, CO: Brewers Publications, 1998.

Mittelman, Amy. *Brewing Battles: A History of American Beer.* New York: Algora Publishing, 2008.

Mosher, Randy. *Radical Brewing: Recipes, Tales & World-Altering Meditations in a Glass.* Boulder, CO: Brewers Publications, 2004.

Narziß, Ludwig. *Abriss der Bierbrauerei.* Weinheim, Germany: Wiley-VCH Verlag, 2004.

Narziß, Ludwig, and Werner Back. *Die Bierbrauerei: Band 2: Die Technologie der Malzbereitung.* 8th ed. Weinheim, Germany: Wiley-VCH Verlag, 2012.

———. *Die Bierbrauerei: Band 2: Die Technologie der Würzebereitung.* 8th ed. Weinheim, Germany: Wiley-VCH Verlag, 2012.

Noonan, Gregory J. *New Brewing Lager Beer.* Boulder, CO: Brewers Publications, 1996.

Ogle, Maureen. *Ambitious Brew: The Story of American Beer.* Orlando, FL: Harcourt, 2006.

Oliver, Garrett. *The Brewmaster's Table: Discovering the Pleasures of Real Beer with Real Food.* New York: Ecco, 2005.

Oliver, Garrett, ed. *The Oxford Companion to Beer.* New York: Oxford University Press, 2011.

Palmer, John. *How to Brew.* 3rd ed. Boulder, CO: Brewers Publications, 2006.

Palmer, John, and Colin Kaminski. *Water: A Comprehensive Guide for Brewers.* Boulder, CO: Brewers Publications, 2013.

Papazian, Charlie. *The Complete Joy of Homebrewing.* 3rd ed. New York: HarperCollins, 2003.

———. "Brewers Association 2016 Beer Style Guidelines." Brewers Association, March 23, 2016. www.brewersassociation.org/wp-content/uploads/2016/04/2016_BA_Beer_Style_Guidelines.pdf.

Pasteur, Louis. *Studies on Fermentation: The Diseases of Beer, Their Causes, and the Means of Preventing Them.* Translated by Frank Faulkner. London: Macmillan, 1879.

Patterson, Mark W., and Nancy Hoalst-Pullen, eds. *The Geography of Beer: Regions, Environment, and Societies.* Dordrecht, The Netherlands: Springer, 2014.

Peck, Garrett. *Capital Beer: A Heady History of Brewing in Washington, D.C.* Charleston, SC: American Palate, 2014.

Pfister, Christian, Rudolf Brázdil, and Rüdiger Glaser, eds. *Climatic Variability in Sixteenth-Century Europe and Its Social Dimension.* Dordrecht: Kluwer Academic Publishers, 1999.

Pilsner Urquell. "Brewery News: Josef Groll." Accessed September 18, 2016. www.pilsnerurquell.com/us/article/josef-groll.

———. "Our Beer Heritage." Accessed September 18, 2016. www.pilsnerurquell.com/us/article/heritage.

Priest, Fergus G., and Graham G. Stewart, eds. *Handbook of Brewing*. 2nd ed. Boca Raton, FL: CRC Press, 2006.

Richman, Darryl. *Bock*. Boulder, CO: Brewers Publications, 1994.

———. "Pilsner Urquell: The Brewery" *Zymurgy* 14, no. 3 (Summer 1991): 30–36.

Rorabaugh, W. J. *The Alcoholic Republic: An American Tradition*. New York: Oxford University Press, 1981.

Rupp, Travis. "Ancient Brewing in the World of Wine." Presentation at the American Homebrewers Association National Homebrewers Conference, Baltimore, MD, June 9–11, 2016.

———. "The Beginnings of Beer in the Ancient World." Presentation at the American Homebrewers Association National Homebrewers Conference, San Diego, CA, June 11–13, 2015.

Scharl, Benno. *Beschreibung der Braunbier-Brauerey im Königreiche Baiern*. Munich: Lindauer, 1814.

Shumway, Daniel. *Utica Beer: A History of Brewing in the Mohawk Valley*. Charleston, SC: American Palate, 2014.

Steele, Mitch. *IPA: Brewing Techniques, Recipes and the Evolution of India Pale Ale*. Boulder, CO: Brewers Publications, 2013.

Strong, Gordon, and Kristen England, eds. "Beer Judge Certification Program 2015 Style Guidelines." BJCP, Inc., 2015. www.bjcp.org/docs/2015_Guidelines_Beer.pdf.

Swinnen, Johan F.M., ed. *The Economics of Beer*. New York: Oxford University Press, 2011.

Tremblay, Victor J., and Carol Horton Tremblay. *The US Brewing Industry: Data and Economic Analysis*. Cambridge, MA: The MIT Press, 2005.

Unger, Richard W. *Beer in the Middle Ages and the Renaissance*. Philadelphia: University of Pennsylvania Press, 2004.

Wagner, Rich. *Philadelphia Beer: A Heady History of Brewing in the Cradle of Liberty*. Charleston, SC: The History Press, 2012.

Warner, Eric. "An Overview of the German Brewing History." *Zymurgy* 16, no. 4 (Special 1993): 11.

———. "The Art and Science of Decoction Mashing." *Zymurgy* 16, no. 4 (Special 1993): 20–23.

Wahl, Arnold Spencer, and Robert Wahl. *Beer from the Expert's Viewpoint*. Reprint edition 2014. Cleveland, OH: BeerBooks.com, 2014.

White, Chris, and Jamil Zainasheff. *Yeast: The Practical Guide to Beer Fermentation*. Boulder, CO: Brewers Publications, 2010.

Yaeger, Brian. *Red, White, and Brew: An American Beer Odyssey*. New York: St. Martin's Press, 2008.

ACKNOWLEDGMENTS

"I'd like to write a book someday."

I get this a lot when I tell people I wrote a book. I used to say it myself. I've learned, though, that the difference between wanting to write a book and having actually written one largely comes down to working with people who are willing to kick you in the ass. I sat on the idea for *Lager* for several years before I finally pitched it to Thom O'Hearn, my acquisitions and content editor at Quarto. But once he picked it up, he offered the structural and logistical support that my scattered, amorphous ideas needed to see the light of day. Thanks for kicking me in the ass, Thom, and thank you for your guidance and editorial wisdom.

I'd also like to thank Luke Trautwein, whose excellent eye and playful disposition led to the beautiful photographs that accompany the recipes. Having worked my way through a handful of black-and-white German brewing textbooks, I can say with certainty that beer writing is much more interesting when it's accompanied by beautiful color photography. Thanks, Luke!

Writing a book is hard. Writing a book by night and weekend while editing the country's premier magazine for homebrewers by day is even harder. There is never a good time to write a book, so you squeeze your life in various places to make room for the monster. The bits that suffer the brunt of the cutbacks invariably involve laundry, sleep, grocery shopping, haircuts, vacations, oil changes, and other forms of personal maintenance. Thank you to my wife Ginny for keeping the world from caving in around us while I burned multiple candles at ends we didn't even know they had. I appreciate your support more than you'll ever know. Our cats, on the other hand . . . I'm not sure they appreciate much of anything.

This book most certainly would not have happened without the help of brewers, media representatives, administrative assistants, and countless other beer industry professionals who took the time to talk with me, answer pesky questions and recipe requests, and provide artwork and beer samples. I owe a debt of gratitude to all of the following individuals: Jessica Lederhos of AC Golden Brewing Co.; Mike Mackay of Avery Brewing Company; Jared Spiker of Bayern Brewing; Michelle Diamandis, Jim Koch, and Ashley Leduc of Boston Beer Company; Rachel Staats of the Brewers Association; Kristi Switzer of Brewers Publications; Samantha Bernstein and Heather Lewis of Brooklyn Brewery; Adam Benson and Jim Mills of Caldera Brewing Company; Horst Dornbusch of Cerevisia Communications; Mari Kemper and Will Kemper of Chuckanut Brewery & Kitchen; Rebecca Holland of Devil's Backbone Brewing Company; Jill Berny of Fort Collins Brewery; Brad Blaser, Dave Coyne, and Jack Harris of Fort George Brewery; Lauren Cosby of Gordon Biersch Brewing Company; Adam Ritterspach of Great Lakes Brewing Company; Don Chapman and Aaron Heaton of Grimm Brothers Brewhouse; Lisa Allen of Heater Allen Brewing; Sarah McGinley of Jack's Abby Craft Lagers; Andrea Allison of Joseph James Brewing Company; Andy Jungwirth of Lakefront Brewery; Tracy Dabakis of Marlo Marketing, on behalf of Narragansett Brewing Company; Peter Bouckaert of New Belgium Brewing Company; Michelle Humphrey and Josh pFriem of pFriem Family Brewers; Annie Johnson of PicoBrew; Tiffany Aveau and Vinnie Cilurzo of Russian River Brewing Company; Bridgett Beckwith and Sarah Moir of Shorts Brewing Company; JT Thompson of Smuttynose Brewing Company; Julie Birrenkott and Brian Elza of Stevens Point Brewery; Jeff Herb and Justin Williams of Tröegs Brewing Company; Amanda Giangiulio of Victory Brewing Company; and Neil Fisher of WeldWerks Brewing Co.

If I have failed to mention someone I should have, the error is due to poor memory and subpar note taking, not to ingratitude.

Finally, thank you to all who have supported my personal metamorphosis from accidental engineer to intentional author. Words are, indeed, far more fun than numbers. You know who you are.

ENDNOTES

INTRODUCTION

1. The modern English words *beer* and *ale* are cognate with the German *Bier* and Danish øl, respectively.

2. Gruit was the blend of herbs, often including things like yarrow and bog myrtle, that flavored and helped preserve ale prior to the widespread cultivation of hops. Today, the term has also come to mean beers that have been brewed with such botanical blends.

3. When I say "one of the strongest beers in the world," I intentionally exclude such rarities as Samuel Adams Utopias, Brew Dog's Sink the Bismarck and Tactical Nuclear Penguin, and Dogfish Head's 120 Minute IPA, which range in alcoholic strength from 20 to 40 percent ABV. Such extreme examples rely on specialized fermentation and concentration techniques to achieve their remarkable levels of alcohol. But as long as we're on the subject, and if we're keeping score, Schorschbock from Brauerei Schorschbräu in Gunzenhausen, Germany, at 57 percent ABV, is fundamentally an eisbock lager.

4. "Top 250 Beers," BeerAdvocate, accessed September 17, 2016, www.beeradvocate.com/lists/top.

5. "Beers of Fame," BeerAdvocate, accessed September 17, 2016, www.beeradvocate.com/lists/fame.

6. For the record, I cannot stomach asparagus, at least not the green kind. White asparagus, however, is a delight.

CHAPTER 1: THE DARK AGES

1. *Sprouted Seeds Gone Bad*—available now for private viewing through in-room pay-per-view.

2. My adaptation of a translation from the University of Oxford (J. A. Black, G. Cunningham, E. Fluckiger-Hawker, E. Robson, and G. Zólyomi, "The Hymn to Ninkasi," *The Electronic Text Corpus of Sumerian Literature*, accessed September 9, 2016, www-etcsl.orient.ox.ac.uk.).

3. In 2014, a team of Egyptologists from Japan uncovered the tomb of an ancient brewer at Luxor dating to around 1200 BCE. Khonso-Im-Heb was likely the head of beer production for the court of Amenhotep III, grandfather of Tutankhamun. The tomb included a fresco portraying, among other things, fermentation and offerings to the Egyptian goddess Mut (Megan Garber, "Discovered: The Tomb of an Ancient Egyptian Beer Brewer," *The Atlantic*, January 3, 2014, www.theatlantic.com/international/archive/2014/01/discovered-the-tomb-of-an-ancient-egyptian-beer-brewer/282801).

4. Travis Rupp, "The Beginnings of Beer in the Ancient World" (presentation, American Homebrewers Association National Homebrewers Conference, San Diego, CA, June 11–13, 2015).

5. To be fair, the Romans weren't the first to set foot in Egypt and insult the local predilection for beer. The Greeks had arrived some three centuries prior when Alexander the Great came on the scene to continue naming cities for himself. Like the Romans, the Greeks preferred wine and considered germinated barley to have gone bad. Poor Greeks.

6. Pliny the Elder, *The Natural History*, trans. John Bostock and Henry T. Riley (London: Taylor and Francis, 1855), accessed October 17, 2016, www.perseus.tufts.edu/hopper/text?doc=urn:cts:latinLit:phi0978. phi001.perseus-eng1:21.50.

7. "Corn" in this context refers to grain in general and not maize specifically. The English word is cognate with the German *Korn*, which refers to any kind of grain. In brewing contexts, we use the term *maize* to name the plant that Americans commonly call corn. (Pliny the Elder, *The Natural History*, trans. John Bostock and Henry T. Riley (London: Taylor and Francis, 1855), accessed October 17, 2016, www. perseus.tufts.edu/hopper/text?doc=urn:cts:latinLit:phi0978.phi001.perseus-eng1:14.29).

8. Richard W. Unger, *Beer in the Middle Ages and the Renaissance* (Philadelphia: University of Pennsylvania Press, 2004), 26.

9. Garrett Oliver, ed., *The Oxford Companion to Beer* (New York: Oxford University Press, 2011), 410.

CHAPTER 2: DUKING IT OUT IN BAVARIA

1. Spain's importing of gold and silver from the Americas didn't help.

2. Horst Dornbusch, "The Reinheitsgebot: Is It Still Relevant?" *Zymurgy* 39, no. 3 (May/June 2016): 50–58.

3. Adapted from Karl Eden, "History of German Brewing," *Zymurgy* 16, no. 4 (Special 1993): 6–8.

CHAPTER 3: BREWERS SEE THE LIGHT

1. If online forum activity is a reliable indicator, I already know I am going to receive hate mail over this paragraph, so let me be clear. Yes, ancient Egyptians and Mesopotamians who sun-dried modified grain would have produced a very pale malt indeed. What I mean here is that most malts dried using direct heat would have been relatively dark, the key words here being *most* and *relatively*. When we discuss historic malt colors, we implicitly reference everything to the color of today's palest malts (less than 2°L), which by historical standards are very pale. It's likely that some maltsters were producing pale malts before the Industrial Revolution, but it's not likely that this was the case across Europe.

   I suspect I'll also hear about the assertion that most beer would have had some smoke character. There is evidence to indicate that some British maltsters were using coke-fired kilns as far back as the seventeenth century, but such technology was by no means adopted universally. Given the rather granular regionality of production, it's probably safe to assume that some maltings would have produced malts with no smoke character, but probably not all of them.

2. Helles continues to pair rather well with hamburgers to this day.

3. English speakers commonly call these steins, but this is an inaccurate term. The term *stein* comes from the German *Steinkrug*, which refers to an earthenware mug (*Stein* means "stone" in German). The hefty, dimpled, liter-sized mugs associated with Bavarian beer halls are made of glass, not stoneware. *Glaskrug* would more accurately reflect the material of its construction, but *Maßkrug*, which emphasizes the mug's liter capacity, is the name that has stuck.

4. The actual situation is somewhat more complex than this. Recent research has revealed that *S. pastorianus* encompasses two distinct genetic groups—Saaz and Frohberg—which have separate origins. Both groups are the result of hybridization between *S. cerevisiae* and *S. eubayanus*, but it appears the two genetic lines arose from different strains of *S. cerevisiae*. Saaz-type yeasts include the original strain isolated at Carlsberg in 1183, while Weihenstephan 34/70, the most popular lager yeast in the world, comes from the House of Frohberg.

CHAPTER 4: THE LAGER DIASPORA

1. George Washington. "To Make Small Beer." From Washington's *Notebook as a Virginia Colonel*, 1757. The New York Public Library, Manuscripts and Archives Division.

2. Daniel Shumway, *Utica Beer: A History of Brewing in the Mohawk Valley* (Charleston, SC: American Palate, 2014), 19.

3. Jeremy Labadie and Argyle Wolf-Knapp, *New Orleans Beer: A Hoppy History of Big Easy Brewing* (Charleston, SC: American Palate, 2014), 25.

4. For comparison, there were approximately thirteen thousand company-owned and licensed Starbucks locations in the United States at the end of 2016.

5. Garrett Peck, *Capital Beer: A Heady History of Brewing in Washington, D.C.* (Charleston, SC: American Palate, 2014), 19.

6. Bill Howell, *Alaska Beer: Liquid Gold in the Land of the Midnight Sun* (Charleston, SC: American Palate, 2015), 32.

7. Howell, *Alaska Beer*, 32.

8. Ellen Merrill, *Germans of Louisiana* (Gretna, LA: Pelican, 2004), 168.

9. At press time, visitors to the Illinois State Military Museum can view the prosthetic wood, cork, and leather leg that Santa Anna used following the loss of his natural one.

CHAPTER 5: THE DRY SPELL

1. Even with an all-time record number of breweries, there's still a long way to go. At the end of 2016, nearly nine thousand wineries called the United States home.

2. Garrett Peck, *Capital Beer: A Heady History of Brewing in Washington, D.C.* (Charleston, SC: American Palate, 2014), 110–111.

3. Jon Abernathy, *Bend Beer: A History of Brewing in Central Oregon* (Charleston, SC: American Palate, 2014), 46.

4. Daniel Shumway, *Utica Beer: A History of Brewing in the Mohawk Valley* (Charleston, SC: American Palate, 2014), 206.

5. Jeremy Labadie and Argyle Wolf-Knapp, *New Orleans Beer: A Hoppy History of Big Easy Brewing* (Charleston, SC: American Palate, 2014), 29.

6. "Number of Breweries and Brewpubs in US." *Brewers Association*, accessed August 21, 2016, www.brewersassociation.org/statistics/number-of-breweries.

7. The Spuds Mackenzie commercials were at their peak when I was in fifth grade, and I remember the tune and the lyrics to this very day.

CHAPTER 6: THE CRAFT LAGER COMEBACK

1. Maureen Ogle, *Ambitious Brew: The Story of American Beer* (Orlando, FL: Harcourt, 2006), 312.

2. Information in this section from Jim Koch in discussion with the author, July 2016.

3. In 1985, Will and his wife Mari joined forces with Andy Thomas to form Thomas Kemper Brewing in Poulsbo, Washington. In 1992, the Thomas Kemper brewery merged with Hart Brewing Company, which eventually became Pyramid Breweries.

4. Will Kemper in discussion with the author, August 2016.

5. "Pliny the Younger Economic Impact Study: Craft Beverage Insights," Sonoma County Economic Development Board, accessed August 21, 2016, www.sonomaedb.org/WorkArea/DownloadAsset.aspx?id=2147518334.

6. Vinnie Cilurzo in discussion with the author, June 2016.

7. Unfortunately, Avery Brewing Company announced at the end of 2016 that it would be retiring the Kaiser as a year-round brew, along with other members of its Dictators and Demons series, including the Czar, Mephistopheles, Samael's, and the Beast (though the Maharaja Imperial IPA is sticking around). The Kaiser might return as a seasonal offering, and it might not, but the folks at Avery were kind enough to supply the recipe, so you can brew your own version of this award-winning imperial oktoberfest at home!

CHAPTER 7: TASTING AND ENJOYING LAGER

1. Also called a Willy becher, and sometimes written as one word: Willibecher or Willybecher.

2. Let us never forget the Mars Climate Orbiter, a more than $300 million spacecraft that fell to pieces in the Martian atmosphere because engineers failed to convert thrust calculations from US customary units to metric. Since rocket scientists aren't leading the charge to an all-metric United States, perhaps we brewers should set the example.

3. "Common" is, of course, a relative term. Only very high-end beer bars and traditional German-style establishments are likely to stock this type of beer glass.

4. A fun variation on the Stange is Firestone Walker's Pivo Pils glass, which looks like a tall Stange with a slight taper in the middle.

5. If you're feeling ironic.

6. Acetaldehyde is commonly found in detectable amounts in some mass-market American light (in the sense of "lite") lagers.

CHAPTER 10: NORTH AMERICAN LAGERS, FOR BETTER AND FOR WORSE

1. Bill Howell, *Alaska Beer: Liquid Gold in the Land of the Midnight Sun* (Charleston, SC: American Palate, 2015), 33.

2. For best results, temperature control is, of course, recommended for ales and lagers alike. The point here is that the novice lager brewer can expand his or her repertoire without necessarily acquiring new equipment.

3. For the purposes of organizing the beer styles in this book, I have classified several American lagers whose names include the word *pilsner* in this category. The ones I have chosen to include here have, to my palate, a more "American" character than the US examples I included in Chapter 8. I encourage you to look for these beers and decide how *you* would classify them!

4. Samichlaus, the iconic strong doppelbock from Austria, could easily have found its way into this section. I chose to include it in Chapter 9 because it's stylistically a bock at heart, and it has a history going back to the 1970s, which predates the modern "imperial everything" trend.

CHAPTER 11: LAGER WORT PRODUCTION

1. Also, why do the British continue to insist on separate hot and cold spigots?

2. Actually, they can do rather well, but they tend to change character.

3. Martin Brungard's values, published in John Palmer and Colin Kaminski, *Water: A Comprehensive Guide for Brewers* (Boulder, CO: Brewers Publications, 2013), 143–144.

CHAPTER 12: FERMENTATION, CONDITIONING, AND PACKAGING

1. I especially like the Brewer's Friend calculator at www.brewersfriend.com/gyle-and-krausen-priming-calculator.

2. If you can do so in a sanitary fashion, you can remove some yeast from the primary fermenter. Otherwise, just use some dry lager yeast like W-34/70 or S-189.

3. Be aware that bottling and capping actively fermenting beer presents the very real possibility of exploding bottles. Before you attempt kräusening, double-check your math using a reliable calculator and err on the side of under-carbonation until you get a feel for the process.

INDEX

ABOUT THE AUTHOR

Dave Carpenter is editor-in-chief of *Zymurgy®*, the official magazine of the American Homebrewers Association (a division of the Brewers Association). A longtime homebrewer and beer writer, he is also author of *The Illustrated Guide to Homebrewing* (Unfiltered Media, 2016) and was formerly a contributing editor for *Craft Beer & Brewing Magazine®*. Dave holds degrees from MIT and the University of Colorado–Boulder and is a BJCP-certified beer judge. He lives with his wife, two cats, and an emergency stash of helles, pilsner, and bock.

PHOTO CREDITS